Decorative Art

Editorial note:
The dates shown in the footers on the reprinted pages relate
only to the year of publication and not to the year of design
for the artifacts included.

Anmerkung der Herausgeber:
Die Jahreszahlen in den Kolumnentiteln geben das Erschei-
nungsjahr der Zeitschrift und nicht das Entstehungsjahr der
Objekte an.

Note éditoriale:
Les dates indiquées en bas des pages renvoient à celles de
publication et non à celles de création des objets concernés.

To stay informed about upcoming TASCHEN titles, please
request our magazine at www.taschen.com/magazine or
write to TASCHEN, Hohenzollernring 53, D-50672 Cologne,
Germany, contact@taschen.com, Fax: +49-221-254919.
We will be happy to send you a free copy of our magazine
which is filled with information about all of our books.

© 2008 TASCHEN GmbH
Hohenzollernring 53, D–50672 Köln
www.taschen.com

Original edition © 2000 Taschen Verlag GmbH
© VG Bild-Kunst, Bonn 2007 for the works by Jacques Adnet,
Herman Bongard, Hugo Gehlin, Ann Greenwood, Dieter Hinz,
Erik S. Höglund, Jaruslak Junek, Lisa Larson, Stig Lindberg,
Tyra Lundgren, Tom Möller, Marcel Mortier, Jais Nielsen,
Edvin Öhrström, Bengt Orup, Arthur Percy, Sigurd Persson,
Eric Ravilious, Axel Salto
© for the works by Charles & Ray Eames:
Eames Office, Venice, CA, www.eamesoffice.com

Design: UNA (London) designers
Cover design: Sense/Net, Andy Disl and Birgit Reber, Cologne
Production: Martina Ciborowius, Cologne
Editorial coordination: Susanne Husemann, Cologne
© for the introduction: Charlotte and Peter Fiell, London
German translation by Uta Hoffmann, Cologne
French translation by Philippe Safavi, Paris

Printed in Singapore
ISBN 978-3-8365-0310-5

50s

Decorative Art

A source book edited by Charlotte & Peter Fiell

TASCHEN

HONG KONG KÖLN LONDON LOS ANGELES MADRID PARIS TOKYO

CONTENTS
INHALT
SOMMAIRE

PREFACE

The "Decorative Art" Yearbooks

The Studio Magazine was founded in Britain in 1893 and featured both the fine and the decorative arts. It initially promoted the work of progressive designers such as Charles Rennie Mackintosh and Charles Voysey to a wide audience both at home and abroad, and was especially influential in Continental Europe. Later, in 1906, *The Studio* began publishing the *Decorative Art* yearbook to "meet the needs of that ever-increasing section of the public who take interest in the application of art to the decoration and general equipment of their homes". This annual survey, which became increasingly international in its outlook, was dedicated to the latest currents in architecture, interiors, furniture, lighting, glassware, textiles, metalware and ceramics. From its outset, *Decorative Art* advanced the "New Art" that had been pioneered by William Morris and his followers, and attempted to exclude designs which showed any "excess in ornamentation and extreme eccentricities of form".

In the 1920s, *Decorative Art* began promoting Modernism and was in later years a prominent champion of "Good Design". Published from the 1950s onwards by Studio Vista, the yearbooks continued to provide a remarkable overview of each decade, featuring avant-garde and often experimental designs alongside more mainstream products. Increasing prominence was also lent to architecture

and interior design, and in the mid-1960s the title of the series was changed to *Decorative Art in Modern Interiors* to reflect this shift in emphasis. Eventually, in 1980, Studio Vista ceased publication of these unique annuals, and over the succeeding years volumes from the series became highly prized by collectors and dealers as excellent period reference sources.

The fascinating history of design traced by *Decorative Art* can now be accessed once again in this new series reprinted, in somewhat revised form, from the original yearbooks. In line with the layout of *Decorative Art*, the various disciplines are grouped separately, whereby great care has been taken in selecting the best and most interesting pages while ensuring that the corresponding dates have been given due prominence for ease of reference. It is hoped that these volumes of highlights from *Decorative Art* will at long last bring the yearbooks to a wider audience, who will find in them well-known favourites as well as fascinating and previously unknown designs.

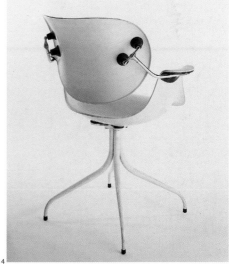

3

4

VORWORT

Die »Decorative Art« Jahrbücher

Die Zeitschrift *The Studio Magazine* wurde 1893 in England gegründet und war sowohl der Kunst als auch dem Kunsthandwerk gewidmet. In den Anfängen stellte sie einer breiten Öffentlichkeit in England und in Übersee die Arbeiten progressiver Designer wie Charles Rennie Mackintosh und Charles Voysey vor. Ihr Einfluss war groß und nahm auch auf dem europäischen Festland zu. 1906 begann *The Studio* zusätzlich mit der Herausgabe des *Decorative Art Yearbook*, um »den Bedürfnissen einer ständig wachsenden Öffentlichkeit gerecht zu werden, die sich zunehmend dafür interessierte, Kunst in die Dekoration und Ausstattung ihrer Wohnungen einzubeziehen.« Diese jährlichen Überblicke unterrichteten über die neuesten internationalen Tendenzen in der Architektur und Innenraumgestaltung, bei Möbeln, Lampen, Glas und Keramik, Metall und Textilien. Von Anfang an förderte *Decorative Art* die von William Morris und seinen Anhängern entwickelte »Neue Kunst« und versuchte, Entwürfe auszuschließen, die »in Mustern und Formen zu überladen und exzentrisch waren.«

In den zwanziger Jahren hatte sich *Decorative Art* für modernistische Strömungen eingesetzt und wurde in der Folgezeit zu einer prominenten Befürworterin des »guten Designs«. Die seit 1950 von englischen Verlag Studio Vista veröffentlichten Jahrbücher stellten für jedes Jahrzehnt ausgezeichnete Überblicke der vorherrschenden

avangardistischen und experimentellen Trends im Design einerseits und des bereits in der breiteren Öffentlichkeit etablierten Alltagsdesigns andererseits zusammen. Als Architektur und Interior Design Mitte der sechziger Jahre ständig an Bedeutung gewannen, wurde die Serie in *Decorative Art in Modern Interiors* umbenannt, um diesem Bedeutungswandel gerecht zu werden. Im Jahre 1981 stellte Studio Vista die Veröffentlichung dieser einzigartigen Jahrbücher ein. Sie wurden in den folgenden Jahren als wertvolle Sammelobjekte und hervorragende Nachschlagewerke hochgeschätzt.

Die faszinierende Geschichte des Designs, die *Decorative Art* dokumentierte, erscheint jetzt als leicht veränderter Nachdruck der originalen Jahrbücher. Dem ursprünglichen Layout von *Decorative Art* folgend, werden die einzelnen Disziplinen getrennt vorgestellt. Mit großer Sorgfalt wurden die besten und interessantesten Seiten ausgewählt. Die entsprechenden Jahreszahlen sind jeweils angegeben, um die zeitliche Einordnung zu ermöglichen. Mit diesen Bänden soll einer breiten Leserschaft der Zugang zu den *Decorative Art* Jahrbüchern und seinen international berühmt gewordenen, aber auch den weniger bekannten und dennoch faszinierenden Entwürfen ermöglicht werden.

5

PRÉFACE

Les annuaires « Decorative Art »

Fondé en 1893 en Grande-Bretagne, *The Studio Magazine* traitait à la fois des beaux-arts et des arts décoratifs. Sa vocation première était de promouvoir le travail de créateurs qui innovaient, tels que Charles Rennie Mackintosh ou Charles Voysey, auprès d'un vaste public d'amateurs tant en Grande-Bretagne qu'à l'étranger, notamment en Europe où son influence était particulièrement forte. En 1906, *The Studio* lança *The Decorative Art Yearbook,* un annuaire destiné à répondre à « la demande de cette part toujours croissante du public qui s'intéresse à l'application de l'art à la décoration et à l'aménagement général de la maison ». Ce rapport annuel, qui prit une ampleur de plus en plus internationale, était consacré aux dernières tendances en matière d'architecture, de décoration d'intérieur, de mobilier, de luminaires, de verrerie, de textiles, d'orfèvrerie et de céramique. D'emblée, *Decorative Art* mit en avant « l'Art nouveau » dont William Morris et ses disciples avaient posé les jalons, et tenta d'exclure tout style marqué par « une ornementation surchargée et des formes d'une excentricité excessive ».

Dès les années 20, *Decorative Art* commença à promouvoir le modernisme, avant de se faire le chantre du « bon design ». Publiés à partir des années 50 par Studio Vista, les annuaires continuèrent à présenter un remarquable panorama de chaque décennie, faisant se côtoyer les créations avant-gardistes et souvent expérimentales et les produits plus « grand public ». Ses pages accordèrent également une part de plus en plus grande à l'architecture et à la décoration d'intérieur. Ce changement de politique éditoriale se refléta dans le nouveau titre adopté vers le milieu des années 60 : *Decorative Art in Modern Interiors.* En 1980, Studio Vista arrêta la parution de ces volumes uniques en leur genre qui, au fil des années qui suivirent, devinrent très recherchés par les collectionneurs et les marchands car ils constituaient d'excellents ouvrages de référence pour les objets d'époque.

Grâce à cette réédition sous une forme légèrement modifiée, la fascinante histoire du design retracée par *Decorative Art* est de nouveau disponible. Conformément à la maquette originale des annuaires, les différentes disciplines sont présentées séparément, classées par date afin de faciliter les recherches. Les pages les plus belles et les plus intéressantes ont été sélectionnées avec un soin méticuleux et on ne peut qu'espérer que ces volumes feront con-

naître *Decorative Art* à un plus vaste public, qui y retrouvera des pièces de design devenues célèbres et en découvrira d'autres inconnues auparavant et tout aussi fascinantes.

6

INTRODUCTION
THE 1950s

7. Pierre Paulin, Wood, Metal and Formica Desk for Édition Thonet, 1956–1958; Erwin & Estelle Laverne, *Lotus* chair for Laverne International, 1958 and *Philips* metal table lamp, c. 1956
8. Arne Jacobsen, *Ant No. 3100* chair for Fritz Hansen, 1951–1952

Homemaking and the American Dream

The 1950s were a period of renewal and optimism that saw post-war austerity gradually replaced by an unprecedented consumer boom. The turmoil of the previous decades gave way to peace and freedom in the West, while vast energies were spent on making much of the world a better place socially, politically, economically and materially. In the decorative arts, national characteristics so prevalent prior to the Second World War became almost obliterated by "constructive pacifism" and its pursuit of universalism and quality. Architecture and design benefited from new applications of wartime research, from anthropometrical data to state-of-the-art materials and methods of construction. New materials such as plastic laminates, fibreglass and latex foam quite literally shaped the look of the 1950s, while designers were inspired by a wide range of themes such as molecular chemistry, nuclear physics, science fiction, African art and abstract contemporary sculpture by such artists as Alexander Calder and Hans Arp. The spiky angular forms of the early 1950s gave way to more organic and biomorphic shapes as the decade progressed.

By the early 1950s, America had moved on from the despair and insecurity that had been associated with the Great Depression and began to experience a period of seeming abundance, driven by a new culture of consumerism. The prosperity of rich metropolitan areas, however, overshadowed the poverty still found in many rural communities and especially among the immigrant and ethnic populations. Designers and manufacturers appealed to consumers' growing aspirations by producing streamlined and forward-looking products that were the embodiment of the "American Dream". These objects of desire were the very antithesis of the "make do and mend" ethos of the 1930s and 1940s, often incorporating a built-in obsolescence which was intended to fuel consumption and, thereby, productivity and prosperity. In the United States, the vast majority of people aspired to a secure job (preferably in a large corporation), a house in a neatly kept suburb, a large family, a large car and an array of labour-saving appliances. The home became the very focus of the American Dream and manufacturers mercilessly targeted this new generation of "homemakers" and consumers.

In European countries such as Britain and Italy, post-war austerity was overcome by common-sense know-how and breathtaking inventiveness. As in America, the home had a special significance during the 1950s as a place of refuge from a world of rapidly advancing technologies, and also as a haven in which to forget the very real threat of nuclear war. In Britain, over 350 schools were provided with model flats for the teaching of "homecraft" to a new generation of homemakers. During the early 1950s, however, buildings, especially in Britain, remained subject to frustrating building regulations and restrictions, while prefabrication (a key to low-cost housing) existed for the most part in theory rather than in practice. It was not until the mid-1950s that Europeans began enjoying the housing boom that had already taken place in America. These new homes in turn required new furnishings, fuelling a revival in the decorative arts which was characterised by technical experimentation. Designers working in the spheres of glass and ceramics drew upon the latest metallurgy research to craft objects both more colourful and expressive in form. Textile designers incorporated newly-developed synthetic materials into their patterns, while silversmiths, especially in Denmark, created ground-breaking sensual organic forms.

New Housing and Ways of Living

On both sides of the Atlantic, the lower middle classes benefited from the large-scale development of smaller houses. Home-ownership rapidly became no longer the province of the rich. In America, Europe and Scandinavia, all of whom instituted post-war housing programmes, housing became widely regarded as a fundamental human right. In Europe, wartime bombing had effectively cleared many slum areas,

8

and from their ashes there now arose new, low-cost, state-aided housing that placed an emphasis on neighbourhood planning. Residential tower blocks, initially developed in Sweden, rapidly grew popular elsewhere too, while construction methods drew increasingly upon industrially manufactured components. Not surprisingly, the greatest advances in public sector housing were made in the most industrialised countries.

These new homes with their smaller living spaces required better planning and led to new ways of living that necessitated new furniture types, such as modular seating, room-dividers, storage walls and sofabeds, as well as new interior layouts, such as open-plan and split-level. Not every country embraced the new Modernism with equal fervour; France in particular remained torn between the old and the new. Gradually, however, the Modern aesthetic gained significant ground over what was termed the "period complex", and by the mid-century the "Contemporary" look was a recognisable and widely-embraced international style. The fact that mass production and mass distribution had reduced prices thereby allowed "contemporary furniture to come into its own".

Journals such as the *Decorative Art* yearbooks, which advocated natural finishes, pattern and texture in architecture, and light, flexibility and colour in interior design, were partly responsible for the mainstream acceptance of furnishings in the modern idiom. New magazines covering domestic issues and offering do-it-yourself tips also helped

alter perceptions and tastes, as did trade fairs and exhibitions such as the annual and hugely popular Ideal Home Exhibition in London, which included an "ideal" three-bedroomed "People's House". Government-funded bodies such as the Council of Industrial Design and the Design & Industries Association also tirelessly promoted Modern design in Britain, while in America, the Museum of Modern Art in New York held exhibitions of "Good Design" from 1950 onwards.

The Contemporary Style

Ironically, the crusade launched by the progressive minority of design critics and museum curators proved all too successful, as Modern design exploded into a popular stylistic trend. The ascendancy of the Contemporary style – or "New Look", as Christian Dior had already termed it in 1947 – fuelled the search by some designers and manufacturers for novelty and gimmicks rather than practical design solutions, to such an extent that white goods were sometimes embellished with knobs and dials that served absolutely no practical purpose. Alarmed by this turn of events, *Which?* magazine was launched in 1957 by the Consumer's Association in Britain as an informative guide to the relative quality of consumer products. The rampant consumerism of the 1950s, however, remained unabated and offered fertile ground for the Pop culture of the following decade.

Although the 1950s cannot be regarded as a permissive period, seeds of anti-establishmentarianism were sown in it – from the rock'n'roll of Elvis Presley and the rebellious anti-heroes portrayed by James Dean and Marlon Brando, to Abstract Expressionism and the formation of CND (Campaign for Nuclear Disarmament). Television and jet travel were opening up new horizons, while satellites were heralding the age of global communications. The unprecedented affluence of the decade, which had been famously summed up by British Prime Minster Harold MacMillan as having "never had it so good", led to significantly higher standards of living by its close. The 1950s were an era of "dream cars, dream kitchens, dream houses" in which mass consumption was promoted as a social and economic necessity.

9

11. Charles & Ray Eames, *ESU 400 (Eames Storage Units)* for Herman Miller, 1950
12. Charles & Ray Eames, *PAW* swivel chair for Herman Miller, 1950

Das schöne Heim und der »amerikanische Traum«

Nach den Entbehrungen des Krieges waren die fünfziger Jahre eine Zeit der Erneuerung und des internationalen Optimismus, mit der eine noch nie dagewesene Konsumwelle einsetzte. In den westlichen Ländern lösten Frieden und Freiheit die gewalttätigen Auseinandersetzungen der vorangegangenen Jahrzehnte ab. Mit enormen Anstrengungen wurde versucht, die sozialen, politischen, wirtschaftlichen und materiellen Grundlagen in der Welt zu stabilisieren und zu verbessern.

In den dekorativen Künsten nivellierten sich die noch vor dem Zweiten Weltkrieg so unterschiedlichen nationalen Positionen zu einem beinahe »konstruktiven Pazifismus«, in dem sich Universalismus und Qualitätsbewusstsein als maßgebende Werte durchsetzten. Architektur und Design profitierten von neuen Materialien und Konstruktionsmethoden aus der Kriegsforschung. Unter den neuen Materialien bestimmten besonders Kunststofflaminate, Fiberglas und Latexschaum den »Look« der fünfziger Jahre. Designer ließen sich aus vielen unterschiedlichen Quellen inspirieren – etwa der Molekularchemie und Nuklearphysik, von Science Fiction, afrikanischer Kunst und den abstrakten Skulpturen zeitgenössischer Künstler wie Alexander Calder und Hans Arp. Die spitzen, kantigen Formen der frühen fünfziger Jahre wurden später von mehr organischen und biomorphen Formen abgelöst.

In den frühen fünfziger Jahren ließen die USA die allgemeine Hoffnungslosigkeit und Unsicherheit der Großen

Depression hinter sich und brachen in eine Zeit scheinbar grenzenlosen Überflusses auf, die von den Bedürfnissen einer neuen Konsumkultur getragen wurde. Der ungeheure Wohlstand der Metropolen überschattete die noch immer erhebliche Armut in den ländlichen Gebieten und unter Immigranten und ethnischen Minderheiten. Gemeinsam versuchten Designer und Hersteller, die Gier der Konsumenten nach stromlinienförmigen und zukunftsorientierten Produkten, die den »amerikanischen Traum« repräsentierten, zu stimulieren. Diese Traumobjekte verkörperten das genaue Gegenteil der Kultur der Improvisation und Sparsamkeit, welche die dreißiger und vierziger Jahre charakterisiert hatte, denn sie hatten eine sogenannten »beabsichtigte Veralterung des Modernen« eingebaut, die den Konsum steigern und dadurch Produktivität und Wirtschaftswachstum sichern sollte. In den Vereinigten Staaten träumten die Menschen von einem sicheren Job (vorzugsweise in der Großindustrie), einem eigenen Haus in einem sauberen Vorort, einer großen Familie, einem großen Auto und einem Heer arbeitserleichternder Haushaltsgeräte. Das Haus stand im Zentrum des »American Dream«, und die neue Generation von »Hausfrauen« und Konsumenten wurde zur Zielscheibe der erbarmungslosen Vermarktungsstrategien von Industrie und Handel.

In Europa überwanden Länder wie z. B. Großbritannien und Italien das Elend der Nachkriegszeit mit gesundem Menschenverstand und einer geradezu atemberaubenden Kreativität. Wie in den USA hatte das Heim auch in Europa eine zentrale Funktion als Zufluchtsstätte vor einer Welt, die zunehmend vom schnellen technischen Fortschritt bestimmt war – ein Ort, an dem man die während des Kalten Krieges sehr reale Bedrohung durch einen atomaren Krieg vergessen konnte. In Großbritannien wurden für mehr als 350 Schulen Modellwohnungen zur Verfügung gestellt, in denen eine neue Generation von Hausfrauen in der Kunst der »Hauswirtschaft und Wohnungsgestaltung« unterrichtet wurde. In den frühen fünfziger Jahren war Bauen in Großbritannien noch immer durch frustrierende Baubestimmungen und -restriktionen eingeschränkt. Fertigbauweise, der Schlüssel zu verbilligtem Wohnungsbau, existierte zwar in der Theorie, war aber noch nicht überall in der Praxis verwirklicht. Erst in der zweiten Hälfte der fünfziger Jahre setzte auch in Europa ein Bauboom ein, der in den USA schon längst stattgefunden hatte. Die für die

12

neuen Wohnungen benötigten Einrichtungen leiteten eine Wiederbelebung in den dekorativen Künsten ein, die durch technisches Experimentieren gekennzeichnet war. Insbesondere Designer von Glas und Keramik experimentierten mit den neuesten Forschungen der Metallurgie, um zu expressiveren Farben und Formen vorzustoßen. Textildesigner begannen, neue synthetische Materialien in ihre Muster zu integrieren, und Goldschmiede, besonders dänische, schufen bahnbrechende organisch fließende Formen.

Neues Wohnen und neue Lebensstile

Auf beiden Seiten des Atlantiks profitierten besonders die unteren Mittelschichten von dem Aufschwung im Wohnungsbau. Privater Hausbesitz nahm zu und war nun nicht mehr nur ein Privileg der Reichen. In den USA, Europa und besonders in den skandinavischen Ländern wurden in der Nachkriegszeit staatliche Wohnungsbauprogramme entwickelt und das Recht auf eine Behausung zu einem fundamentalen Grundrecht des Menschen erhoben. In Europa hatten die Bomben während des Krieges Städte und Slums zerstört, und auf den Trümmern waren mit staat-

lichen Mitteln finanzierte, neue preiswerte Wohnsiedlungen entstanden. Durch die Anwendung von Konstruktionsmethoden mit seriengefertigten industriellen Baukomponenten setzten sich in den Städten allmählich auch mehrstöckige Wohntürme – ursprünglich in Schweden entwickelt – überall durch. Es war also kein Zufall, dass sich der staatliche Wohnungsbau am stärksten in den Industriestaaten entwickelte.

Die Einrichtung der neuen Wohnungen, die weniger Wohnfläche hatten, erforderte eine bessere Planung und führte zu neuen Lebensstilen, für die zweckmäßige Möbelformen – aus Kastenelementen zusammengesetzte Sitzgelegenheiten, Raumteiler, Schrankwände und Sofabetten – ebenso typisch waren wie neue Grundrissgestaltungen für offenere Wohnformen oder Zwischenstockwerke. Nicht alle Länder assimilierten den neuen Modernismus mit gleicher Begeisterung. Insbesondere Frankreich schwankte lange zwischen dem Alten und dem Neuen. Nach und nach setzte sich aber die moderne Ästhetik gegen die sogenannten »Stilmöbel« durch, und um die Jahrhundertmitte wurde dieser »zeitgenössische« Look als internationaler Stil überall akzeptiert. Massenproduktion und Massendistribution hatten das ihre getan und den »zeitgenössischen Möbeln« über sinkende Preise zum endgültigen Durchbruch verholfen.

Zeitschriften wie die *Decorative Art* Jahrbücher, die als Befürworter von materialgerechter Verarbeitung sowie von natürlichen Mustern und Texturen in der Architektur und zukunftsweisenden Konzepten flexibler, heller und farbiger Innenraumgestaltungen eingetreten waren, trugen wesentlich zu einer breiten Akzeptanz moderner Wohnformen und Raumausstattungen bei. Die zahlreichen neuen Wohnzeitschriften und Do-It-Yourself-Bücher, die Möbelmessen und -ausstellungen, allen voran die jährlich stattfindende und äusserst populäre »Ideal Home Exhibition« in London, die ein »Modellhaus« mit drei Schlafräumen vorstellte, bewirkten, dass sich Sensibilität und Geschmack änderten. Auch staatliche Institutionen wie das Council of Industrial Design und die Design & Industries Association kämpften unermüdlich für zeitgenössisches Formempfinden in Großbritannien, und in den USA organisierte das Museum of Modern Art in New York schon seit 1950 Ausstellungen zu dem Thema »gutes Design«.

13

14. Poul Henningsen, *PH6* lamp for Louis Poulsen, probably early 1950s
(contemporary reissue based on earlier unrealized design)
15. Verner Panton, *Cone* chairs for Plus-Linje, 1958
16. Nils Landberg, *Tulpan (Tulip)* glasses for Orrefors, 1956
17. Erwin & Estelle Laverne, *Champagne* chair for Laverne International, 1957

Der zeitgenössische Stil

Ironischerweise war der ursprünglich von einer fortschrittlichen Minderheit von Designkritikern und Museumskuratoren begonnene Kreuzzug für »gutes Design« so erfolgreich, daß es als stilistischer Trend immer populärer wurde. Die allgemeine Akzeptanz des »zeitgenössischen Stils« – oder »New Look«, wie ihn Christian Dior schon 1947 genannt hatte – führte dazu, daß Designer und Hersteller sich mehr auf die Suche nach Novitäten und Schnickschnack als auf funktionale Designlösungen spezialisierten; etwa in dem sie weiße Möbel mit Knöpfen und Scheiben verzierten, die absolut keine praktische Funktion hatten. In Reaktion auf diese alarmierende Wende wurde in Großbritannien 1957 von der Consumer's Association zum Schutz der Verbraucher die Zeitschrift *Which?* als Informationsorgan zum Qualitätsvergleich von Gebrauchswaren ins Leben gerufen. Aber das hemmungslose Konsumverhalten der Verbraucher blieb davon unberührt und bereitete der Pop-Kultur der folgenden Jahrzehnte einen fruchtbaren Boden.

Obwohl man die fünfziger Jahre kaum als eine Zeit unbegrenzter Freizügigkeit bezeichnen kann, wurden damals schon die Weichen für das spätere anti-autoritäre Verhalten gestellt – vom Rock'n'Roll eines Elvis Presley und rebellierenden Anti-Helden, verkörpert durch James Dean und Marlon Brando, bis zum Abstrakten Expressionismus und der Gründung antinuklearer Bewegungen. Fernsehen und Flugreisen öffneten neue Horizonte und Satelliten leiteten schließlich das Zeitalter globaler Kommunikation ein. Der unübertroffene Überfluss dieses Jahrzehnts, den der ehemalige Premierminister Harold MacMillan treffend mit den Worten »wir hatten es nie so gut« charakterisierte, resultierte am Ende des Jahrzehnts in einem allgemein höheren Lebensstandard. Die fünfziger Jahre waren die Ära der »Traumautos, Traumküchen, Traumhäuser«, in der Massenkonsum zu einer sozialen und wirtschaftlichen Notwendigkeit wurde.

14

15

INTRODUCTION
LES ANNÉES 50

18. Unknown designer, Leather & Walnut chairs for Malatesta & Mason, c. 1950
19. Piero Fornasetti, Canisters for Fornasetti, c. 1955
20. Arne Jacobsen, AJ (Visor) floor lamp for Louis Poulsen, c. 1956

Monter son ménage avec le rêve américain

Les années 50 correspondirent à une période de renouveau et d'optimisme, l'austérité de l'après-guerre s'effaçant progressivement devant un essor de la consommation sans précédent. En Occident, le tumulte des décennies antérieures céda la place à la paix et à la liberté, tandis qu'on dépensait une énergie considérable à faire du monde un endroit plus vivable socialement, politiquement, économiquement et matériellement. Dans le domaine des arts décoratifs, les caractéristiques nationales, très marquées avant la Seconde Guerre mondiale, furent pratiquement annihilées par le « pacifisme constructif » dans sa quête universaliste de la qualité. L'architecture et le design bénéficièrent des nouvelles applications développées par la recherche militaire, des données anthropométriques ainsi que des matériaux et méthodes de construction de pointe. Les nouvelles matières telles que les plastiques laminés, la fibre de verre et la mousse de latex conditionnèrent le look des années 50. Les designers puisaient leur inspiration dans des sources aussi diverses que la chimie moléculaire, la physique nucléaire, la science-fiction, l'art africain ou la sculpture abstraite contemporaine telle que la pratiquaient des artistes comme Alexander Calder ou Hans Arp. Les formes angulaires et hérissées du début de la décennie cédèrent peu à peu le pas à des silhouettes plus organiques et biomorphiques.

Au début des années 50, l'Amérique s'était enfin débarrassée de l'atmosphère d'angoisse et d'insécurité associée à la Grande Dépression et entamait une période d'apparente abondance qu'alimentait la nouvelle culture du consumérisme. Toutefois, la prospérité des riches métropoles cachait la misère qui affligeait encore de nombreuses communautés rurales ainsi que les populations d'immigrants et les minorités ethniques. Les designers et les fabricants entretenaient les aspirations grandissantes des consommateurs en produisant des objets aux lignes épurées et tournés vers l'avenir qui incarnaient le « rêve américain ». Ces objets de désir étaient l'antithèse même de la mentalité de « débrouille et bricolage » des années 30 et 40. Ils étaient souvent conçus de sorte à devenir rapidement obsolètes afin de pousser à la consommation et, donc, d'entretenir la productivité et la prospérité. Aux Etats-Unis, la grande majorité des gens aspirait à un emploi stable (de préférence dans une grande entreprise), à une maison dans une banlieue bien entretenue, à une famille nombreuse, à une grosse voiture et à tout un éventail d'appareils mé-

19

20

nagers limitant les corvées domestiques. La maison devint le centre même du « rêve américain », et les industriels ciblaient sans merci cette nouvelle génération de ménages et de consommateurs.

Dans des pays européens tels que la Grande-Bretagne et l'Italie, l'austérité d'après-guerre fut surmontée par un savoir-faire reposant sur le bon sens et par une créativité époustouflante. Comme en Amérique, la maison occupa un rôle particulièrement important tout au long des années 50. Elle constituait un refuge où l'on se sentait à l'abri d'un monde où les technologies progressaient rapidement et où l'on pouvait oublier la menace bien réelle d'une guerre nucléaire. En Grande-Bretagne, plus de 350 écoles furent équipées d'appartements modèles où l'on enseignait comment tenir sa maison à une nouvelle génération de futures femmes d'intérieur. Cependant, au début des années 50, le secteur du bâtiment, surtout en Grande-Bretagne, était encore soumis à des régulations et des restrictions frustrantes. Le préfabriqué (la solution pour un logement bon marché) existait plus en théorie qu'en pratique. Il fallut attendre le milieu de la décennie pour que les Européens commencent à connaître le grand essor de l'immobilier qui s'était déjà produit aux Etats-Unis. Tous ces nouveaux logements nécessitaient de nouveaux ameublements, ce qui suscita un regain des arts décoratifs caractérisé par l'expérimentation technique. Les créateurs travaillant dans le domaine de la verrerie et de la céramique se tournèrent vers les récentes recherches en métallurgie pour façonner des objets plus colorés et plus expressifs. Les stylistes du textile intégrèrent de nouvelles matières synthétiques à leurs tissus. Les orfèvres, notamment au Danemark, inventèrent des formes organiques sensuelles révolutionnaires.

Nouveaux logements, nouveaux modes de vie

Des deux côtés de l'Atlantique, la petite bourgeoisie bénéficia de la construction à grande échelle de petites maisons. Devenir propriétaire de son logement n'était plus l'apanage des riches. En Amérique, en Europe et en Scandinavie, où l'on avait instauré des programmes de logements d'après-guerre, l'accession à la propriété fut bientôt considérée comme un droit fondamental. En Europe, les bombardements avaient détruit de nombreux quartiers insalubres. Des cendres de ces derniers surgirent de nouveaux logements bon marché, subventionnés par l'Etat, et mettant l'accent sur l'urbanisation des quartiers. Les tours d'habitation, qui firent d'abord leur apparition en Suède, devinrent rapidement populaires dans les autres pays tandis que les méthodes de construction reposaient de plus en plus sur des composants fabriqués industriellement. Naturellement, les plus grandes avancées dans le domaine des habitations financées par le secteur public se produisirent dans les pays les plus industrialisés.

21

22

Ces nouveaux logements plus petits nécessitaient une meilleure organisation de l'espace. Cela entraîna l'apparition de nouveaux modes de vie qui requéraient de nouveaux types de meubles tels que des sièges modulaires, des cloisons amovibles, des placards encastrés, des canapés convertibles, ainsi que de nouveaux plans, tels que des espaces ouverts ou sur plusieurs niveaux. Ce modernisme ne fut pas accueilli partout avec la même ferveur. La France, notamment, resta déchirée entre le moderne et l'ancien. Toutefois, l'esthétique moderne gagna progressivement du terrain sur ce qu'on appelait le « complexe d'époque » et, vers le milieu du siècle, le « style contemporain » était devenu un style international très répandu et immédiatement reconnaissable. En faisant baisser les prix des produits, la production et la distribution de masse lui avaient permis de « s'imposer ».

Les magazines, tels que les annuaires de *Decorative Art*, qui prônaient les finitions naturelles, les motifs et la structure en architecture, ainsi que la lumière, la flexibilité et la couleur dans la décoration d'intérieur, étaient en partie responsables de l'acceptation générale d'un langage moderne en matière d'ameublement. Les nouveaux magazines qui proposaient des thèmes de la vie domestique et des idées à réaliser soi-même ont aussi contribué au changement des perceptions et des goûts. C'est aussi le cas des salons et expositions, comme par exemple la très populaire Ideal Home Exhibition annuelle de Londres, qui exposa une maison « idéale » à trois chambres. Les organisations financées par le gouvernement, telles que le Council of Industrial Design et la Design & Industries Association, ne cessaient de préconiser le design moderne en Grande-Bretagne. Pendant ce temps, aux Etats-Unis, le Musée d'Art Moderne de New York organisait des expositions de « bon design » dès 1950.

Le style contemporain

Ironiquement, la croisade lancée par la minorité progressiste des critiques de design et des conservateurs de musée fut dépassée par son succès : le design moderne explosa et devint une tendance stylistique populaire. L'ascendance du style « contemporain », ou du « New Look » comme Christian Dior l'avait déjà baptisé dès 1947, incita certains designers et fabricants à rechercher la nouveauté et l'anecdotique à tout prix plutôt que des solutions pratiques, au point de gros appareils électroménagers étaient parfois embellis de poignées ou de cadrans qui ne servaient strictement à rien. Alarmée par cette nouvelle tournure, l'Association Britannique de Consommateurs lança en 1957 le magazine *Which ?* pour informer les lecteurs sur la qualité relative des produits de consommation. Néanmoins, le consumérisme galopant des années 50 continua sur sa lancée, préparant le terrain à la culture pop de la décennie à venir.

Bien que l'on ne puisse vraiment considérer les années 50 comme une décennie permissive, elles semèrent les graines de la contestation de l'ordre établi, du rock and roll d'Elvis Presley et des antihéros rebelles incarnés par James Dean et Marlon Brando, à l'expressionnisme abstrait et à la formation de la C. N. D. (Campagne pour le Désarmement Nucléaire). La télévision et les transports aériens ouvrirent de nouveaux horizons, alors que les premiers satellites annonçaient déjà l'ère de la communication planétaire. La prospérité sans précédent de la décennie, parfaitement résumée par la célèbre réplique du Premier ministre britannique Harold MacMillan – « On n'a jamais été aussi riche » –, déboucha sur une hausse significative du niveau de vie. Les années 50 furent l'époque des « voitures de rêve, cuisines de rêve et maisons de rêve », durant laquelle la consommation de masse fut promue au rang de nécessité sociale et économique.

23

houses and apartments | Häuser und Apartments | Maisons et appartements

The house of Mr and Mrs Warren Tremaine, in Santa Barbara, has a structural solidity, deriving from reinforced concrete, and is enriched by the detachment of roof slab from the frontal girders. Each lintel girder has a uniform span of sixteen feet of the continuous lower openings, comprising doors, windows and sliding plate-glass fronts framed in anodized aluminium. Between girders and roof extends a tier of swing-in windows which, when open, form a glass shelf. Continuous fluorescent tube lighting illuminates the ceiling. Ventilation takes place at ceiling height, where it is most effective.

Exterior and interior borderline is obliterated by a system of radiant floor heating extending to outer terraces. Living areas, covered and roofless terraces are combined in one flowing space, extending on the one hand to a roof deck of panoramic view and on the other to an underground gallery of graphic exhibits leading to a plate-glazed pool and play porch equipped with its own cooking facilities.

HOUSE AT SANTA BARBARA

Despite such a conception of the private house, no suggestion of freakishness or novelty has been permitted in its design. Architect: Richard J. Neutra.

OPPOSITE, TOP: Looking from the radiantly heated dining terrace into the living quarters whose sliding glass walls have been pushed aside. All furniture was designed by the architect.

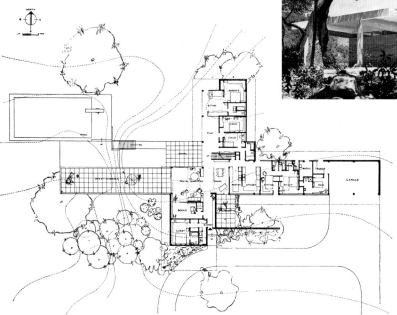

The terrazzo-paved ocean terrace, radiantly heated, extends west of the social quarters to a view of the ocean at its end. (Photos: Julius Shulman).

TOP: The roof slab cantilevers at the end of the house at Santa Barbara, California. ABOVE: A view from the north where old oak trees and rock outcroppings limit the building site. LEFT: The owner's private sitting-room. Note the cutting of the overhang to preserve the tree.

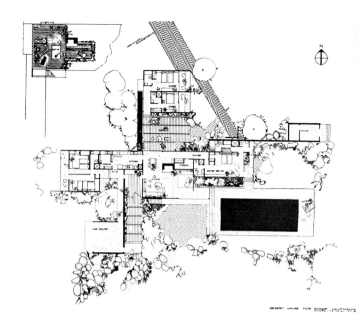

A HOUSE IN THE

COLORADO DESERT

This four-courter house, designed by Richard J. Neutra, has Utah stone masonry walls sandwiched to structural cores to take horizontal and earthquake strains, and is sited to be sheltered from north winds. All exterior walls have mica-glaze Cemelith finish. LEFT: Part of the master suite, showing the wall-hung storage furniture of birch and the continuous curtains

of light canary yellow. OPPOSITE, RIGHT: A view of the outdoor-indoor living-room with its vertical aluminium blinds, protecting against wind, sun and sandstorm when closed. Opened, they allow air movement on hot days and give a view of the mountains beyond. ABOVE: A view in late afternoon, looking towards the master bedroom across the lawn patio.

BELOW, LEFT: The bedroom wing from the swimming pool, and RIGHT: a view from the south over the oasis plantation. Large natural boulders give privacy to the entrance. The garage wall was made without mortar joints in softly coloured stratified Utah stone. (Photos: Julius Shulman).

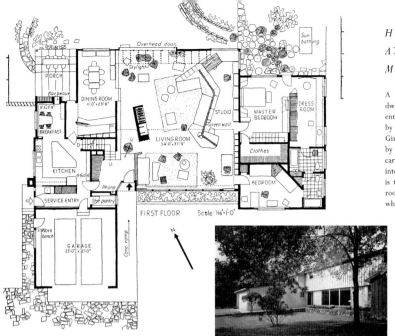

HOUSE AT GROSSE POINTE MICHIGAN

A conversion from two existing dwellings, with the addition of an entirely new section to link them, by the architect-owner, Alexander Girard. Built-in furniture designed by the architect and made by local carpenters forms a basic part of the interior scheme. The main feature is the spacious pine-beamed living-room 20 × 30 ft, shown below, where a curved screen divides the

studio from the living area. The walls are black-stained fir-plywood, with grey concrete floor, cold cathode indirect lighting, natural rugs and dark brown sofas with red and yellow cushions. The natural orange brick fireplace in the same room is seen here. Note the variations in ceiling and the rise to the dining area. A cantilevered staircase (BELOW) in the master-bedroom leads to the children's room above, EXTREME RIGHT: Another view of the master bedroom. The bedspread is orange, the carpet sand-coloured.

ABOVE: A counter with black linoleum top and white enamelled front, standing on pipe legs can be used as a food bar or as a serving surface in the dining-room. Tables in foreground of solid cherry-wood. LEFT: The kitchen with its three-way island table covered with black linoleum, fitted with a maple cutting board and designed for convenience from all angles of working. (Astleford photos).

RIGHT AND BELOW: Two views of a small top storey apartment in Paris furnished with antique and modern pieces, the latter in natural oak and cane. The curtains and bed draperies are straw-coloured chintz patterned in mauve and carmine.

BELOW: Recessed shelving, the beading painted in *tête de nègre*, is a feature in this French lounge. Ivory walls form a background to the rust-coloured curtains and upholstery in *tête de nègre*. (Collaborator: Jacques Levy-Ravier)

THE PARISIAN APARTMENT

BELOW: This French living-room has a red brick fireplace and green coverings to the large settee and chairs. A pleasant splash of colour is given by the orange lacquered base of the floor lamp.

The decorative schemes on these two pages are by Jean Royère (FRANCE).

The residence of Mr and Mrs Charles P. McGaha. LEFT: Looking towards the living room. Exterior finish is redwood siding painted blue. Special planting areas have been retained and framed by split brick and lighted for night effects by wrought iron crook-staff bells. BELOW: A pool-side view of the house and its terrace made of redwood blocks set in cement. Black wrought iron furniture on terrace with cushions and backs covered in red, white and blue striped sail cloth.

WICHITA FALLS — TEXAS

ABOVE: The entrance gate is radio-controlled by walkie-talkie units at the gate and in the house. RIGHT: The St Charles kitchen containing steel cabinets lacquered light blue; Hotpoint garbage disposal and dishwasher; and built-in electric range and oven by Thermador. The floor is blue and white rubber tile.

The daughters' dressing-room furnished in a scheme of green and red lacquer, and a mirrored wall which gives an impression of size. Chairs covered in quilted chintz, one in red, the other in green.

BELOW: The games room with chairs and sofa upholstered in unborn calfskin, and draperies hand-painted with the motif of the Katchina dolls made by the Hopi Indians. Poker table covered with russet leather and fitted with individual drawers for players' poker chips. The free shape rug and ceiling are in strawberry ice-cream colour.

ABOVE: The dining-room has a blue lacquer table with blue plastic top, and the blue lacquer chairs are covered in rose-copper leather. The buffet, also in blue lacquer, has a cork top. The carpet is sea-green. Through the archway is the flower room, with a hand-woven reed screen to the window.

RIGHT: In Mrs McGaha's dressing room the walls are deep aquamarine, the carpet is grey-green, and the split reed screens lacquered red, handwoven with threads of black, white and gold. The dressing table unit is lacquered the same colour as the walls and contains a built-in sewing machine which can be raised to table level. Both chairs are of solid Lucite covered in quilted Italian silk printed in Switzerland with blue, yellow, red and beige predominating. Interiors designed by Paul Laszlo. Executed by Laszlo Inc (USA).

Dr Treweek's redwood house overlooking the lake is one of a pair designed by the same architect whose aim was to merge the house harmoniously into the natural surroundings of eucalyptus trees. CENTRE: A view along the flagstone-paved terrace to the kitchen door. BOTTOM: The living-room, which occupies a

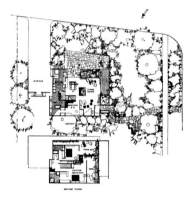

LOS ANGELES, CALIFORNIA

large area of the lower floor, has a free standing fireplace in narrow grey flagstone. Behind it is the dining area. A bay towards the north windows comprises the music area, and contains the piano, radio, gramophone, books and television. BELOW: The built-in dressing table, made of birch, has a mirrored fold-down lid, and is fitted with a brown Formica top on the outside. The wall panelling is of light bleached birch, fitted with mirror on one side. Architect: Richard J. Neutra (USA).

This British Columbian home makes use of the many building timbers available in Canada in its exterior and interior. The wall to the left is of striated plywood yellow-greyed off, with a horizontal spandrel to the studio wall of 1 in. by 6 in. cedar V-joint painted dark grey green. All posts, beams and window frames are white, and the door greyed-off cobalt blue.

The three interiors are all of the same room. The fireplace is of rough split granite boulders in soft colours varying between grey, pink, green and rust, with white cement joints. Wall fitments and panelling of Western birch plywood with white fir framing to the shelving. In the left-hand picture is seen the 'Modernfold door' (grey-green fabric on a concertina steel frame) which leads to the studio.

A view from the fireplace. The wall on the left is covered with burlap glued to rough plywood and painted grey pink, and the door is flush plywood. A mushroom-coloured broadloom carpet covers the plywood floor. Architects: Gardiner & Thornton, MRAIC, ARIBA (CANADA).
(Photo: Graham Warrington)

VANCOUVER,
BRITISH COLUMBIA

Photos below and right: Courtesy of Architectural Review

FLATS AT TWICKENHAM

The exterior of the block of six flats known as 'Box Corner', Twickenham, Middlesex, is of pleasant-looking golden brown brick, with pattern of projecting red brick, and panels of oiled cedar boarding assuming a natural unevenness of colour. The balconies also have cedar balustrades. In general, the paintwork is white with turquoise blue reveals to the main door architrave. Internally, the staircase balustrade between floors is metal painted pale grey with polished mahogany capping, and the brick wall is golden brown, dark stained headers making a formal pattern. The stairs and passage flooring is of blue and pale grey rubber tiles. In each flat the living-room is divided from the balcony by a glazed screen (the upper part clear, the lower translucent) in painted softwood with a shelf unit in polished hardwood. The first floor flat illustrated has contemporary furnishings from Dunns of Bromley. Architects: Eric Lyons FRIBA and G. Paulson Townsend LRIBA (GB)

Mr and Mrs William Perleberg have a large living-room, in their Californian home, divided from the dining-area by handwoven reed screens. It is furnished in soft tones of beige and grey with accents of red and brown. The upholstered pieces are in beige plaid with a brown stripe; the dining chairs and table in bleached walnut. TOP RIGHT: Bill Perleberg Junior's room with built-in television, radio and bookshelves, and striped chintz for the upholstery and draperies. BELOW LEFT: The master bedroom with a raised fireplace of travertine marble and sliding doors below giving a view of the garden. In front of it, a glass-topped table on Lucite base. The quilted bedspread is of rose silk matching the rose carpet, and the sofa is in quilted red and white silk handprinted. BELOW RIGHT: Washbasins, in the dressing-room/bathroom fitted to a centre partition, form an island with access from either side. The ceiling has sun-ray, infra-red and daylight lamps. A further illustration is shown on page 38. House and interiors designed by Paul Laszlo (USA)

A STUDIO HOUSE IN JAPAN

Although this is a new house (and it appears modern enough to Western eyes) it nevertheless follows traditional Japanese principles in domestic architecture; principles which take into account the need for standardized features employed in such a manner as to give variety in unity. It was built for Mr Ryuzaburo Umehara to the designs of Professor Isoya Yoshida. The austerity of the interior appointments may amount to starkness in comparison with Western ideas, but the rooms are not bare. The design, as in all Japanese houses, makes a virtue of economy, giving pleasure in its quiet refinement, clean lines and absence of furniture as well as in its relation to the garden of which it forms a part. The exterior of the house is painted light yellow; the wooden uprights dark brown with Japanese tiling on the roof, and green rock plates forming the terrace. In the studio (ABOVE) the clay wall is dull red, and there are sliding doors which push back to the right-hand wall. The platform in the alcove (LEFT) is lacquered dark brown with pillars of keyaki and vertical wooden uprights lacquered vermilion.

The large living-room in this City apartment is dominated by the two-piece sofa, 13-ft long, designed especially for television viewing, covered in hand-woven white chenille shot with gold. A black lacquered angle table, low coffee table, and a painting by Hans Moller complete the group. Facing the sofa is the television cabinet, its 24-inch screen concealed by slide-in doors. The bookshelves architecturally connect living-room to dining alcove and are in platinum walnut. The armchair is covered in coral fabric. Living-room walls are grey with a purple section to the left of the couch. In the dining alcove, the grey walls again have a purple section to the right of the buffet and coral coverings to the platinum walnut chairs. The wood sculpture by Milton Hebald stands on a black lacquer pedestal flanked by hand-printed curtains on grey and silver ground by Donelda Fazakas. The two small illustrations (RIGHT) show the bleached mahogany chests in the bedroom, the centre drawer section of which is fitted for jewellery and similar items; and a close-up view of the black lacquered table seen in the top illustration with its lamp on a sculptured wood base and reed shade designed and made by James L. McCreery. In the master bedroom the bedhead and bedspread are of light blue satin, the former framed in hand-sculptured bleached mahogany, the same wood being used for the side tables and chests. On this floor is a gold-coloured carpet, blue, beige and gold being repeated in the sheer gauze draperies and grass cloth on the walls. Designers and makers: Wor-De-Klee Inc. (USA)

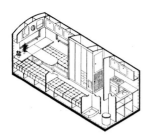

bunk converted
into table

A HOUSE ON WHEELS

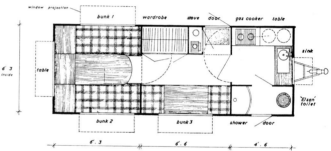

window projection · bunk 1 · wardrobe · stove · door · gas cooker · table

6' 3" inside

table

6' 3" — 6' 6" — 4' 6"

bunk 2 · bunk 3 · shower · door

sink · 'Elson' toilet

This trailer was designed as a home for two, with a third bunk when required. Its over-all size was limited by regulations and weight for towing by a 20-h.p. car: the kitchen was placed forward because its heavier equipment would make the trailer tail-heavy if placed at the rear. Outside walls painted flat pale grey, roof silver painted, window frames bright chromium with green and white sunblinds, and red and white curtains. Carpet is pale grey, with yellow, green and white bunk covers over rubber mattresses. Kitchen has white walls and cupboards, grey linoleum, zinc and teak table tops. Light either from the 12-volt car battery or from the butane-gas cylinders used for cooking and heating.
Architects: Tayler & Green FFRIBA Makers: Bertram Hutchings Caravans Ltd (GB)

A HOUSE IN NORFOLK

'Värmland', in the East Anglian city of Norwich, replaces a bomb-destroyed house. Built of rustic Fletton bricks sprayed with *Snowcem*, it embraces both structurally and in the interior details many Scandinavian features, from the corner fireplace in the living-room to the Swedish rugs and Danish light fittings. The front porch has a glass brick screen, a circular window, and the name of the house in a coloured coat-of-arms plaque. The rear elevation shows another glass brick screen on the first floor, and the sun terraces. Internally, the entrance hall is carpeted in cherry red, the door panel is of acid burnt glass with Swedish handles, and the wallpapers (John Line & Sons Ltd) are blue and white with a star motif. The L-shaped living-dining room has beech parquet flooring with Swedish rugs predominantly blue in colour, the decorations are in grey and geranium red, and the fabrics are blue, white and red. In the kitchen, the cupboards have been recessed over the working surfaces which are faced with Formica: the cabinets have sliding doors of Masonite, white enamel finish. The small illustration shows an Australian walnut cocktail cabinet with built-in Electrolux refrigerator. Designer: Raymond King. Executive architect: Thomas F. Trower FRIBA (GB)

OTHAM, KENT

This house, set on a sloping orchard site of about one acre, and designed for the architect's own use, is of Kentish Rag-stone multicolour bricks and blocks rendered with a pale blue-grey cement: interior walls are white. All large panes of glass are in Insulite double-glazing, and the living-room (*top left*) has full-height glass, the sliding door running on a rubber-covered track. Floors are of solid concrete with embedded wire radiant heating, covered with gunmetal fitted carpet. The contemporary upholstered furniture, by Hille of London and Dunn's of Bromley, is in black, pale yellow and warm grey fabrics. The bedroom scheme is in pale blue with a specially designed upholstery and sycamore bedhead. Another view of the living-room is shown at *lower left*: the shelving and walls are white, with macassar ebony and mahogany fronts to the cupboards. This bookcase, the bedhead, low yew tables and mahogany dining chairs were made to the architect's own designs by F. W. Clifford Ltd. Architect: Brian Peake, FRIBA (GB)

Designing a doctor's house presents special problems since it is desirable that the accommodation necessary for the practice should be separate from the living quarters.

The ground floor in this house—built for Dr and Mrs Oswald-Smith on a site only 40 feet wide—is occupied almost entirely by the doctor's consulting rooms, but includes garage space for two cars. Above is a projecting living-room, facing south. The interior (*top, left*) has an olive-green fitted carpet, white walls and white venetian blinds to a ceiling-height window. It is furnished in natural mahogany with upholstery in a warm grey/beige fabric. The tiled fireplace (*left*) is built into a background wall of grey, white-pointed brick, the extended surround forming a frame for a niche. RIGHT: Natural mahogany stairway with bamboo screen and grey brick wall. *Bottom right:* Dividing the living-room from staircase lobby is a fitted 'sideboard' in natural mahogany with panels of pale blue Warerite and reeded glass; a service hatch is included. The two bedrooms (one of which is illustrated bottom left) are on the top floor, and have fitted cupboards and built-in dressing tables. The exterior (*top, right*) is finished in grey, white-pointed brick with in-filling panels rendered in pale grey cement. Window frames are painted white, the front door pale yellow. Architect: Brian Peake, FRIBA (GB)

Designed by Mr Leslie Gooday, ARIBA, for his own use, this house at Sheen was built to a floor area of only 1,245 square feet within which are accommodated three bedrooms, living room, studio, bathroom, dressing-room, hall, kitchen, utility room and garage. RIGHT: Exterior of Uxbridge flint bricks with 15° pitch copper roof on timber trusses. BELOW: Lounge and raised dining area. The insulated ceiling slopes up from the fireplace to about 12 feet with the dining area ceiling at a lower level. Window wall is of Pirana pine in grooved 4-inch strips. BOTTOM, CENTRE and RIGHT: Corridor dressing-room, equipped with dressing table, wash basin and fitted wardrobe, and brick-walled kitchen with cantilevered table. Furnishings are in *House & Garden* colours and David White-head fabrics (GB) *Courtesy 'The Architect & Building News'. Photos: J. R. D. Heming*

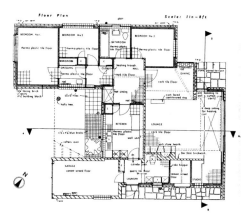

SHEEN, LONDON, SW14

BEVERLY HILLS, CALIF.

Mr Neutra's sound principles of designing a house to the 'biology of the landscape' and to the 'biology of the humans who are here to cast anchor' are embodied in the home illustrated on this page. The problem involved was mainly to fit the house to a very steep hillside and to provide some level outdoor sitting areas. An outdoor patio was one of the stated requirements and a balcony facing west was developed in addition.

The house hugs the hillside and is reached by a gently sloping path ending in a flight of steps up to the wide entrance porch. A trellis on which growing vines are trained affords interest and shade to the entrance. The living-room faces south-west overlooking a canyon on one side and, on the other, opening directly, through wide glass doors which slide apart, on to the spacious patio. This device visually enlarges the living-room space and enables meals to be taken outdoors, if desired, with the minimum of inconvenience. Beyond the patio a terraced garden planted with shrubs and bushes leads the eye up the hillside. At the fireplace end of the room are metal-covered cupboards for wood storage, and a record cabinet and record shelves are ranged under the windows. Architect: Richard J. Neutra, FAIA (USA)

In this Canadian home built for Mr and Mrs L. J. Lefohn, the living-room brick fireplace wall of a novel design is thrown into relief by lights inset in the Luan mahogany-panelled ceiling. Couch and chair, also of Luan mahogany, are upholstered in a grey rough fabric with a light rust geometric design. RIGHT (Top): Dining-room. Walls are light cocoa, ceiling grey; mahogany furniture with bleached oak contrasting surfaces; chair coverings cotton Celanese in a soft yellow shade. CENTRE: Hall table of ¾-inch armourplate glass on drift-wood grey tree stump with flat lacquer finish. Light fitting of spun aluminium on Luan mahogany stem. Coral pink partition wall, grey carpet. BELOW (Right): Recreation room panelled and furnished in bleached Philippine mahogany, upholstery in tan and chartreuse. White tiled floor, streaked beige, with copper dividing strips; draperies in off-tones of floor colours. Tempera mural (*shown below*), painted by the architect, based on Nootka Indian art. The house was designed and furnished by Robert R. McKee, B.Arch, MRAIC. Furniture makers: Segal's Studio, Ridgewood Studios Ltd and the Progressive Manufacturing Co (CANADA)

NEW CANAAN, CONN.

A house in Connecticut planned with an integral continuity between interior and exterior. The bluestone flagged court is repeated in bluestone flooring throughout, sliding windows replace doors; ceilings are natural cypress. An unpainted asbestos cement board facia gives unity to the exterior (*left*). The desk (*centre*) is of painted wood with Marlite sliding panels to bookshelf. Kitchen: Teak counters, other surfaces white. Dining-room: Teak table, foreground wall blue, background yellow. Grey Marlite sliding panels open onto the Living-room with its white-painted brick fireplace against a blue wall. The Travertine-topped table, leather lounge chairs on black frames and grey tweed-covered Knoll couch suggest a masculine atmosphere. House and furniture designed by Marcel Breuer, A I A (USA)

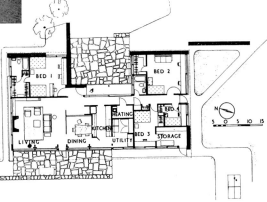

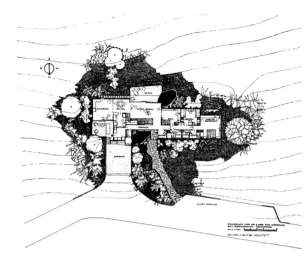

SAN BERNARDINO - CALIFORNIA

This house was designed for Dr and Mrs Max Goodman and their two young sons, and is built on a height overlooking the town towards the south. It occupies not more than 2700 sq. feet, but by planning the living room, den, dining bay and solarium as one visual unit, a sensation of uninterrupted space is created; this is further emphasised by the corrugated light pine ceiling continuing, through glass partitions underneath, onto the roof overhang, where it is reflected in a strategically placed pool. The living-room is carpeted in moss green, curtains are brick. BELOW is the children's playroom and/or solarium, which has a built-in television set fitted with a birch covering door, a birch-panelled wall, Vinylite cork floor covering, and a wall seat upholstered in white plastic. Architect: Richard J. Neutra, FAIA (USA)

SANTA FE - NEW MEXICO

This house was remodelled, restored and added to by the designer to serve as a home for his family, as an office and as a workshop. Previously it was of three different periods, the oldest dating back over two hundred years. It is a good example of a successful partnership between old and new styles: for instance, the twentieth-century fibre glass plastic chairs, by Charles Eames, do not look at all incongruous in a setting of adobe and pumice white-plastered walls hung with folk carvings, and native red stone flooring. The pine dining table is suspended from ceiling and floor by steel and nylon cables. Opposite it is a mural (*shown bottom*) executed by the architect in brilliant casein colours. The living-room is all white with bright colour accents such as the fireplace seat upholstered in magenta and orange Peruvian wool fabrics. In the kitchen is an impressive perforated masonite pine-framed utensil rack.

Architect: Alexander Girard, AIA (USA)

(Photos: Charles Eames)

The houses illustrated on this and the opposite page are built in the environs of Buenos Aires, and both are designed to give protection against, and to obtain the maximum benefit from, the hot climate of the Argentine. The home of Mr Francisco Hirsch is built of brick, with a wide overhanging roof and a recessed porch and loggia. Each window is fitted with sun blinds which are rolled up under neat white panels when not in use. The chimney and the low garden wall are of Mar del Plata stone; the decorative wrought-iron gate was designed by Mrs. Hirsch.

A winding stairway in shades of green terrazzo leads off the main hall, which has yellow walls and a vaulted roof in blue; background linen draperies are brick red. The sitting-room (*below and far left*) has grey and yellow walls and is furnished in natural peterebi wood, with chairs upholstered in Nile green and yellow linen— the sofa in grey, yellow, and black cotton tweed. The last two colours are repeated in the shades of the adjustable floor lamp beside it. Floor and hearth are in green terrazzo; the latter is framed in black palissander and rests on a dark peterebi base, extended on either side as an ornamental shelf. By the window are two wall cabinets. The first contains *objets d'art*; the second (which forms a continuous unit with the small table below it) is a fitted bar with sliding doors and interior lighting. Furniture and fittings are by Adams SRL, lighting by Ilum, SC. Architect: Federico Wermer (ARGENTINA)

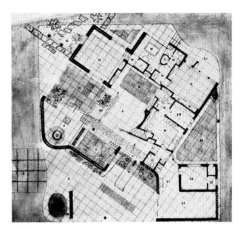

SAN ISIDRO - ARGENTINA

Built in the centre of a 'V' shaped site, the house faces north, (equivalent to a southern aspect in the northern hemisphere). The square plan of the roof and floor gives a parallel frontage to the street, while the main rooms are orientated at an angle of 37° to obtain the greatest value from the sun; co-ordination is achieved by cuttings in the roof line. Exceptionally wide eaves protect the walls from the summer heat. Basically, the floor area, both inside and out, consists of 3 × 3 foot squares of polished terrazzo, serving as a pattern for the distribution of the walls, while oak, marble, linoleum and other materials emphasise the special character of individual areas.

At left is the central patio which has a sliding roof of double iron plate with sun shutters opening in any direction. The main living-room, with slatted cedarwood wall, lies immediately behind it. Exterior walls are in a variety of finishes, and a glass mosaic by the painter Carybé decorates the entrance. BELOW, *left to right*: Entrance bridge spanning an ornamental fish pond; bedroom window wall with fitted mosquito frames; corner of the living-room—fireplace in cement and refracted brick. Designed by architect Martin Eisler for Mr. Alfred Silbermann (ARGENTINA)

SYDENHAM - LONDON, S.E.26

This five-bedroom house was designed by the architect for his own use. It is situated off a quiet road in one of the London suburbs, and has an enclosed garden with fruit trees. Living and sleeping accommodation are in the two-storey block, and a hall, cloakroom and study in the single storey, which runs at right angles to the former with a double garage at the end. Excluding the garage, the total area occupied is 1500 square feet. The two-storey block has 11-inch cavity walls of buff facing brick, and the single storey is in 9-inch brickwork, colour washed in blue and in white.

On the ground floor is a combined living-dining room with french windows opening onto paved terraces on the south side. The kitchen opens directly off the dining recess and has direct access to it via a hatch inset in a wood-panelled wall. Other walls are in fairfaced brickwork or are distempered in light colours, the surface area being broken up with small niches. Flooring is concrete on hardcore finished with Marley tiles. The lower flight of the staircase, which rises directly from the tiled hearth, has precast reinforced concrete treads cantilevered from the adjoining wall with a metal handrail painted white; the upper flight is in polished hardwood. Heating is provided by a Weatherfoil unit housed beneath the stairs; supplementary warmth in the living area is radiated from a new type of pressed metal free-standing open fire, designed in America, which is seen in the illustration at right. Architect: Edward D. Mills, FRIBA (GB) *(Courtesy: The Architect)* *(Photos: Colin Westwood)*

An eighty-year old house in Amsterdam was converted and furnished by the designer for his own use. *Above* is the kitchen-dining area which, together with lounge-study and hall, occupies the ground floor. The whole space is planned as one unit with flooring of warm brown Java teak; shelving or cabinets and ceiling colour change define the limits of each area. Here, for instance, a black plastic-topped storage cabinet, supporting a white-painted shelf fitment with sliding glass panels, divides off the kitchen. The doors facing the kitchen are painted red and white, and on the dining side are three sliding panels giving easy access to the interior. The dining table top of Silesian marble rests on black-enamelled steel legs. Chair frames are in grey-enamelled steel, with washable plastic upholstery in a darker tone.

In the lounge the ceiling height fireplace of Calacatta marble flanked by grey painted walls, rises from a black Belgian stone hearth. Upholstery is in dark brown and in blue; draperies are yellow *Velours d'Utrecht*, carpet black. Dividing off the hall is a cabinet with black and white sliding glass doors on which stands a sculpture *The Political Prisoner* by Ben Guntenaar. Knock-down adjustable bookshelves on white-enamelled steel frames divide lounge from study, and include a built-in radio.

The kitchen has three stainless steel sinks, above which is a storage unit with glass drawers and glass-fronted cupboards. All gas, electricity and water piping is hidden behind yellow and white *Eternit* enamelled panels which are screwed onto a removable framework. A powerful ventilator removes all cooking odours. Architect: J. Penraat, GKF, KIO (HOLLAND)

The trend which divides interiors into areas rather than rooms, and therefore tends to dispense with any particular division, is often thought to be unsuitable to cold or variable climates. In fact it is a trend which is growing throughout the world and is found in high latitudes as well as those in equatorial zones. It would appear that a low density of population, rather than an amenable climate, induces a favourable attitude toward open plan housing and intelligent methods of heating.

It is difficult to see the connection between the partitioning plan of a house and the number of people living within a given area of territory, although the external proportions and number of floors will obviously be influenced by population density. Nevertheless, countries such as Canada, the United States, South America, the Scandinavian group, Australia—all with comparatively widely dispersed populations—have given a lead in the design of houses in which the internal volume is utilised to the utmost, opened out and kept warm instead of being closed off into chilly rectangular boxes.

In densely populated countries like Britain, where little plots of land are jealously fenced off against neighbours, the idea of seclusion invades, unnecessarily, the interior of the house itself and imposes its own very severe restrictions on liberal interior design. Such a way of thinking is usually supported by localised and inadequate heating arrangements, which make the small room, with all its inconveniences, the only possible way to keep warm in winter.

In the review of houses which follows, the examples from larger countries, it will be noticed, reveal a habitually freer and more open design, an appreciation of the æsthetic values of building materials and textures, and a greater awareness of the physical proportions and structural surfaces of the house itself.

VANCOUVER – CANADA

In Canada timber is a readily available and widely used building material: it is also very well suited to the climatic conditions of the country. Another great advantage is that Canadian cedar, used in its natural state, makes a perfectly satisfactory wall finish; thus a considerable saving can automatically be effected by its use.

The house illustrated here is a low cost one. To keep his structure economical and easy to build, the architect used post-and-beam construction and building materials cut to standard sizes. The main framework is of posts spaced at 4-foot intervals. Beams connect the tops of the posts and support the roof planks, which are extended to form a wide protective overhang.

The whole of the living area is planned as a single unit. A semi-transparent framed screen—somewhat reminiscent of Japanese sliding screens—divides off the dining end. It stands clear of the floor and thus does not destroy the unity of the interior, which is furnished in an alternating scheme of light and dark finishes. Architect: A. King, MRAIC (CANADA)

An artesian borehole, a beautiful view over distant hills, indigenous trees, and a river with a series of dams are the setting for this house, situated in a lovely valley about 10½ miles west of Pretoria

It was built by the architect for his own use and is christened 'Hakahana', meaning 'quick', because he and his wife had to act speedily to get a roof over their heads and to establish a farm. The rear block—a tubular steel structure with non-loadbearing walls—was completed within a month, and was their temporary home: it now houses guestrooms, studio/games room, and garage.

In designing the main house, the readily available

(continued below)

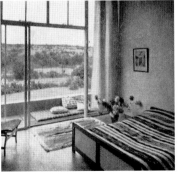

water supply played an important part— 'we wanted to see it all the time, to hear it running'. This desire materialised into a swimming pool at two levels abutting directly onto the living room, which has a picture window at water level. This creates a sense of coolness in summer; in winter the concrete-hooded fireplace and slate walls retain the heat and keep the room cosy. Opposite is a bar with steps leading up to the dining room. The bedrooms, raised high above ground level, jut out from the house and command a magnificent view

Exterior walls are plastered grey; a mural by a native woman of the Mapoch tribe decorates one wall. Architect: H. W. E. Stauch, MIA (SOUTH AFRICA)

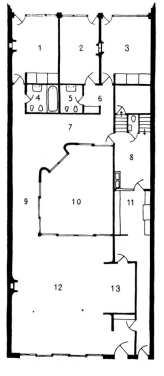

MAR DEL PLATA – ARGENTINA

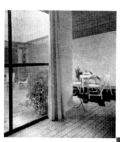

This is a seaside home in a fashionable summer resort on the shores of the Atlantic. It is built on a long, narrow plot, with a garden at one end, and a central patio—glass-walled on three sides (*No. 10 on plan*). A gallery (9) links the living-room (12/13) with the library (7) and bedrooms (1/2/3); the kitchen and service quarters (11/8) lie behind the patio.

The house is built of local grey stone and red brick. The front entrance (*top left*) gives direct access to the large living-dining room, which is paved in red brick and has a cedarwood ceiling. A wide window, framed within lemon curtains, has sliding panels opening onto a small terrace, and another, opposite, leads onto the patio. The living area is furnished in black wrought iron, with sofas upholstered in a natural handwoven fabric, armchairs in black leather; the floor rug is a black cowhide.

The use of local stone for the dining recess (other walls chalk white) gives it a separate individuality, further emphasised by the lower level unstained wooden ceiling. Dining table and chairs are veneered mahogany.

At left is a corner of the gallery and (*below*) one of the bedrooms in a cool green-and-white colour scheme; the bedhead unit is in walnut. All three bedrooms have direct access to the garden. Architect: Walter Loos (ARGENTINA)

ST. NAZAIRE - FRANCE

Illustrated on this page is a country home on the coast of Brittany. The garden looks down on to the estuary of the Loire and commands a fine view across the open water and out to sea. The house itself—a long, low-built structure with a tiled sloping roof and gable windows to the upper floor—faces this view. French windows give direct access from the living-room to the garden. There is also a summer dining-room, the whole front of which can be thrown open to the garden terrace, and here one can sit on long summer evenings enjoying the constantly changing pattern of the river traffic.

A corner of the living-room is shown at left. The settee and armchair are upholstered in velvet, and the low table in the foreground is in thick plywood with a straw marquetry patterned surface under glass. The dining end of this room is at a slightly higher level and is separated from the main area by a gold-studded black wrought-iron screen, carrying light fittings at varying heights on both sides. (Other details in wrought-iron include the main door grille and flanking lamp posts, and the staircase balustrade.) Dining table and chairs are in light oak with black, grey and yellow plastic covers to chairs.

The summer dining-room is furnished in bleached cane, which makes an effective contrast to the red-tiled floor and walls. The light fittings, two of which are shown flanking the beige-hooded brick fireplace, are also backed by bleached cane mounts.

The bedroom curtains in sky blue, green and violet and door panels of the same fabric are designed by Paule Marrot. All other fittings and furniture are designed by the architect, Jean Royère (FRANCE)

This home, shared by himself and his parents, was planned by a young Australian architect while still at Sydney university. It is built on a steep slope overlooking Botany Bay, and has an open-plan central section, containing living, dining, kitchen and utility areas, with bedrooms and garage in side wings. By this arrangement the living room has the winter sun and, with ceiling-height windows along two sides, commands a magnificent view. On the lower ground level is a self-contained unit used for dancing or games, or as a guest room.

The exterior of the house is white; interior decoration and furnishings (selected by the architect) are in a varied but carefully blended choice of colours; ceilings hardwood, on Oregon pine beams. *Below:* Bookshelves and storage cupboards in the vestibule. *Below Right:* Dining table, backed by film projection screen and loudspeaker disguised as a free-standing cupboard and room divider. Architect: Ross Thorne (AUSTRALIA)

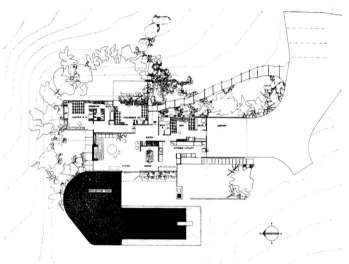

A winding drive up a mountain side leads to this house—the home of a busy country doctor and his wife and two teenage boys. The surrounding landscape is arid and desert-like; not, perhaps, an ideal site, yet possessing its own rugged beauty of outline and individual interest.

The long, low, wood-frame house is planned to 'fit the biology of the landscape'. Exterior walls are plastered, interior birch-panelled, with a redwood ceiling linking living, dining and kitchen areas. One wall of the living room is in glass, and immediately in front of this is a large pool carrying the interior image outside so that house and surroundings become one. It also engenders a cool and restful atmosphere, which is fostered by the choice of grey and charcoal for furnishings and upholstery in the living room. A more colourful note is introduced at the dining end, with blond birch table and chairs, and upholstery and match-stick curtains in light green. A small bar counter (*top left*) linking kitchen and dining corner is used for breakfast and light meals.

Radiant heat coils are embedded in the concrete flooring, and there is a large grey stone fireplace in the living room for additional warmth in winter. Architect: Richard J. Neutra, FAIA (USA)

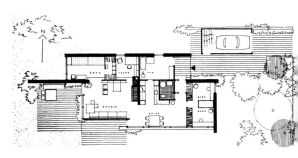

'One of the most difficult tasks facing an architect is the designing and building of his own house', says Mr. Udsen, whose home this is on the outskirts of Copenhagen. And indeed it requires perhaps even more self-discipline than when working to the requirements of others.

The site, about half-an-acre in extent, is a fairly wooded one, and as it was desired to have an informal 'easy to keep' house, an open plan was decided on with the kitchen in direct contact with the whole living area and with the children's room.

The house is built of Bloustrød bricks on a wood frame construction with a weatherboard facing just below the roof line. Flooring is cement painted with Zellaphen and carpeted with fibre runners except in the kitchen. Here a cork surface has been applied, which is comfortable to walk on and easy to keep clean. The ceiling is in natural boarding, doors and cabinet work in oil-finished Oregon pine.

Instead of the closed-in stove, traditional on the Continent, there is a central raised hearth, large enough to take a log fire, with a brick chimney piece extending to the ceiling and containing a built-in niche for wood storage. This feature forms the main interior division, with bookshelves acting as other partition 'walls'. Interior furnishings are simple, with low-slung canvas chairs and couches, and bright-coloured patterned floor rugs.

The parent's bedroom, facing west, leads directly off the living room and is meant on occasion to serve as an extension to it. The outer dividing wall is continued outside, and an indoor climbing plant placed at the corner carries the eye out to the garden. The children's room is placed at the other end of the living room for 'a long distance from the children's to the parents' bedroom is of great advantage when the children are above the baby age'.

Nokatene pipes cemented into the floor provide a comfortable and economic type of heating. Architect: Bertel Udsen, MAA (DENMARK)

This house, by its open plan and built-in furniture, aims at a feeling of space within relatively small area. It stands on a corner site and is bordered on three sides by pines, Swedish conifers and silver birch. Large windows creating 'picture areas' of trees and sky link these surroundings with the interior and ensure that the house forms an integral part of the site.

The hall is paved in heather-colour quarry tiles, the whole living area in wood-blocks, with furniture and fittings in teak. Lighting, placed at strategic points, emphasises individual areas within the open plan, and a visual link between upper and ground floor is provided both internally and externally by the white metal staircase.

Lime-yellow in varying proportions according to the mood required is used as the main colour link. It provides: a welcome in the porch and hall; with orange/red, black and white, a lively dining scheme; a cheerful kitchen, with lime-yellow ceiling and door, white walls, black/white plastic-tiled floor, black/green and white serving hatch, orange/red door to drying cupboard, paintwork of wood units in wisteria and white, and working surfaces in grey/white Formica. In the living room it is used for

KIDDERMINSTER —

WORCESTERSHIRE

window curtains and upholstery, creating a sunny effect against grey/green paintwork and wall areas, and pine-black carpet. Bedrooms and guest room are in quieter tones, but lime-yellow continues as an accent in curtains and wallpaper.

Skirting and other radiators fed by a solid fuel boiler supply an efficient central heating system. For focal interest there is a coal fireplace in the living area at knee height with a quarry tile hearth forming a continuous seat round two walls.

Interior decorations are by the owner, Mrs. Leonard Griffin. Architects: S. N. Cooke & Partners, FF/RIBA (GB)

This house, designed by the architect for his own use, is on Point Piper, a headland overlooking Sydney harbour. Because of space restrictions and the steep slope, it is built on three levels with a seven-foot drop between each, the main living area being centrally placed.

A striking feature is the imaginative use of colour throughout, commencing with the garden facade in white framing, deep turquoise eaves, and black terrazzo-paved terrace. In the dining room the warm tones of the red-upholstered teak furniture make an effective contrast to the white checkerboard storage wall with up-and-down sliding doors; strip panelling above is in Queensland maple. Accenting the pleasure of good food and wine is a background vista of sea and sky reflected in a sunken pool in turquoise/blue/lavender mosaic tiles at the terrace end.

Lounge and dining room interconnect, and the whole area (43½ feet) is carpeted in a soft pinky-grey. Panelling in warm brown maple contrasts with the bleached silvery maple finish of the gallery and recessed bookcase wall; opposite is a 17-foot window wall giving a clear view of the harbour. The bedroom is in muted shades of grey, white and black, highlighted with deep gold bedspread and vivid turquoise ceiling. The bathroom in pink, with grey-patterned Italian tiling. has neat overhead storage shelves. Architect: L. McDonald Downie (AUSTRALIA)

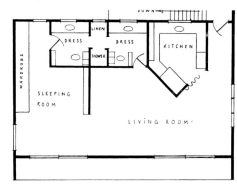

LINEN

DRESS · DRESS · KITCHEN

SHOWER

WARDROBE

SLEEPING ROOM

LIVING ROOM

DOWN

CORONA DEL MAR – CALIFORNIA

'It has always been my theory that architecture and interior design are influenced more by the economic conditions existing in a country than by æsthetic thinking: this house is an outstanding example' states the architect, who planned it primarily as an 'easy-to-run' seashore home for Mr and Mrs Ray Melin, and to accommodate family or other visitors at weekends.

It was therefore designed as two separate self-contained units. The main living area, on the upper level, is reached by an exterior stairway of heavy oak treads housed in logs. It consists virtually of one large room, divided by sliding panels, with the kitchen separated by a screen-curtain.

Interior walls are celadon green, ceiling white-washed board; the linoleum floor covering in a woven pattern of white, grey, and charcoal, is stain and dirt resistant. Upholstery is likewise in soil-resistant vinyl 'breathable Naugahyde'; the bridge table chairs in split cane on an iron frame are a practical design for seashore living. In addition to central heating, the whole area is warmed by an open, pivoting fireplace in baked enamel.

In the kitchen, efficient planning includes hanging refrigerator and freezing units, while air-conditioning removes cooking odours and permits the closely related kitchen-living area. Architect: H. W. Grieve, AID (USA)

PACIFIC COAST –
CALIFORNIA

The design of this house with its feeling of 'expanding into outer space' is the result of careful planning by the architect to overcome the limitations of a somewhat restricted and precipitous site. It had the advantage, however, of a panoramic view reaching southward to the waters and horizon of the Pacific coast. To enjoy this, the main living quarters are raised above ground level; at the same time, a strip of clerestory windows and transparent 'bubble' openings inserted below the level of the cantilevered roof, open up the interior to the wooded mountainside. Complete integration of the house with its surroundings is thus achieved, and the space limitations of the site successfully overcome.

Built on a stainless steel-clad framework, the long, stretched house is reflected in a swimming pool at the south-east end, where, as part of the planning consideration, provision was made for accommodating holiday visits from four married sons of the owners, Mr and Mrs Joseph Staller.

Illustrated on the right is the glass-walled south facade overlooking the wide coastal landscape down to the sea. The sloping two inch-plank insulated roof, supported on laminated beams and timber frame, projects well out to afford protection from the hot

Californian sun. The master bedrooms are situated to the west of the entry stair and ante-room; downstairs are two secondary bedrooms connecting with the pool-porch. A corner of one of the bedrooms with built-in fittings designed by the architect, is shown above, left.

Screened by the central white spur wall, the living area and den, separated by a double fireplace, lie at the eastern end, and open with wide sliding doors and glazed openings onto a spacious balcony terrace over the pool. Several steps up and hillward is the deck of the dining area and breakfast room with a sliding glass partition in between. At the far end sliding glass doors open onto a small courtyard. A deep-texture fitted carpet covers the whole floor area. The fireplace in white Texas shellstone has a pivotal position in the centre of the living space which seems to expand laterally to the outer world. Architect: Richard J. Neutra, FAIA (USA)

LUXURY FLAT – NEW YORK

This open plan setting was entirely redesigned from a conventional 5½-room apartment by an architect who conceives rooms as vistas not contained by the restraints of four walls, but rather as a continuous effect with distant horizons; a play of lights, shapes and shadows; a contrast in colours, textures and surfaces.

At the entrance, a dropped illuminated ceiling, rheostatically controlled for desired lighting effects, establishes a welcoming and serene atmosphere.

Space for musical interests and books, seating for both formal and informal entertainment, a well-stocked bar and 'wine cellar' were some of the requirements to be met. To create the necessary space, bookcases concealing desk and storage space were floated between beams; a fitted bar, interior lit, and accessible to both living and dining areas, built into the entrance hall; and a large area created and redesigned into a modern living room and antique drawing room separated by an illuminated dividing screen. A large geometric pattern handwoven carpet spanning this area brings unity to both rooms. Though furnished in entirely different styles, they have common elements in teak panelling and draperies of handwoven Siamese silk. To save space, radio and record equipment are housed in a floating wall cabinet in oiled-teak designed by the architect, as are the sculptured settee and chair; these are upholstered in Dreyfuss fabrics. Dining furniture is in high-polished dark cherrywood with mosaic inlay. Colour schemes inter-relate, the colours ranging from browns to muted rusts, putty and sand greys, with charcoal and gold accents. Architect: Vladimir Kagan, AID. Executed by Kagan-Dreyfuss Inc. (USA)

HAMPSTEAD - LONDON

THE problems facing an architect are many: not least, as in this case, of 'infiltrating' a house of modern design into an old-established high class residential area. It is built on land formerly used as tennis courts, with only a 60-foot frontage onto a road containing houses of mixed character but which, in the eyes of the local authorities, formed an architectural unit not to be disturbed.

The occupants are a widow and teenage daughter, and in addition to the main living area there are four bedrooms, two bathrooms, and a study. The house is placed at right-angles to the road, so that all rooms (except the study) face south to a rural and well-wooded aspect; there is thus no sense of being overlooked by the adjacent houses. Exterior walls are faced in local red brick and yellow London stocks, with double-glazed Insulite units framed in white-painted timber forming a window wall on the south side.

Illustrated below is the well-chosen colour scheme of the living/

dining/hall area, planned as one visual unit carpeted throughout in gunmetal grey, with the ceiling in Unitex softboard panelling. A semi-solid partition with inset cupboards screens the dining area from the inner hall, and a sliding panel provides privacy from the living room if desired. At the far end is a two-way fitting with direct access to the kitchen, where the equipment is grouped into separate areas for cooking, laundry, and breakfast; the main colour scheme is grey and yellow.

The bedrooms look out to the south-west through ceiling-height windows and are provided with built-in cupboards and dressing table with a large wall mirror. In the bathrooms, windows at ceiling level ensure privacy and good light; the mosaic-tile surround is in blue/white or yellow/white. Heating is by a thermo-statically-controlled system embedded in the floors. Furnishing and interior decoration are by the architect, Brian Peake, F R I B A, M S I A (GB)

AMSTERDAM · HOLLAND

THIS flat is in a new glass-fronted block built on the banks of the Amstel in the heart of old Amsterdam. It is occupied by a leading Dutch furniture designer and interior decorator, and is furnished in a style reflecting his lively appreciation of the aesthetics of industrial design. With a fresh, simple colour scheme, he has created a home in which he can both work and live: to use his own expression 'a liveable sphere.'

The large studio/living room is divided by a metal folding door faced in ivory plastic; the whole room can thus be used when receiving clients, or the studio end can be shut off for working. A dark blue fitted wool carpet covers the entire floor area; this balances the light-toned colour scheme with walls papered in Japanese grasscloth, white paintwork, and door panels in red, olive green, or lemon yellow. The dining group is in teak, the silver-grey upholstered suite in brass and teak combined. Adjoining the limestone fireplace is a brass-edged hanging bookshelf, lined in white plastic with top surface in red.

The kitchen, just glimpsed through the open door, has a black colovinyl floor, blue-tiled walls, white-lacquered cupboards, and working surfaces faced in red Formica.

Architects Bart van Kasteel and J. A. Landman; the flat is furnished and decorated by A. A. Patijn (HOLLAND)

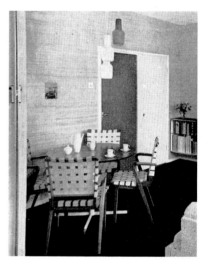

SØLLERØD KRAT - DENMARK

THIS house is one of several designs submitted by various architects for the planned development of a rural area with three-bedroom family houses of simple construction. It is a very successful design, since it is not only visually pleasing from the outside, but is well-planned inside for family living, with the rooms all grouped around and opening into a common dining-hall.

It is built mainly of cement-rendered lightweight concrete, but the whole wall area on the south side surrounding two bedrooms and the long, oblong living room is a glass and steel-frame construction with the window base faced in asbestos cement, painted blue. Forming a visual extension to the living room, is a sheltered walled terrace with a pergola-like timber roof which extends out over the window wall and links the two ends of the house; this is in plain, untreated pine, in contrast with the dark solignum-treated centre roof panelling. Behind the terrace is a carport.

The interior is simply furnished with metal frame furniture designed by Poul Kjærholm, and made by E. Kold Christensen. Both floor and ceiling are boarded in natural pine. Thermo-statically-controlled radiators placed under the windows maintain an even temperature throughout. Architects: Henrik Iversen and Harald Plums (DENMARK)

SHOSHONE - CALIFORNIA

This house, set against the backdrop of a black volcanic mountain which underlines the simple geometric form of its roof line, is situated on the edge of the Nevada desert. The owner is the supervisor of Indio County in the adjoining State of California.

The surroundings are dramatic: nearby lies the famous death valley, nearly 300 feet below sea level, and Mount Whitney, the highest mountain in America, rising to 14,495 feet. The house is designed to 'coalesce' with this landscape: side wings stretch out into the desert, and the 30-foot long living-dining room, together with the adjoining glass-walled sunroom, opens out through sliding doors to a sheltered terrace overlooking a golf course and the mountains beyond. Built-in fittings keep the floor space uncluttered, increasing the sense of continuity with the exterior. Alongside, sharing the view, are three bedrooms, two of which, with built-in shelves and desk, are used as study/bedrooms by the teenage son and daughter of the family. These rooms face east, and are shaded from the heat and glare by the deep overhang of the roof. *Below:* Night view of the interior. In the background is the long verandah entrance, off which is a guest room with its own walled patio. Architect: Richard J. Neutra, FAIA (USA)

HELSINKI - FINLAND

The rural setting of this block of two-storey terraced flats makes it difficult to realise that they lie within a twenty-minute bus journey from the heart of a capital city. They are in fact built on the shores of the Finnish Gulf amidst the beautiful archipelago surrounding Helsinki. Though the block is a modern nickel-steel frame and concrete construction, it yet retains something of a traditional character in the white-painted fascia extending along the top.

There are in all seven three-bedroom flats, divided from one another by a buttress wall, and each having its own private beach. Above is the main living area: this comprises a combined sitting-dining room and kitchen, which can be separated from one another by sliding panels or curtains, with a central built-in wardrobe fitting dividing off the bathroom and dressing room. The central heating system is contained in the floor, and the teak-framed wide window wall has three thicknesses of glass for insulation against the cold in winter.

At ground level, with direct access to a small terrace, are the sauna' (Finnish steam bath), a small dressing room and study, spare room, and garage.

Boldness of construction, a sound feeling for material and an organised simplicity in the interior furnishing, combine to produce an atmosphere of serenity and repose in keeping with the exterior surroundings. Architect: Viljo Rewell (FINLAND)

Basic to the architectural tradition of Japan are the simplicity of form and proportion based on a module of 2:1, and expressed most obviously in the *tatami* (wadded mats).

In this tradition is the home of Ryuzaburo Umehara, a major artist. The architect designed it to provide a setting with a feeling of open space, and reflecting colours which would conjure up the spirit of Kyoto, Peking and Paris—towns of which the artist had special memories.

The fifteen rooms are laid out on a big, simple plan with posts and beams in stained lauan, and bone-white ceilings.

1 Front entrance, with threshold paved in aqueous rock which is continued into the entrance hall and parlour linking the garden to the interior. Exterior walls, stucco; fittings, steel sash; interior walls, beige brush-finish.

2 The salon, opening directly onto the garden, has pale blue brush-finish walls, red-lacquered shelf, and zelkova-boarded floor.

3, 4 Entrance hall and parlour.

5, 6 Intercommunicating ten-mat rooms with sliding screens and a transome grille in cypress, lacquered dark brown. In 6 can be seen the *tokonoma*, a traditional recess for the display of a special work of art. Beside it is the *tokowaki*, also traditional, a built-in cupboard with sliding doors. Architect: Isoya Yoshida, Academy of Arts (JAPAN)

I

2

TOKIO - JAPAN

3

4

5

6

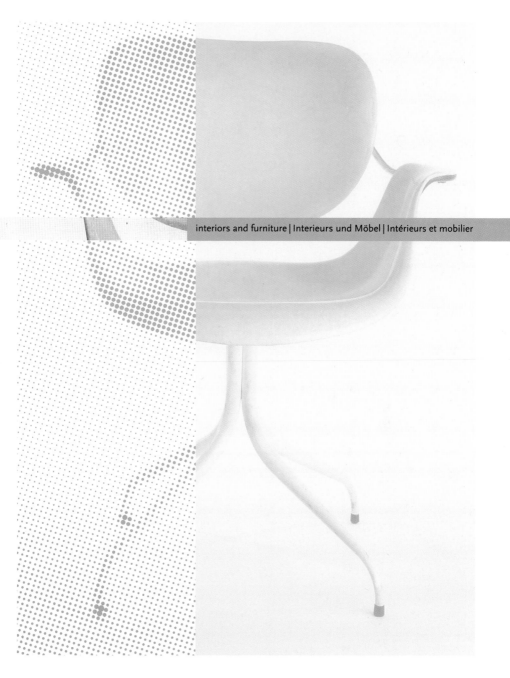

interiors and furniture | Interieurs und Möbel | Intérieurs et mobilier

Furniture in solid oak, with the chair and drop front of the combined bookcase and writing desk covered in calfskin, designed by Catherine Speyer and made by Rena Rosenthal Inc.

Built-in wall cabinet in natural mahogany comprising desk unit, radio and phonograph unit, loudspeaker, and record storage, designed by Felix Augenfeld. The handles are aluminium, as also are the tubular legs, which are fitted with an invisible screw device for adjusting height. Benches and chairs are upholstered in yellow leather, and the floor covered in silver-grey broadloom.

(Photo: Ben Schnall).

iving-room designed by Alexander Girard, showing the natural stone fireplace.
The furniture is in birch against walls of pine.
Sofa upholstered in dark brown fabric, with the armchair in orange.
(Astleford photo).

Mahogany bar cabinet designed by Felix Augenfeld, with
sliding doors, partly covered in white leather and partly of
perforated aluminium sheet. Legs and knobs of aluminium.
Counter top and back wall of travertine. (Photo: Ben Schnall).

Living-room furniture designed by George Nelson and made
by Herman Miller Furniture Company. Black-and-white
rug on the floor by V'Soske Inc.

LEFT: Living-room furniture designed and made by Jens Risom. Silk drapery designed by Alexander Girard. (Polish folk sculpture lent by the Polish Embassy.)

OPPOSITE: Sitting-room in the house of Mrs Herman Kiaer modernized by William Platt, architect, and decorated by Joseph Mullen. The pine panelling makes an unusual background for the modern painting by David Pack but harmonizes pleasantly with the general colour scheme. The recessed bookshelves and console table below were also designed by Joseph Mullen. (Courtesy: *Town and Country*).

Small dining-room in a New York penthouse apartment designed by Felix Augenfeld using Herman Miller furniture combined with custom-made pieces. The storage unit is of primavera with a red lacquer front. On the right are hanging rubber foam cushions covered with red and white print. Multi-coloured print forms the draperies against the black and grey marbleized rubber tile flooring. (Photo: Ben Schnall).

ABOVE—LEFT: *Intruder* wing chair upholstered in fawn tapestry from the 'Helios' range. CENTRE: *Sabu* covered in 'Ormiston' printed linen designed by Marion Mahler and made by Donald Bros Ltd.

RIGHT: *Cavalier* upholstered in rust wool tapestry supplied by Heal's Wholesale and Export Ltd. All three chairs designed by Howard B. Keith, MSIA and made by H. K. Furniture Ltd. Available in both birch or beech with light, medium or dark finish to woodwork. (Photos: John Gay). BELOW: Sitting-room furniture designed by Laurence A. J. Rowley and made by The Rowley Gallery. The curved bookcase is in English sycamore, polished ivory colour: it has drawers on the other side, thus making a desk. Cabinet in the background also in sycamore, designed to accommodate music and gramophone records. Lamp standard of bamboo enriched with gilt leaf.

Occasional chair in Honduras mahogany designed and made by S. A. Lord, of the High Wycombe School of Art. Woodwork finished in natural colour. Covering of wool tapestry made in the School.

Sitting-room at Hyde Park Corner, London, designed by A. V. Pilley, FRIBA, and executed by A. Francis & Co Ltd. Walls and fitment covered with natural raffia cloth, panel wall of untreated acoustic Celotex tiles. Bookshelves painted gloss white and battleship grey. Chair upholstery Indian red against a light cream lambs' wool carpet on the plywood parquet floor. (Photo: John Furley Lewis).

Chair designed by Ernest Race, FSIA, and produced by Ernest Race Ltd. Made on an electrically welded steel rod frame with vertical coil springing and rubberized hair stuffing. The legs are of polished beech, the covering is blue and white cotton tapestry.

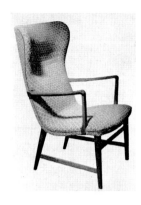

BELOW: Corner of a sitting-room designed by Oskar Riedel.
The upholstered corner fitment can be converted
into an emergency bed by the placing of an additional line of stools.
Cupboard mounted above the stove is
designed to house china and is accessible from both sides.

BELOW: Sitting-room designed by Eduard von der Lippe,
furnished in walnut.
Chimney breast is supported by two iron columns and an iron frame,
the fireplace being faced with Delft tiles on right and left.
(Photo: Courtesy of *Die Kunst und Das Schöne Heim*)

EXTREME LEFT: Lounge chair in natural-coloured
mahogany, covered with grey and green hand-woven
fabric, designed by Harbo Sølvsten and made
by the firm of Harbo Sølvsten.
LEFT CENTRE: Chair with interlaced leather covering,
designed by Axel Larsson and made by Svenska
Möbelfabrikerna.
Curtain, *The Lilies*, designed by Elsa Gullberg and
made by AB Elsa Gullberg Textilier och Inredning.
LEFT: Trolley chair and stool in birch, designed
by Carl Johan Boman and made by O. Y. Boman AB.
Hand-woven covering in green, yellow and white,
designed by Lea Wehmanen-Tennberg.
RIGHT: Chairs in beech,
designed and made by Fritz Hansens Eftfl,
covered with hand-printed 'Graucob' textiles.

Sitting-room designed by Eduard von der Lippe,
showing the fireplace opening framed in brass surrounded by blue and white Delft tiles
topped with red marble. Plain sand-coloured walls contrast with
the multi-coloured carpets and textiles.
(Photo: Courtesy of *Die Kunst und Das Schöne Heim*).

Living-room designed by Bernard Durussel showing a smoking chair, and ash and pipe tray on the left,
a low table for books or magazines (see also illustration below, left),
and a chair designed for restfulness, all in natural oak.
Curtains (above) in blue cotton with white and dark blue stripes designed by Bauret: (below) by René Mauler.
Chairs upholstered in blue wool fabric.
The walls are white, the flooring black tiles covered with a black apeskin rug.
RIGHT: Tubular armature chair with natural heavy oak seat and back designed by Bernard Durussel.

Cupboard in polished ash, with Havana leather doors,
ornamented with gilt studs.
BELOW: Lady's writing table in polished ash and chair
upholstered in pale yellow. All designed by Jean Royère.
Curtain in background is of multicoloured chintz.

Table and chairs in polished ash, designed by Jean Royère.
The table has a green opaline top
and the chairs are covered in green fabric.
Background curtain, plum coloured with a twisted rope design.
BELOW: Sideboard designed by André Renou and Jean-Pierre Genisset
and made by La Crémaillère, mounted on a base of
transparent glass and covered in natural parchment. The handles are of
rope fixed to the drawers with brass studs. Picture by Suzanne Fontan.

Suggestion for a bedroom, furnished in the contemporary manner, by Hugh Casson.
It lays emphasis on the colour value to be derived from suitable choice of a mixture of textiles
for curtains, bedspreads and chair covers in a room of small dimensions.
Reproduced by courtesy of Morton Sundour Fabrics Ltd.

OPPOSITE PAGE: Dwarf wardrobe, dressing table and chair, the latter covered in printed linen,
part of a bedroom suite in waxed walnut, waxed oak or waxed mahogany,
designed by Christopher Heal, MSIA, and made by Heal & Son Ltd.

BELOW, LEFT: Bedroom in the *Corrientes* style by Comte SA
The two-tiered bed and all the furniture is in native South American woods, left in their natural colours.
BELOW, RIGHT: Bedroom furniture designed by Professor Karl Nothhelfer and made by Holig-
Homogenholzwerke. Bed and cupboard designed to fit into a sloping wall section.
Under the window is a combined work-table and chest. (Courtesy: *Die Kunst und Das Schöne Heim*).

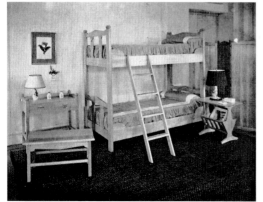

BELOW: Dressing table in sycamore with green hide covered and padded centre designed by C. Addison and made by Thomas Justice & Sons Ltd.

AT BOTTOM: Bedside table in painted wood with wax polished finish designed by Laurence A. J. Rowley and made by The Rowley Gallery Ltd. The triangular shape and ball castors enable the table to be placed in any convenient position. Top section is a useful hinged flap. Electric lamp, made to swivel, is controlled by a miniature press switch. Shade of pleated nylon enclosed at bottom to counteract glare.

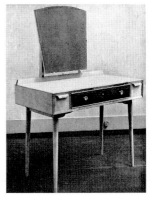

Bedroom scheme in birch and pine designed by Alexander Girard. The bedhead is covered in green grass cloth: the bedspread of bright yellow. Black linoleum top to the writing desk and bedside table. (Astleford photo).

Bedside trolley on wheels, designed by Edward H. Pinto and made by Compactom Ltd. Framework is old gold anodized aluminium inlaid with Santa Vera. Flaps and lower tray of laminated plastic, veneered with buff linette Formica.

1 and 2. *Unad* writing-dressing table in blackbean with English cherrywood front; the chair in beech. *Unad* sideboard and table with hand-made coffee table in beech and dining chair all designed by The Story Design Group (Ian Henderson, Director of Design) and made by Story & Co. Ltd. *Simplon* settee and *Intruder* chair made by H. K. Furniture Ltd.

3. Mahogany rail-back settee with Dunlopillo seat covered in Scottish tweed by Wilson & Glenny Ltd, and table with Formica top made by A. H. McIntosh & Co. Ltd. Chair made by John McGregor & Sons Ltd, of formed plywood with tweed upholstered seat. All three pieces designed by Dennis Lennon, M C, A R I B A. Handmade rug by the Highland Home Industries Ltd. (*Courtesy: Scottish Furniture Manufacturers Ltd.*)

4. Settee with back and seat of pressed aluminium upholstered in foam-rubber and covered in Scottish tweed by Wilson & Glenny Ltd, designed by Dennis Lennon, M C, A R I B A, and made by John McGregor & Sons Ltd. (*Courtesy: Scottish Furniture Manufacturers Ltd.*)

2

5. Radiogram, low for use from an armchair or mountable on high legs designed by Neville Ward, B Arch A R I B A, M S I A, and Frank Austin, M S I A, and made by Wylie & Lochhead Ltd.

(*Scottish Furniture Manufacturers Ltd.*)

OPPOSITE: Interior furnished by Liberty & Co. Ltd. Wall desk in natural birch made by Fin mar Ltd. Windsor armchair in birch made by The Furniture Industries Ltd. Upholstered chair designed by Howard Keith, M S I A, and made by H. K. Furniture Ltd. Tray-top table in Chilean rauli and birch by Ronald Harford & Henry Long. Skane wing chair with striped covering by Trimwel Products Ltd. Lamp by Merchant Adventurers Ltd.

(*Colour photo: Peter Luling.*
Courtesy: Good Housekeeping.)

6. Unit chairs which, placed together, form a seat made by John McGregor & Sons Ltd, and covered in *Old Glamis* fabric by Donald Bros Ltd. Coffee table with mahogany legs and a lip of mahogany round the veneered sycamore top made by A. H. McIntosh & Co. Ltd. Bookcase in mahogany lined with sycamore made by Andrew Thomson & Sons Ltd. All designed by Jacques Groag, Dipl.Ing. Arch, F S I A. (*Courtesy: Scottish Furniture Manufacturers Ltd.*)

3

4

5

6

1

2

1. Chest with drawers in Australian cedar framed in silver ash on a myrtle stand designed and made by S. Krimper (Collection of the National Gallery of Victoria).

2. Couch, 7 ft. long, in walnut and primavera with 6-in. mattress-type foam-rubber cushion to seat, both back and seat cushions removable and zippered; and matching table of two shelves hung from wooden frames all designed by Joseph Salerno and made by Corvilla Furniture Inc.

3. Writing desk, settee and nesting tables in Queensland blackbean, designed and made by S. Krimper. Cushions covered in linen: Indian rug on the floor.

3

4. Dining-room furnished by Dunn's of Bromley. Bookcase-cupboard unit and dining table in oak designed by Geoffrey Dunn. Table chair by Geoffrey Dunn and E. Clinch, MSIA. Small table in chestnut by A. B. Reynolds. Two upholstered chairs designed by Howard Keith, MSIA, and made by H. K. Furniture Ltd. Textile designed by F. H. K. Henrion, FSIA, and produced by A. & J. Finch Ltd.

4

5

5. Living-room group designed by Edward J. Wormley and made by Dunbar Furniture Manufacturing Co. Settee of moulded laminated plywood with a covering of Swiss printed linen, and mahogany chairs covered in hand-woven metallic cloth by Dorothy Liebes. Cabinet of mahogany with pandanus cloth panels, and glass table combined with metal and Finnish birch birl.

6. Occasional chairs in natural oak of even height to fitted table, and wrought-iron floor lamp designed by J. H. Tabraham and made by D. S. Vorster & Co. (Pty) Ltd.

6

8

7

7. Mahogany and maple table with engraved plate-glass top designed by P. Döhler and made by P. Döhler Workshops.

8. Living-room designed by Paul T. Frankl Associates. Table of $\frac{3}{4}$-in. bleached cork on a plywood frame, settee covered in hand-loomed silk by Maria Kipp with cushions in Morton Sundour's Red Rowena. Lamp bases of split bamboo matting and shades wound with white cotton cord. White textured wool carpet on the floor.

1

2

3

1. Garden room designed by Jean Royère with green lacquered furniture upholstered in woven raffia. The circular rug is of white wool.
2. Interior designed by Allan Gould and executed by Functional Furniture Manufacturers.
3. Low coffee table on a base of macassar ebony with plate-glass top and an undershelf for magazines designed and made by Bernard Durussel. Ceramics by G. Jouve.
4. Living-room furnished in oak by Jean Royère with the chair and settee covered in plain green fabric. Curtains are white with the motif in violet and grey.
5. Suite in maple and teak upholstered in blue hand-made woollen fabric, with grey seats, designed by Finn Juhl and made by Søren Willadsens Mobelfabrik A/S.

4

5

6

7

8

6. Living-room designed by Donald Deskey Associates for the Bigelow-Sanford Carpet Co., as a setting for their 'permaset process' carpeting.

7. Recreation room designed by Twitchell & Rudolph and built by Associated Builders Inc. Sliding glass walls with fish net curtains. (*Photo: Ezra Stoller.*)

8. Furniture in ash with table legs of forged iron designed by Jean Royère. Chair coverings in red cotton with the motif in yellow and grey. Window seat upholstered in green cotton fabric.

9. Fireplace faced with old tiles and surrounded with travertine; glass-topped table on iron frame, and chairs in beige fabric designed by Jacques Dumond. Tapestry above fireplace by Jean Lurçat.

10 and 11. Living-dining-room in the Frank Mitchell home designed by Semmens-Simpson and built by Pike & White Construction. Chesterfield and two chairs upholstered in turquoise fabric with a white leaf motif. Black lacquer dining table with white shag rug below and white covering to dining chairs.

9

10

11

1. *Unad* furniture in blackbean and cherrywood, and *Hepple* dining chairs designed by The Story Design Group (Ian Henderson, Director of Design) and made by Story & Co. Ltd. *Fern Leaf* chintz curtains in brown, plum, green, grey and white. Lamp with green glass base and Le Klint shade.

2. Sideboard and table designed by Booth & Ledeboer F and ARIBA, and chairs designed by W. H. Russell, FSIA, all made by Gordon Russell Ltd. Sideboard doors of narrow reeded boards with handles of Bombay rosewood. Table reducible in length by removal of centre panel, which can be stored on runners fixed between the rails.

3. Dining group by The Dunbar Furniture Manufacturing Co., with mahogany dining table (extendable by the insertion of an aproned leaf) and chairs covered in hand-woven metallic fabric by Dorothy Liebes. 'Long John' in foreground is of sap-striped walnut and the settee is covered in striped textured damask. Swiss printed linen curtains.

4. Mrs. Chiyo Uno's Western-style living-room designed by Professor T. Satow with wax-polished cedar sideboard and *sen*-wood tables and chairs made by Ginza-kensetsu Co. Ltd. Walls covered with pale yellow *basho* cloth; white ceiling; cherry parquet flooring, wax-polished; and dark blue Persian pattern carpet.

5. Dining table and chairs in walnut and primavera designed by Joseph Salerno and made by Corvill Furniture Inc. The zipper-covered foam-rubber chair cushions rest on sailcloth slings laced to the frame.

6

7

8

6. Country dining-room designed by Jacques Adnet and executed by Cie des Arts Français with furniture in elm, and simple pottery and glassware to suit the scheme. *(Colour photo: Alec Murray.)*

7. Table, chairs and built-in bookcase-cupboard in polished beech designed by Nils Enström and made by A B Ferd. Lundquist & Co. Hand-woven carpet by Ingrid Hellman-Knafve.

8. Blackbean and cherrywood *Unad* furniture designed by The Story Design Group (Ian Henderson, Director of Design) and made by Story & Co. Ltd.

1

2

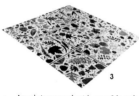

3

4

5

8

6

7

1. Armchair covered with grey felt and table of forged iron with natural coloured top designed by Jean Royère. Wallpaper painted by Leonor Fini.

2. Mahogany writing table and oak chair, designed by Peter Brunn and made by Peter Brunn Workshops.

3. Table top with pressed leaves under plate-glass designed by Martin Eisler.

4. Oak writing table, chair and carpet designed by Jacques Dumond.

5. Oak coffee table with two nesting tables designed by Catherine Speyer and made by Rena Rosenthal Inc. Large table has sea twill under glass top.

6. Coffee table of plate-glass, walnut and Italian twine designed by Martin Freedgood and made by Bernhard & Hayes Inc.

7. Pearwood table by Paul T. Frankl Associates for Johnson Furniture Co.

8. Nest of tables, rauli legs and frames, tops of sapele mahogany, brass feet. Designed for The British Leather Federation by Hulme Chadwick, ARCA, and made by Frank W. Clifford Ltd.

9. Glass-topped cocktail table with walnut legs pierced with brass shafts designed by T. H. Robsjohn-Gibbings. Made by The Widdicomb Furniture Co.

10. Mahogany coffee table with tiled top designed by Vladimir Kagan and made by Kagan Woodcraft Inc.

9

10

11. Writing table and chair in Australian silky oak and Chilean rauli designed and made by Ronald Harford and Henry Long for Heal & Son Ltd. The chair has small arms to allow easy movement of the body.

12. *Boomerang* table available in oak, walnut or mahogany, 12 in. high, designed by A. M. Lewis, MSIA, and made by Liberty & Co. Ltd.

13. Magazine table in bleached cork on wooden frame designed by Paul T. Frankl for Johnson Furniture Co.

13

14

15

16

17

14. Magazine tree with walnut shelves and birch trunk, available also in mahogany, designed by Edward J. Wormley and made by Dunbar Furniture Manufacturing Co.

15. Magazine rack with plate-glass dividers designed by Ernst Payer and made by Harvey G. Stief Inc.

16. Magazine rack in sorrel walnut designed by T. H. Robsjohn-Gibbings. Made by The Widdicomb Furniture Co.

17. Nested tables with sap-striped walnut tops on mahogany bases (available in sets of three or four tables) designed by Edward J. Wormley and made by Dunbar Furniture Manufacturing Co.

18. Hand-painted tiled-top coffee table of oak, natural pickled finish, designed by Vladimir Kagan and made by Kagan Woodcraft Inc., for Kagan-Dreyfuss Inc. The tiles are treated to resist heat and liquor marks.

19. Oak drop-leaf table, natural pickled finish, designed by Vladimir Kagan and made by Kagan Woodcraft Inc., for Kagan-Dreyfuss Inc. Candlestick and lamp also designed by Vladimir Kagan.

20. Free form coffee table designed by Arthur A. Klepper, and made by Wor-De-Klee Inc. Available in oak, mahogany, walnut or birch.

18   19   20

1

1. Kitchen designed by William T. Snaith of Raymond Loewy Associates with Frigidaire, double-oven range, American kitchen cabinets and Goodyear Wingfoot Vinyl flooring, all Loewy-designed. Fireplace made by Peter de Guard. (*Photo: George Karger, Pix Inc. Courtesy: FLAIR.*)

2. Snack bar or kitchenette designed by Cecil & Presbury Inc., and made by Sylvania Electric Products Inc., providing a spacious counter, shelving, grille and small refrigerator behind the coral leather cupboard doors. Paintwork also in coral.

2

3

3. Dining-kitchen designed by Booth & Ledeboer F and ARIBA, and made by Wooldridge & Simpson Ltd. Off-white painted fittings and African mahogany bench tops. Wall tiling pale cream, eggshell finish. Equipped with Aga cooker and stainless steel sink. (*Photo: John Maltby.*)

4

4. Kitchen designed by Alyne Whalen. Storage cabinet painted inside in a brilliant blue-green with brass wire sliding doors. All fitments painted white exteriorly with counter tops of grey Formica. Floor of pale grey marbelized asphalt tile. Dining floor adjoining of brown asphalt tile.

5. Kitchen built round a *Kitchen Pride* sink made by The Crane Company, with a built-in breakfast nook on the far right and a utility room (not shown) on the left.

6. *Zintec* steel cabinets, bonderized and stove enamelled cream, and stainless steel sink, with the steel counter tops covered with Formica in a kitchen designed by Ezee Kitchens Ltd.

7

5

8

6

9

7. Kitchen scheme designed and carried out by Sylvania Electric Products Inc. Walls light blue; curtains grey, red and white; shelf covering light grey; mottled blue and white floor; and *Admiral* electric cooker.

8 and 9. Kitchen schemes designed by The General Electric Home Bureau, using cookers, refrigerators and other units made by The General Electric Company. Indoor-outdoor kitchen (left) has an outside fireplace for charcoal broiling.

1

2

3

4

8

9

10

11

15

16

17

18

22

23

24

25

5

6

7

1. Cane back, wooden frame. Dunbar Furniture Manufacturing Co. 2. Natural Makore mahogany. Designer: T. R. L. Robertson. Makers: A. H. McIntosh & Co. Ltd. 3. Stuffover. Designers: Neville Ward, B Arch., A R I B A, M S I A, and Frank Austin, M S I A. Makers: H. & A. G. Alexander & Co. Ltd. 4. Teak and cane. Designers: Aage Windeleff and David Birnbaum. Maker: Axel I. Sørensen. 5. Upholstery, webbing straps. A. F. Styne, A I D, for Advance Design Inc. 6. Maple, tweed upholstery. Designer: Paul T. Frankl for Johnson Furniture Co. 7. Teak. Designers: Aage Windeleff and David Birnbaum for Axel I. Sørensen. 8. Steel, beech and Dunlopillo. Ernest Race Ltd. 9. *Ax* chair, laminated beech and solid wood. Designers: Peter Hvidt and O. Molgaard Nielsen. Makers: Fritz Hansens Eftfl. 10. Moulded plastic on tubular frame. Robert Nickel (Institute of Design, Chicago). 11. Natural walnut, striped grey cotton velvet. Bernard Durussel. 12. English walnut and dark green goatskin. Designer: Edward Barnsley. Made by Charles Bray. 13. Lacquered birch designed by Nils Enström. A B Ferd. Lundquist & Co. 14. Beech and plywood. Designer: Borge Mogensen for The Danish Co-operative Wholesale Society. 15. Lacquered birch. Designer: Bertil Fridhagen for Svenska Möbelfabrikerna, Bodafors. 16. Natural Makore mahogany, foam-rubber back. Designer: T. R. L. Robertson for A. H. McIntosh & Co. Ltd. Covering by Arthur H. Lee & Sons Ltd. 17. Lacquered steel frame, plaited cane, by R. Guys. 18. *Antelope.* Welded steel and plywood. Makers: Ernest Race Ltd. 19. Elm with white-painted back and woollen cover. Designer: Carl-Johan Boman for O/Y Boman A B. 20. Elm or beech, and check wool. Designer: Axel Larsson for Svenska Möbelfabrikerna, Bodafors. 21. Pink beech, cane and blue-grey leather. Designer: W. H. Russell, F S I A, for Gordon Russell Ltd. 22. Fibreboard on tubular frame. Designers: Joan Robinson and William Geer (Institute of Design, Chicago). 23. Metal frame, canvas seat. Designers: Nathan Lerner and Group (Institute of Design, Chicago). 24. Plated steel tubing and zippered fabric. Designer-maker: Eva Zeisel. 25. Birch, sorrel finish. Designer: T. H. Robsjohn-Gibbings for The Widdicomb Furniture Co. 26. Moulded plastic, tubular frame, adjustable. Designer: Arpad Augusztiny (Institute of Design, Chicago). 27. Walnut, muslin cover, foam-rubber. John Ossian for John Scalia Inc. 28. Oak frame, metal-sprung cushions, by Renan de La Godelinais.

12

13

14

19

20

21

26

27

28

Mural in *papier collé* by Alexander Girard,
AIA. Sofa and arm chair designed by
George Nelson and covered in grey fabric by
Moss-Rose. Plastic shell chair and moulded
ash plywood coffee tables designed by
Charles Eames. Furniture Makers: Herman
Miller Furniture Corporation. Gold
coloured heavy wool pile rug by V'Soske.
Floor covered in black and white Vinyl
cork by Dodge Vinyl Corporation (USA).

Cabinet bookcase with wing divider in
dark mahogany (or any other wood to
order). Light mahogany chair with covering of brown textured fabric. Designer:
Irina A. Klepper. Makers: Wor-De-Klee
Inc (USA).

BELOW: Dining-living room divided by a bamboo screen arranged by Frederick Manning. Natural oak sideboard, oak shelf and 'flying' bookcase, and two one-arm chairs of light oak (together forming a settee) (BRITISH); oak dining table and chairs (SWEDISH); and a natural elm bureau (DANISH). From Bowman Bros Ltd (GB).

Queensland walnut bookcase, writing table, occasional table and screen bookcase designed by A. Greenwood, MSIA. Small chairs designed by A. J. Milne, MSIA. Makers: Heal & Son Ltd. Curtains of Heal's *Spring Harvest* printed linen. Easy chair by H. K. Furniture Ltd (GB).

Living-room and a corner of the studio in the North Vancouver home of Mr and Mrs Bruno Bobak, furnished by the owner. Of post and beam construction, with red cedar walls and a white ceiling. Birch furniture with a cedar base to the sink unit and terracotta linoleum to floor. Posts and beams painted grey. Designer: Douglas Shadbolt (CANADA). (*Photo: Peter Varley*)

Coffee table with ¾-in. glass top on a light grey mahogany base. Available also in dark mahogany and in oak, walnut and birch, light or dark finishes. Designer: Irina A. Klepper. Makers: Wor-De-Klee Inc (USA).

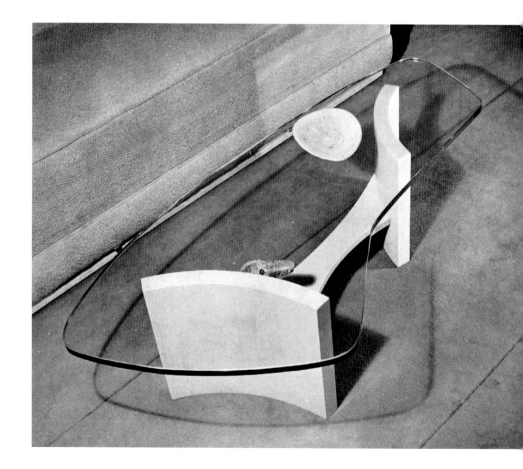

Metal and glass coffee table of 1-in. thick plate glass 42-in. by 18-in. supported on highly polished brass frame. Designer: Brice of Auerbach Associates. Makers: Charak Furniture Co Inc (USA).

Coffee table, prototype (not yet in production) made in ¾-in. plywood with glass top and ebonized undershelf. Designer and maker: Jacques de Tonnancour (CANADA).

Light grey mahogany occasional table inset with tiles of rough textured ceramic by Key-Oberg. Available also in dark mahogany, oak, walnut or birch, in light or dark finishes, with tiles to blend. Designer: Arthur Klepper. Makers: Wor-De-Klee Inc (USA).

Occasional table with metal plant container, laminated top of Japanese tamu on beech underframe. Designer: K. McAvoy. Makers: Liberty & Co Ltd (GB).

Nimbus coffee table with four fitting 'boomerangs', available in oak, mahogany or walnut. Designers: A. M. Lewis and K. McAvoy. Makers: Liberty & Co Ltd (GB).

BELOW: *Octopus* coffee table in mahogany and sycamore, natural waxed finish. Designer: Peter Brunn. Makers: Peter Brunn Workshop (GB). (*Photo: John Fry*)

Coffee table in brushed oak on polished bronze legs, inset with five hand-painted ceramic tiles which act as coasters for glasses. Designer: Vladimir Kagan. Makers: Kagan-Dreyfuss Inc (USA).

Corner of a room for two boys with a bleached oak desk fitment and sofa beds (the room contains two, separated by a table) covered in plaid cotton and rayon Greeff fabric. Heavy cotton draperies with *Trees* design by Dan Cooper. Knoll *Prestini* covering to chairs, cotton and rayon in red and oatmeal. The wooden sculpture on left by Walter Midener: free form wire, stone, wooden and ceramic sculptures by Anita Weschler. Furniture designer: Irina A. Klepper. Makers: Wor-De-Klee Inc (USA).

LEFT: Chair mounted on steel rod base held in position by four bolts, shell moulded in fibrenyle plastic with latex foam headrest and seat cushion, covered in brown pile fabric with the outside back in contrasting material. Designer: Dennis Young, ARCA, MSIA. Makers: Design London Educational and Industrial Ltd (GB).

Mahogany occasional table with chessboard inlay, made by A. H. McIntosh & Co. Ltd; and chairs made by Steadfast & Co Ltd, upholstered in tartan plain tweed made by Wilson & Glenny Ltd, all designed by Jacques Groag, Dipl. Ing.Arch, FSIA. *Thistle* decanter and glasses made by Edinburgh & Leith Flint Glassworks Ltd. Rugs by Highland Home Industries Ltd (GB).
(*Courtesy: Scottish Furniture Manufacturers Ltd*)

Easy chair, spring stuffed loose seat cushion, covered in green tapestry. Designer: A. J. Milne, MSIA. Makers: Heal & Son Ltd (GB).

Sectional chairs, frames of birch stained to any required colour, cotton print covered in rose, mustard and black on white ground. Designers and makers: Advance Design Inc (USA).

Extension dining table (shown extended) of korina, and walnut chairs covered in black, grey and white handwoven fabric. Designer: Vladimir Kagan. Makers: Kagan-Dreyfuss Inc (USA).

Occasional chair, birch frame, covered in gold and ivory on brown ground weavecraft. Designer: Bill Evans. Makers: Advance Design Inc (USA).

ntruder settee with arms and legs of beech or birch polished to sycamore, walnut or mahogany, covered in pinky-beige wool and cotton tapestry designed by Marianne Straub. Furniture designer: Howard B. Keith, MSIA. Makers: H. K. Furniture Ltd (GB).

Front view of the chair shown opposite, top left. The steel legs are stove enamelled in light blue and have rubber pad toes. Designer: Dennis Young, ARCA, MSIA. Makers: Design London Educational and Industrial Ltd (GB).

Chair on walnut legs covered in ivory textured fabric with cushions of red oriental silk. Designer: Donald Cameron. Makers: Rena Rosenthal Inc (USA).

BELOW: A living-room in Stockholm furnished by Emilio Del Junco (CUBA) with Swedish and American pieces. The book shelving is adjustable on metal wall guides. *(Courtesy : Domus)*

Living-dining room arranged by Dunn's of Bromley with a *Simplon* settee and easy chair (Designer: Howard B. Keith, MSIA. Makers: H. K. Furniture Ltd); *Freydun* dining table available in oak or mahogany (Designer: Geoffrey Dunn); *Freydun* dining chairs in beech or mahogany (Designer: E. L. Clinch, MSIA); Occasional table in oak or mahogany (Designer: Jacques Groag, Dipl. Ing. Arch, FSIA); and cane canterbury (Designer: Geoffrey Dunn) (GB).

(Courtesy: Good Housekeeping)

Siesta in deep textured corn yellow tapestry made by Tibor Ltd. Designer: Howard B. Keith, MSIA. Makers: H. K. Furniture Ltd (GB).

Beech frame, upholstered in cloth made by Richard Johnson. Designer: Bertil Fridhagen. Makers: Svenska Möbelfabrikerna (SWEDEN).

Stelvio in black and grey Welsh wool tapestry. Designer: Howard B. Keith, MSIA. Makers: H. K. Furniture Ltd (GB).

Birch frame covered in blue, red and white striped woollen fabric. Designer: Carl-Johan Boman. Makers: OY Boman AB (FINLAND).

White birch, clear cellulosed. Mustard yellow upholstery. Detachable legs. Designer: A. V. Pilley, FRIBA. Makers: C. Jay Cole & F. A. Cole Ltd (GB).

Futura. Collapsible stool of red beech with plastic web seat. Makers: AB Nordiska Kompaniet (SWEDEN).

'Knock-down' chair in bleached birch upholstered in dark blue wool. Designer: Dirk van Sliedregt. Makers: Jonkers Meubelfabriek (HOLLAND).

Oak frame with loose cushion seat. Available also with loose back. Designer: Steve Tourre. Makers: Mueller Furniture Co (USA).

Mahogany frame, covered in Tabergs Yllefabrik. Designer: Svante Skogh. Makers: AB Svenska Möbelfabrikerna (SWEDEN).

White lacquered iron frame, with hairlock stuffing and handwoven covering. Designer: Nils Enström. Makers: AB Ferd. Lundquist & Co (SWEDEN).

Honduras mahogany and Canadian birch moulded laminated sections, lemon yellow whipcord cover. Designers: Jane Drew and Maxwell Fry, FFRIBA with Neil Morris. Makers: Morris of Glasgow (GB).

Sorrel-finish walnut chair and ottoman, foam-rubber upholstery covered with beige linen. Designer: T. H. Robsjohn-Gibbings. Makers: The Widdicomb Furniture Company (USA).

Hayes. Beech legs, oatmeal linen covering. Designers: Geoffrey Dunn and Mollie Benham. Makers: Dunn's of Bromley (G B).

Mahogany frame, moulded plywood back and foam-rubber seat, covered in horse blanket tweed. Designers: Norman A. P. Whicheloe and Nigel Walters. Makers: Primavera (G B).

Hardwood frame, lacquered black. Fixed seat, loose back. Covering of light green textured silk. Designer: Paul Laszlo. Makers: Laszlo Inc (U S A).

Elm frame upholstered in blue woollen fabric. Designer: Olof Ottelin. Makers: O Y Stockmann A B (FINLAND).

Electrically - bent rattan chair. Designer: Dirk van Sliedregt. Makers: Gebr. Jonkers (HOLLAND).

Walnut legs and arms, upholstered in green and gold damask. Designer: Erno Fabry. Makers: Fabry Associates Inc (U S A).

Natural beech or birch. Makers: A B Nordiska Kompaniet. Designed by their Design Department (SWEDEN).

Sycamore frame, seat and back in coral and ivory Regency stripe velvet. Designer: Roff Marsh, FRIBA, AMTPI. Makers: D. Burkle & Son Ltd (G B).

Back and arms of pre-formed plywood, steel frame, back and seat of foam-rubber covered in lime yellow fabric. Designer: Robin Day ARCA. Makers: S. Hille & Co Ltd (G B).

White birch, clear cellulosed, seat and back webbed and padded. Mustard yellow upholstery. Detachable legs. Designer: A. V. Pilley, FRIBA. Makers: C. Jay Cole & F. A. Cole Ltd (G B).

Steel underframe with leather-covered sponge rubber seat, moulded plywood back and arms. Designer: Robin Day, ARCA. Makers: S. Hille & Co Ltd (G B).

Plywood seat, mahogany underframe, covered in Scottish tweed. Designer: Dennis Lennon, M C, ARIBA. Makers: John McGregor & Sons Ltd, for Scottish Furniture Manufacturers Ltd (G B).

LEFT: Chairs covered in red and blue repp, and aperitif table, all in waxed cherrywood. The table has a space between the glass top and the base for magazines or papers, and a container for plants or flowers at one end. Walls veneered in natural Swedish pine, floor covered in slate blue linoleum and a white long pile wool carpet. Interior decorator: Bernard Durussel (FRANCE).

RIGHT: Man's room furnished in pickled oak, the bed mounted on large rubber castors to facilitate movement; bed cover of brown and beige tweed; curtains of natural silk shantung with valance of Puerto Rican fibre hand-woven by Geraldine Funk; carpet beige and olive tweed mixture; chair covered with quilted chintz, olive green, brown and beige. Designer: William Pahlmann (USA).

Sofa beds with natural cane backs (which collapse to make three-quarter size bed) covered in olive green, coral and brown tweed. Coffee table with glass top, two drawers and a centre magazine space, mounted on large brass and rubber castors. Chair covered in quilted glazed chintz in olive-green and beige on coral ground. Lime green shaded reed light on ceiling pulley. Designer: William Pahlmann (USA).

Living-room with 7 ft. 6 in. sofa bed and upholstered lounge chair, both of foam rubber construction. The metal frame cocktail table has a glass top and base of Finnish birch burl. Designer: Edward Wormley. Makers: Dunbar Furniture Corporation (USA).

BELOW: Living-room furniture, fabrics and carpet designed by William Pahlmann. Coffee table of walnut with burl top. Sofa covered with hand-woven Peruvian linen *Rio Grande* design; white silk gauze curtain printed with *Still Trees* design, both made by Schumacher Fabrics. Roll reed blind to window of natural coloured yarn with gold and copper Lurex woven by Grace Ritchie Clarke Studio. Furniture makers: Grand Rapids Bookcase & Chair Co (USA).

RIGHT: Work table with four drawers and a knitting locker, and sewing chair both in light mahogany. Designer: Olof Östberg. Makers: The Swedish Homecraft Association (SWEDEN).

(*Courtesy: The Swedish International Press Bureau*)

Sideboard of Jugoslavian beech, the long drawer with compartment fitted for cutlery. Designer: A. J. Milne, MSIA. Makers: Heal & Son Ltd. Curtain of *Matura* printed linen. Designer: Roger Nicholson (GB).

LEFT: Commode covered in topgrain hand-tooled leather on a bleached mahogany base. Hand-wrought brass ring handles. Makers: Charak Furniture Co Inc (USA).

BELOW: Sideboard in mahogany and rosewood, the doors decorated with incised lines showing the light coloured veneer below. Handles of brass. Designers: Booth & Ledeboer, F & ARIBA. Makers: Gordon Russell Ltd (GB).

Triva cabinet in mahogany and birch with moulded handles and fitted with two adjustable shelves or sliding trays on each side. Designer: Elias Svedberg. Makers: A B Nordiska Kompaniet (SWEDEN).

Amber-toned mahogany chest, the drawers and door openings formed by a grooved wooden overlay which forms part of the design and acts as decoration. Designer: Harvey Probber. Makers: Harvey Probber Inc (USA).

Four-door cabinet in dark walnut with panels of bleached Hungarian ash. Designer: Donald Cameron. Makers: Rena Rosenthal Inc (USA).

Natural pickled oak tambour-doored double chest, 8 ft. 6 in. long. Designer: Vladimir Kagan. Makers: Kagan-Dreyfuss Inc. Lamp, plate, sculpture and painting also from Kagan-Dreyfuss (USA).

Pencil-striped walnut suite, the table and sideboard tops faced with heatproof and washable Warerite; chairs with cane or tapestry backs to match seats; *Ormiston* linen on wall designed by Marion Mahler and made by Donald Bros Ltd. Furniture designer: E. L. Clinch, MSIA. Makers: Bowman Bros Ltd (GB).

ABOVE: Birch table, top clear cellulosed, with legs of aerofoil section (detachable for transport) fixed to the table frame with coach screws. Designer: A. V. Pilley, FRIBA. Makers: Walter F. Baker Ltd (GB). Chairs from the Continental factories of Thonet Bros Ltd.

LEFT: Dining table, chairs and sideboard in polished ash, chair coverings of natural morocco. Tapestry on rear wall by Jean Lurçat. Table in foreground of ash with black slate top. Easy chairs covered in dark green velvet. Designer: Jacques Dumond. Makers: Ets Gazel et Cie (FRANCE).

BELOW: Extending dining table, sideboard and side table in oak.
Designers: Booth & Ledeboer, F & ARIBA. Makers: W. Rowntree
& Sons Ltd. Beech chairs with loose seats covered in cotton tapestry.
Designer: E. L. Clinch, MSIA. Makers: Goodearl Bros Ltd (GB).

ABOVE: Dining table and chairs in natural mahogany with brass feet.
Designer: Dennis Lennon, MC, ARIBA. Makers: Joseph Johnstone
Ltd for Scottish Furniture Manufacturers Ltd (GB).

BELOW: Hand-made Queensland walnut furniture, the chairs with
stuffed seats and backs covered in fawn hide and the cupboards lined
with sycamore. Curtains of *Chrysanthemum* printed linen designed by
Michael O'Connell. Furniture designer: A. Greenwood, MSIA.
Makers: Heal & Son Ltd (GB).

RIGHT: Bookcase with sliding glass doors; bureau with mirror fitted to top drawer if desired; and folding table, all in oak. Table available also in walnut. Makers: D. Meredew Ltd (GB)

ABOVE: Radiogram and chairs in sapele mahogany, and light oak table on grey steel legs with terra-cotta linoleum top. Chair upholstery of Dunlopillo foam rubber covered in yellow wool and mohair mixture. Designers: J. H. Tabraham (radiogram) and D. S. Vorster (chairs and table). Makers: D. S. Vorster & Co (Pty) Ltd (SOUTH AFRICA)

Television - radio - phonograph-record album cabinet, usable as one fitment or as separate units, in cordovan or blonde finish mahogany with perforated coloured masonite sliding doors to television and record cabinets. The drapery is Laverne's *Maze*, white satin with the design in black. Designer: F. B. Arthur. Makers: F. B. Arthur Modern Interiors (USA)

Chelsfield dining-suite in Pal Dao walnut with elm doors to sideboard and Caton fabric in red or olive-green on chairs. Coffee table available in natural oak, walnut or mahogany. Designer: Ian Audsley MSIA. Makers: G. W. Evans Ltd (GB)

RIGHT: Storage cabinets of Douglas fir plywood. Designer: Fred Brodie MRAIC. *Rushtex* and steel-framed chairs designed by Robin Bush and Earle A. Morrison. Makers: Earle A. Morrison Ltd (CANADA).

BELOW: Combination sideboard and cocktail cabinet in mahogany, sliding doors of Brazilian rosewood, top of black plastic, inside of swing door white lacquer, mixing surface and back of Cipollino marble, and chromium legs. Designer: Felix Augenfeld (USA)

Corner of a man's room, the cabinets and matching chair in varnished wild cherrywood. Designer: Jean Royère (FRANCE)

Free-form Regency coffee table in yew, with brass ferrules. Designers and makers: Charak Furniture Company (USA)

Mahogany table, natural cellulosed finish. Designer: Dennis Young, ARCA, MSIA. Makers: Design (London) Educational & Industrial Ltd (GB)

Patio with Mesa table, strapped sofa covered in *Bark* linen, side chair in *Strata* linen, and curved cocktail couch in linen tweed. Designer: T. H. Robsjohn-Gibbings. Makers: The Widdicomb Furniture Company. Courtesy: The Marble Institute of America (USA)

Mesa table in walnut, Sienna finish. Designer: T. H. Robsjohn-Gibbings. Makers: The Widdicomb Furniture Company (USA)

Coffee table with ¾-inch glass top on a sculptured walnut, oak or mahogany base. Designer: Vladimir Kagan. Makers: Kagan-Dreyfuss Inc (USA)

Low table in walnut or birch, 54 inches long, available also with Micarta top in yellow, grey or green, convertible into a bench by the addition of a 1½-inch reversible foam rubber pad. Designer: Jens Risom. Makers: Jens Risom Design Inc (USA)

Pear-shaped table made of cork veneered to a wood base. Designer: Paul T. Frankl. Makers: Johnson Furniture Company (USA)

Plant table in African mahogany (available also in walnut or beech) with plastic plant tray. Top slides over plant tray to make a plain table if required. Designer: T. Gibbs. Makers: Primavera (GB)

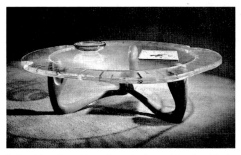

Coffee table, sculptured base of natural walnut and free-shaped Lucite top, the outer edge frosted with an irregular pattern of colour. Designer: Paul Laszlo. Sculpture: F. F. Kern. Makers: Laszlo Inc (USA)

Walnut cocktail table with centre recess for magazines. Designer: T. H. Robsjohn-Gibbings. Makers: The Widdicomb Furniture Co (USA)

Television set in macassar ebony with *Sycamore Q* front; *Esbac* chair
(LEFT) with moulded plywood seat and back on quarter-inch mild steel
frame, foam rubber cushioning; *I.C.A.* chair (RIGHT BACKGROUND) and
two-seated chair on laminated frames with foam rubber upholstery;
magazine rack in mahogany and birch laminations. Designer: Neil
Morris (*I.C.A.* chair in conjunction with Jane Drew and Maxwell Fry,
FFRIBA). Makers: Morris of Glasgow (GB)

Walnut chairs covered in black and white calfskin, walnut cocktail
table with black *Trolonit* top, brass-edged, and built-in walnut settee
covered in handwoven woollen fabric. Designer: Paul G. R. Baum-
garten. Maker: P. Döhler (GERMANY)

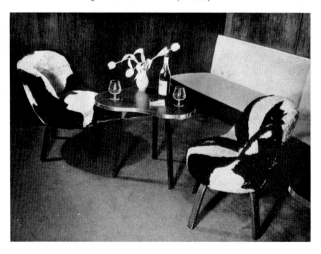

RIGHT: Combination chest-bureau in oak, walnut or mahogany on beech base with matching chair. Designer: Børge Mogensen. Makers: Søborg Møbel-fabrik (DENMARK)

BELOW: Living-room with walls of Philippine mahogany, cane panelled doors and red tile floor, radiant heated. The long bench under the window has a metal frame and slate top painted chartreuse, the same colour being re-peated in the Micarta top of the table. Sofas covered in printed linen, easy chairs in white linen, curtains of printed silk gauze. All upholstered and modern furniture (except the two iron and rush chairs) by William Pahlmann Associates Inc (USA)

Cocktail cabinet of petiribi fronted with walnut, the serving shelf faced with Formica. The inner shelves have handles at both ends and can be used as trays. Makers: A.I.M. (ARGENTINA)

Walnut cabinet faced with a paper map of London. Designer: Josef Frank. Makers: Svenskt Tenn (SWEDEN)

BELOW: Waxed oak chest with polished brass handles. Designer: René Jean Caillette (FRANCE)

Cabinet in walnut and birch with sliding glass doors. Designer: T. H. Robsjohn-Gibbings. Makers: The Widdicomb Furniture Company (USA)

Beech sideboard with routed decoration on the Indian laurel door panels. Designer: Kelvin McAvoy, exclusively for Liberty & Co. Ltd (GB)

LEFT: Cabinet in Honduras mahogany and English beech, finished in the natural colours of the woods. Designer and maker: Arthur Edwards of the High Wycombe College of Further Education (GB)

French walnut cabinet with burr maple drawer fronts, natural colour with satin lacquer finish. Designer: T. R. L. Robertson DA. Makers: A. H. McIntosh & Co. Ltd (GB)

LEFT: Cabinet in smoked oak, mahogany and beech, or teak and beech, oil-finished. Designer: Poul M. Volther. Makers: Fællesforeningen for Danmarks Brugsforeninger Møbler (DENMARK)

TOP: Multi-purpose units in natural oak—television set, record cabinet, linen storage chest and cocktail bar with built-in lighting. Designers and makers: Kim Hoffmann & Stephen Heidrich (USA)

CENTRE: Radiogram in wengé, coffee brown with thin light brown stripes, and a glass top fitted into a copper frame. Tambour front to lower cupboard. Designer: Dirk van Sliedregt. Makers: H. H. de Klerk & Zoon (HOLLAND)

BOTTOM: Combination bar-television cabinet in walnut with pull-out bar unit behind the tambour fronts. Black Formica base to bar section, and marble inlay on top left-hand for additional mixing space. Designer: Vladimir Kagan. Makers: Kagan-Dreyfuss Inc (USA)

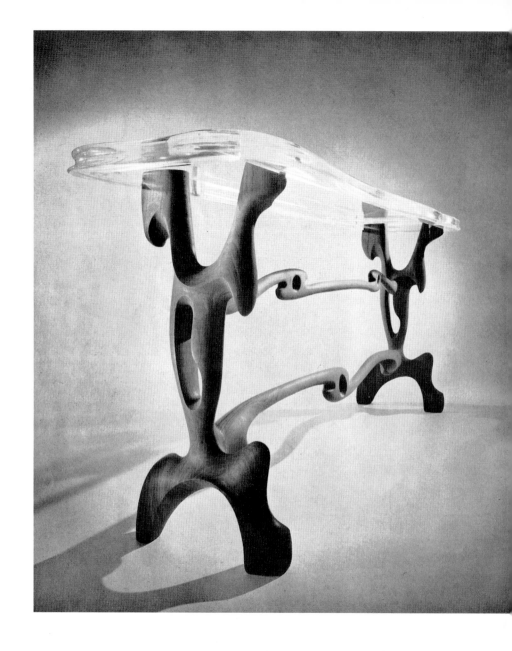

Wall table with free-form clear Lucite top on base of sculptured walnut, natural finish. Designer: Paul Laszlo. Sculpture: F. F. Kern. Makers: Laszlo Inc (USA)

Drop-leaf table, elm or mahogany top on birch underframe. Designers: AB Nordiska Kompaniet Design Studios. Makers: AB Nordiska Kompaniet (SWEDEN)

Stacking tables, beech frames with plywood tops surfaced in plastic of different colours, or in various wood veneers. Designer: Robin Day, ARCA. Makers: S. Hille & Co. Ltd (GB)

Occasional table in oak, mahogany or straight-grained walnut with moulded plywood top. Designer: Ewart Myer. Makers: Horatio Myer & Co. Ltd (GB)

Glass-topped table, 36 inches diameter, of 1-inch thick polished plate-glass supported on *Armourplate* fins bedded into a hardwood base. Designer: Sven Sternfeldt, LRIBA. Makers: Pilkington Bros Ltd (GB)

Waxed Japanese oak table with glass top on tri-foil column fitted into an oak plinth. Designer and maker: H. W. Grieve (USA)

Natural waxed-finished oak tray table with cork top edged walnut. Designer: Peter Brunn, MSIA. Makers: Peter Brunn Workshops (GB)

Children's work table with a shelf for satchels, etc. The working surfaces are topped with Formica in the Linette range of colours. Designer: Pierre Leconte (FRANCE)

LEFT: Warerite surface incorporating a photographic design veneered on to a laminated wood base, finished with black Warerite edge-veneer, polished mahogany frame and brass ferrules. Designer: Richard Levin, MSIA. Makers: F. W. Clifford Ltd (GB)

Chair in a combination of cherrywood and elm. Designer: David W. Pye. Maker R. Lenthall (GB)

BELOW: Folding laminated blonde birch plywood chair on ⅝-in tubular steel legs painted black and fitted with grey rubber feet. Designer: Russel Wright. Makers Shwayder. From Modernage Furniture Corporation (USA)

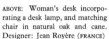

ABOVE: Woman's desk incorporating a desk lamp, and matching chair in natural oak and cane. Designer: Jean Royère (FRANCE)

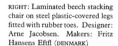

RIGHT: Laminated beech stacking chair on steel plastic-covered legs fitted with rubber toes. Designer: Arne Jacobsen. Makers: Fritz Hansens Eftfl (DENMARK)

LEFT: Armchair with frame and arm-pads of ash, formed plywood seat and back cellulosed celadon green. Designer: J. A. Williams, while a student at the Royal College of Art (GB)

BELOW: Natural cane-backed chair with fixed padded seat, in birch stained blonde, black, cordovan or mahogany. Designer: E. J. Brussel. Makers: Advance Design Inc (USA)

Lounge chair in natural red oak and black lacquer, supplied with seat and back insets of cane, natural oak wythe, or in muslin for covering with fabric. Designer: Edward D. Stone. Makers: Fulbright Industries (USA)

Oak frame with cane seat and back. Designer: Marcel Gascoin. Makers: Amenagement Rationel de l'Habitation et des Collectivités (FRANCE)

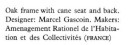

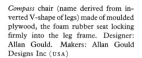
Compass chair (name derived from inverted V-shape of legs) made of moulded plywood, the foam rubber seat locking firmly into the leg frame. Designer: Allan Gould. Makers: Allan Gould Designs Inc (USA)

BELOW: Reclining chair in natural ash. Designer: Dipl-lng Arch Schneider-Esleben. Makers: Gebrüder Thonet A.G. (GERMANY)

Wire shell on black metal legs, fitted with removable two-piece or single cushion in leather or fabric. Designer: Charles Eames. Makers: Herman Miller Furniture Company (USA)

RIGHT: Natural cherrywood frame with yellow and black striped woollen covering made by 'De Ploeg'. Designer: Th. Ruth. Makers: Wagemans & Van Tuinen N.V. (HOLLAND)

LEFT: Oak frame, 36-inch high back, seat covered in brown, white and beige hand-woven fabric. Available also in walnut and mahogany. Chair designer: Vladimir Kagan. Fabric designer: Hugo Dreyfuss. Makers: Kagan-Dreyfuss Inc (USA)

BELOW: *Woodpecker* chair with vertical coil springs to seat and foam rubber 'swell' to back, on legs of polished beech. Designer: Ernest Race FSIA. Makers: Ernest Race Ltd (GB)

Knock-down chair in birch with *No-sag* springs in seat and back. Covering of machine-woven fabric with piped edges and buttoned back. Designers: Nordiska Kompaniet Design Studios. Makers: A.B. Nordiska Kompaniet (SWEDEN)

RIGHT: Dining chair on oak, walnut or mahogany legs with hair, spring and foam rubber cushioning and covering of brown, white and beige hand-woven fabric. Chair designer: Vladimir Kagan. Fabric designer: Hugo Dreyfuss. Makers: Kagan-Dreyfuss Inc (USA)

Settee and arm-chair in Royal Danish beech, finished in mahogany, walnut or natural colour, the settee covered in gold-coloured woollen fabric and the chair in similar striped material. Designers: Peter Hvidt and O. Mølgard-Nielsen Makers: France & Daverkosen (DENMARK)

Demountable chair, floor lamp with two-way adjustable light, and low table with two asymmetric shelves. Designer: René Jean Caillette (FRANCE)

Cali-quilt sofa sleeper constructed of fabric, foam rubber and felt quilted together to four-inch thickness for seating or sleeping, convertible into double bed by lowering the back which has an additional leg for stability. Cocktail and step-table of Sahara mahogany. Sofa makers: Cali-quilt. From Modernage Furniture Corporation (USA)

Day-bed on walnut base covered in natural jute and linen fabric. Coffee table of walnut inset with white Micarta. Steel chair with natural saddle leather seat. Designer: Allan Gould. Makers: Allan Gould Designs Inc (USA)

Occasional chair in natural cherrywood, handsprung with hair stuffing, covered in nigger brown wool tapestry checked in red and white. Designer and maker: F. W. Boyd of High Wycombe College of Further Education (GB)

Large, low armless chair, show-wood frame of walnut or birch, with foam rubber seat and back. Designer: Jens Risom. Makers: Jens Risom Design Inc (USA)

Birch frame, Sienna finish, foam rubber upholstered seat and loose back cushion. Designer: T. H. Robsjohn-Gibbings. Makers: The Widdicomb Furniture Company (USA)

Chair in English oak with foam rubber upholstery covered in a striped and floral printed duck. Designer: P. Yabsley MSIA. Maker: P. Yabsley with the assistance of D. Wellstead (GB)

Show-wood frame of agba, natural cellulosed finish, upholstered in green and red lined fabric over Latex foam cushioning. Designer and maker: Dennis Young ARCA MSIA for The British Rubber Development Board (GB)

Upholstered chair with arm-tips of teak, covered in beige fabric with a green cushion. Designer: Hans J. Wegner. Maker: A. P. Stolen (DENMARK)

Chair constructed of a series of 'S' bends of formed plywood riveted to make a curved back. Legs of stove-enamelled aluminium. Seat and cushion of foam rubber. Designer: Ernest Race FSIA. Makers: Ernest Race Ltd (GB)

Birch frame, Sienna finish, with blue *Strata* linen covering over foam rubber. Designer: T. H. Robsjohn-Gibbings. Makers: The Widdicomb Furniture Company (USA)

Esprit chair, beech frame in natural, walnut or mahogany finishes, outside back and platform covered in similar fabric to front but in reverse colours. Tension-sprung back and seat with 'high crown' rubber foam seat cushion. Designer: Howard B. Keith MSIA. Makers: H. K. Furniture Ltd (GB)

Wing chair, welded steel rod frame, legs of turned beech, seat with vertical coil springing and back stuffed with rubberized hair. Designer: Ernest Race FSIA. Makers: Ernest Race Ltd (GB)

Oak and teak chair, light grey seat and green back. Designer and maker: Knud Juul-Hansen (DENMARK)

Upholstered chair on teak frame, upholstered in red and white fabric. Feet tipped with brass. Designer: Bertil Fridhagen. Makers: Svenska Möbelfabrikerna, Bodafors (SWEDEN)

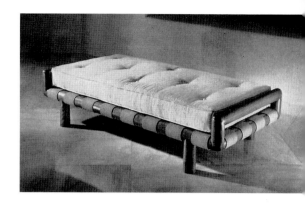

Stool formed of sections of solid red oak bent into a series of ribs. Available also in black lacquer. Designer: Edward D. Stone. Makers: Fulbright Industries (USA)

Strapped birch sofa, Sienna finish, with foam rubber mattress covered in linen tweed. Designer: T. H. Robsjohn-Gibbings. Makers: The Widdicomb Furniture Company (USA)

American walnut stool with seat upholstered in fabric designed by Marianne Straub. Designer: Peter Brunn MSIA. Makers: Peter Brunn Workshops (GB)

ABOVE: Bench of slatted red Arkansan oak, 62 in long, on black lacquered legs. Designer: Edward D. Stone. Makers: Fulbright Industries (USA)

Stool made of vivaró (a native Argentinian wood) with coloured stringing. Makers: A.I.M. (ARGENTINA)

Electrically-bent rattan chair.
Designer: Dirk van Sliedregt.
Makers: Gebr. Jonkers
(HOLLAND)

ccasional chair with Rushtex seat and
ack, on oak or walnut frame. Designer:
arle A. Morrison. Makers: Earle A. Mor-
son Ltd (CANADA) *Photo: A. David Rogers*

ELOW: Natural mahogany terrace chair
vith rush seat and back. Designer: Dennis
ennon MC. ARIBA. Makers: Scottish
urniture Manufacturers Ltd (GB)

'Knock-down' chair, plywood frame
with laced cotton webbing seat and back
in yellow, red or black. Designer: Dirk
van Sliedregt. Makers: N. V. Utrechtsche Machinale Stoel- en Meubelfabriek (HOLLAND)

Rattan chair with green and white linen
cushions. Designer: Olavi Hanninen. Makers:
O/Y Stockmann AB (FINLAND)

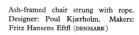

LEFT: Black-lacquered European beech with seat
and back of woven Hong Kong grass. Designer:
Harold Bartos. German-made for Modernage
Furniture Corporation (USA)

Ash-framed chair strung with rope.
Designer: Poul Kjærholm. Makers:
Fritz Hansens Eftfl (DENMARK)

Settee and easy chair on mahogany frame, upholstered in yellow over 'Epeda' springs: the Dunlopillo cushions are covered in a fine yellow check on black ground fabric. Designer: Svante Skogh. Makers: Ernst Hjertqvist & Co. (SWEDEN)

BELOW: Settee and armchair from the *Hilleplan* range covered in a variety of exclusive fabrics with foam rubber cushions on hand-sprung bases. The centre table is of Derbyshire fossil stone on a laminated timber frame. Designer: Robin Day, ARCA, FSIA. Makers: Hille of London Ltd (GB)

BELOW: *Pandora* settee covered in contrasting woollen fabrics; outside oatmeal, inner back and cushions grey and white spot. Tension-sprung back upholstered over rubberized hair. Deep foam rubber cushions. Designer: Howard B. Keith, MSIA. Makers: H. K. Furniture Ltd (GB)

Python settee with beech frame, hand-sprung back and tension-sprung seat. Pocket spring interior cushion. Covered in Tibor or Whitehead fabrics. Designer: A. J. Milne, MSIA. Makers: E. Horace Holme Ltd (GB)

ABOVE: Three pieces shown at the Dansk Kunsthåndværks Forårsudstilling 1953. The settee and chair have foam rubber cushioning and were designed by Folke Pålsson and Erik Ole Jørgensen. Teak table with beech surface finish designed by Poul M. Volther. Makers: Fælles-foreningen for Danmarks Brugsforeninger Møbler (DENMARK)

Settee and chair in natural cherrywood, upholstered in *Gent*, a moss-textured hand-woven woollen fabric, main colour corn, arms and piping anthracite. Table surfaced Formica with cherry legs lacquered black. Designer: Th. Ruth. Makers: Wagemans & van Tuinen NV (HOLLAND)

BELOW: Interior with pine slatted ceiling and oak-faced fireplace canopy. Settee and chair covered in green-and-yellow-striped fabric. Handmade rug with yellow and off-white design on deep red ground. Interior designer: Frederick Manning. Furniture and furnishings by Bowman Bros Ltd (GB)

ABOVE: Corner of a salon. Low folding table of polished pearwood with black Formica surface. Chairs, also of pearwood, are upholstered in yellow *satin de laine*. Walls are light grey. Designer: Jacques Dumond (FRANCE)

Informal arrangement for a study-cum-sitting room. Settee (upholstered in rib-cord), writing table and magazine/book-holder are harmoniously designed in natural birch. Green carpeting, light grey walls and red-lacquered triangular occasional table add colour. Chairs are Swedish. Designer: A. A. Patijn. Makers: Meubelfabriek Swanborn (HOLLAND)

Cocktail wall cabinet in painted whitewood set against a wall distempered light grey. The two-metre long shelves are of palissander; floor is dark grey. Designer: William Penaat. Makers: Metz & Co. (HOLLAND)

Living-room furnished with *Bertoia* form-wire chairs on rod frames finished black oxide, white vinyl or white enamel. The dining chairs are contour shaped with canvas or foam rubber seat pads in tangerine, black, lemon or turquoise; the pivoting diamond-shaped lounge chairs also have removable foam rubber cushioning covered in Prestini cotton fabrics in five colours. The high-back chair (*far left*) and ottoman (*right*) are designed for deep comfort with black oxide seat contour and base cushioned with foam rubber. Designers: Florence Knoll and Knoll Planning Unit. Makers: Knoll Associates Inc. (USA)

Piano in mahogany with satin-finish brass lyre, ferrules and tops to the legs. The slender tapered legs are not entirely straight: they curve in accordance with the classical precedent of entasis. Designer: Walter Dorwin Teague Associates. Makers: Steinway & Sons Inc. (USA). (Entasis—the slight swelling outline given to the shaft of a column to correct apparent concavity.)

Free-standing triple-sectional cupboard with shelves. Total height 6 feet 10¾ inches, the cupboards each measuring 27½ inches wide by 15¾ inches deep. Top, sides and door handle of centre cupboard are teak; front and back panels and frame are lacquered black. Designer: David Rosén, N.K. Design Studio. Makers A/B Nordiska Kompaniet (SWEDEN)

BELOW: Armchair on bentwood frame with leather seat. Table legs are also bentwood with teak or jacaranda top. Designer: Yngve Ekström. Makers: ESE-Möbler (SWEDEN)

Occasional table in brown and pollard oak with corded magazine racks. The flap of the centre cupboard lifts and slides under the top. Designer and maker: H. J. Perkins (GB). RIGHT: Hand-made desk and chair in mahogany. Chair back and Dunlopillo seat covered in a Primavera fabric. Desk designer: A. J. Stiff, chair by A. Noble. Makers: Primavera (London) Ltd (GB)

Drop-front cocktail cabinet of Burma teak on ladder mount, the front veneered in Ceylon satinwood with inlay motif in flowered satinwood, ebony and tamarind. Designer: J. Jonklaas, MSIA. Makers: The Decorators & Furnishers Ltd (CEYLON)

ABOVE: Wire magazine holder, 8-gauge frame with 12-gauge circles. spray-painted in a variety of colours. Designer: John Crichton. Maker: Tom Beer (NEW ZEALAND). LEFT: Drop-side table in plane, 22 inches wide by 3 feet long extended. Designer: Marianne Boman. Makers: O/Y Boman AB (FINLAND)

BELOW: Steel-framed four-drawer writing desk in mahogany or birch. Drawers of primavera walnut with clear lacquer finish, lined with birch. Designer: Peter Cotton, ACID. Makers: Perpetua Furniture Ltd (CANADA) (*Photo: Graham Warrington*)

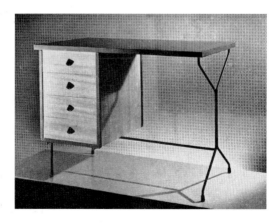

LEFT: Free-standing bookshelves of teak with cherrywood shelves and deep base drawer. Designed and made by Knud Juul-Hansen (DENMARK)

Cabinet in teak with carved decoration on the doors. The writing table has a teak top on grey-lacquered legs. The black granite top of the occasional table in the foreground is supported on oiled pinewood legs. Designers: Sven Engström and Gunnar Myrstrand. Makers: A/B Skaraborgs Möbelindustri (SWEDEN)

Living-room in the extendible house built by Simms Sons & Cooke Ltd. Architect: W. M. Carter, ARIBA. Off-white Indian rug, flame textured curtain fabric, and light grey wallpaper. Occasional table and standard lamp in natural mahogany. Outside backs of settee and chairs in light grey fabric, seats and inside backs in dark brown and grey; natural mahogany legs and arms. Designer: Robert Mabon. All furniture and fittings supplied by Dunn's of Bromley (GB)

BELOW: Teak and cherrywood reading desk, chair and writing table with glass-topped extension. Chair designed by Erik Buck; desk and table designed and made by Knud Juul-Hansen (DENMARK)

ABOVE: Three-piece sectional settee and corner table in oak, finished a butternut tone. Upholstery of 'knubette' (Respirovinyl) plastic in red, lime, emerald green or grey. Designers and makers: T. Baumritter & Co. Inc. (USA)

RIGHT AND BELOW: Walnut-topped cocktail tables on polished brass legs. Designer: T. H. Robsjohn-Gibbings. Makers: The Widdicomb Furniture Company (USA)

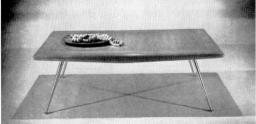

BELOW: White birch sideboard with dark mahogany doors and birch-framed electric clock. Wall brackets are copper. Sideboard designer: S. Asscher. Maker: Asscher Interiors (HOLLAND).

BELOW: Settee, designed by Lea Nevalinna, of white painted birch covered with a black-and-white-striped handwoven fabric. Tables, designed by Eila Meiling, have natural teak tops on black painted metal legs. Adjustable metal frame lamp-stand designed by Eero Paatela. Furniture makers: TE-MA (FINLAND). BELOW (Right): Glass-topped stone-shaped coffee-table with cut-out recess for ash-tray or vase. Supports are double cones of rosewood, waisted, with a solid cast brass stretcher. Designer: Edward Wormley. Makers: Dunbar Furniture Corporation (USA)

Living-room of Vancouver apartment designed and decorated for his own use by Mario Prizek. Walls and ceiling in various tones of sandalwood brown; deep terra-cotta asphalt tiled floors with black tiled borders. Carpet in oyster white. Settee covered in deep brown heavily textured flax fabric, and chair in the same material in chartreuse. Draperies are of wine grown jersey. Table lamps have mahogany bases with copper base caps and deep tangerine corduroy shades
Furniture designers: Morrison-Bush Associates Ltd (CANADA). *(Photo: Graham Warrington)*

Small three-drawer chest (20⅝ inches high) with birch or walnut top and welded angle frame on legs of chrome-plated steel. Side panels in neutral or brightly coloured combination. Designer: Charles Eames. Makers: Herman Miller Furniture Co (USA)

Black wrought-iron hanging wall mirror with opaque white glass pivoting shelves, overall 25 inches high by 14 inches wide, 8-inch deep shelves. Designer: Paul Mc-Cobb. Makers: Bryce Originals (USA)

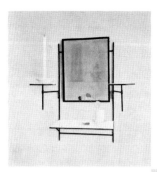

Glass-topped dressing table of Manilla rattan, with under shelf and stool seat executed in pulp wrapping cane. Designer: René Jean Caillette. Maker: Chevallier (FRANCE)

ABOVE: Low, three-tier dressing table in varnished sycamore, the drawers being faced with rose embossed fabric. Stool covered in white fur. Gilded metal light brackets. Designer: Jean Royère (FRANCE)

RIGHT: Bedroom scheme with bedcover and matching curtains of Vantona *Starlight* design, available in Tudor rose, jade green, royal blue or autumn gold. Makers: Vantona Textiles Ltd. *Esprit* chair in cherry red wool tapestry. Designer: Howard Keith, MSIA. Makers: H. K. Furniture Ltd (GB)

A bedroom in a New York apartment, designed also as a retreat for the non-television addict. Well-chosen materials, colours and finishes have created a pleasing, uncluttered interior within a restricted space of 14 feet by 14 feet. The light oak headboard extends from wall to wall; storage chest, cupboards, shelving and even reading lamps are built into it, thus providing ample surface space. Walls and carpet are a warm light grey; the bedspread is in a brown and gold heavy woven fabric with bright accents of coral and brown in the drapery to tone. Designed and furnished by Wor-De-Klee Inc. (USA)

Double-sided nursery toy unit on wheels in multi-ply with ivory enamel finish and black plastic handles. Shut down lids, pull-down side flaps and drawer opening on both sides give easy access to a child. Designed and made by A. J. Eves, BA (GB)
(Photo: Marchant)

Writing bureau in makoré and beech in two sections, with deep low slung drawers and intervening space for papers. Designed and made by C. Dorosz, student at the L.C.C. Technical College for Furnishing Trades (GB)

Radiogram cabinet in Burma teak, the front veneered with Ceylon satinwood and mahogany. Designer: T. Jonklaas, MSIA. Makers: The Decorators & Furnishers Ltd (CEYLON)

RIGHT: Corner cupboard in waxed oak with cane-panelled doors. Designer: Jean Royère (FRANCE)

Work-table in walnut, consisting of self-contained table and sewing box lined with English plane. Designer and maker: Kenneth D. Lampard (GB)

Small cabinet in cherrywood with flat polished brass circular key plate and brass-tipped hinges. Designer: B. Helweg-Möller. Maker: Jacob Kjær (DENMARK)

LEFT: Combined bookcase and cupboard in African walnut; laminated cupboard doors veneered in Queensland walnut with sycamore handles and sliding glass panels to top section. Designer: Neil Morris. Makers: H. Morris & ((GB)

Chest with leather-bound metal frame, front veneered acajou. Copper handles are also bound with leather. Designer: Jacques Adnet. Makers: Compagnie des Arts Français S/A (FRANCE)

LEFT: Easy chair with wide arms and sloping back. Welded steel rod frame mounted on ball-bearing castors with hard rubber wheels, upholstered in grey tweed. Designer: Ernest Race, RDI, FSIA. Makers: Ernest Race Ltd (GB)

RIGHT: *Ditzel* easy chairs on smoked oak frames with exteriors covered in a dark brown woollen fabric and interiors lined a natural shade. Designers: Nanna and Jørgen Ditzel. Makers: A. P. Stolen (DENMARK)

RIGHT: Chair on metal frame finished black. The moulded seat and back are padded with foam rubber and are covered in a strong, hard-wearing fabric. Designer: Hans-Harald Molander, N.K. Design Studio. Makers: A/B Nordiska Kompaniet (SWEDEN)

BELOW: 'Knock-down' chair for assembly with six screws, the moulded seat finished blue on beech legs. Designer: Yngve Ekström. Makers: A/B Södra Snickeri- & Möbelfabriken (SWEDEN)

BELOW: *Sunlite* contour lounge chair with aluminium alloy tube frame and removable nylon covering in royal blue, green, red or gold. Designer: Julien Hebert. Maker: Siegmund Werner Ltd (CANADA)

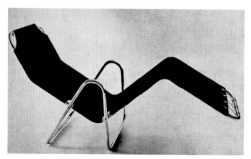

(Photo: Michel Brault)

The *Ditzel* chair of woven wicker on a sturdy mahogany frame. Designers: Nanna and Jørgen Ditzel. Maker: L. Pontoppidan (DENMARK). From Dunbar Furniture Corporation (USA)

Moulded chair finished mahogany on iron legs sprayed white plastic; the latter are designed so as to be secured to the seat by one screw only. Designer: Yngve Ekström. Makers: A/B Södra Snickeri- & Möbelfabriken (SWEDEN)

The *Bombay* chair of heavy woven rattan with spar varnish finish, frame of black wrought iron. Designer: John Risley. Makers: Ficks-Reed Company (USA)

Moulded plastic and fibreglass chairs in red, sea-green, yellow, elephant grey, off-white and other tones on metal legs or wire strut bases. Designer: Charles Eames. Makers: Herman Miller Furniture Co. (USA)

Settee upholstered in yellow and grey check cotton over Latex foam cushioning. Legs of natural polished beech. Designer: Ernest Race, RDI, FSIA. Makers: Ernest Race Ltd (GB)

RIGHT: Prototype chair with curved ladder back and seat upholstered in foam rubber. Designer: Poul M. Volther. Makers: Fælles-foreningen for Danmarks Brugsforeninger Møbler (DENMARK)

LEFT: Cradle-shaped lounge chair with beech legs, upholstered in fawn corduroy velvet with cushion and studs in red corduroy. Designed by Kelvin McAvoy for Liberty & Co. Ltd (GB)

BELOW: Natural petiribi table and chair covered in natural linen with hand-painted design in green on a light brown ground; alternative colourings white and yellow on black ground. Textile designer: Margot Portela Parker. Furniture designers and makers: Adams, SRL (ARGENTINA)

BELOW: Oak chair with moulded back-rest of laminated beech faced with Pacific walnut. Designer: David Fowler, MSIA. Makers: D. Meredew Ltd (GB)

ABOVE: Black metal-framed natural cane chair with inset Dunlopillo cushion; the cushion cover is removable. Designer: Dennis Lennon, MC, ARIBA (GB)

BELOW: Occasional chair covered in *Lucerna* handwoven fabrics in a variety of colours. The back is supported on a resilient laminated spine. Designer: Robin Day, ARCA, FSIA. Makers: Hille of London Ltd (GB)

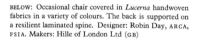

ABOVE: Nesting *Kangaroo* rocker and low table of welded steel rod enamelled white and graphite. Table top of natural teak. Designer: Ernest Race, RDI, FSIA. Makers: Ernest Race Ltd (GB)

LEFT: Slat-backed chair from the *Hilleplan* range with mahogany frame on beech legs. Seat and back cushions are reversible, the seat cushion being supported on tension springs. Designer: Robin Day, ARCA, FSIA. Makers: Hille of London Ltd (GB)

Corner of a Finnish living-room. Settee
covered in white woollen fabric with loose
cushion in brown and white; occasional
table in plane with hinged magazine rack;
black metal-frame chair with orange-brown
fabric cover. Designer: Marianne Boman.
Makers: O/Y Boman AB (FINLAND)

RIGHT: 'Long-Tom' stool in beech (length
40 inches), with seat covered in Heal's
Fitzroy fabric. Designers: Le Grest & Co.
(GB). The sycamore table illustrated is
designed by David Joel Ltd, for Heal's
of London (GB)

White rattan wing chair with open diamond pattern back support and arms. The matching rattan ring-base table has a glass top supported on five knobbed legs enclosed within a circular hoop. Designer: Jean Royère. Maker: Jean-Paul Gauberti (FRANCE)

Glass shelving 2 feet 3 inches long by 7 inches wide on oak, ash or acajou supports. Designer: René Jean Caillette (FRANCE)

Living-room furnished in mahogany with extendible combined bookcase and cupboard units lining one wall. Settee and armchair covered in handwoven fabrics. Standard lamp of brass with grey painted metal shade and ceiling lamp of white opalescent glass designed by Lisa Johansson-Pape. Furniture designer: Olof Ottelin. Maker: O/Y Stockmann AB (FINLAND)

'Knock-down' chair in Danish beech. Seat of foam rubber on flat helical springs, free-swinging back. Designer: Sigvard Bernadotte. Makers: France & Daverkosen (DENMARK)

LEFT: Walnut dining chair with foam rubber upholstered seat covered in linen. Designer: T. H. Robsjohn-Gibbings. Makers: The Widdicomb Furniture Co. (USA)

LEFT: Dining chair in Honduras mahogany, with seat and back covered in a red-spotted white woollen fabric. Designer: A. A. Patijn. Makers: Meubelfabriek Zijlstra (HOLLAND)

LEFT: *Dux* armchair on beech frame finished teak. Seat and back are covered in Danish *Plyds* fabrics black warp with yellow weft, with headrest in grey rep. Designer Alf Svensson. Makers: Ljungs Industrier AB (SWEDEN)

RIGHT: *Python* armchair with beech frame, hand-sprung back and tension-sprung seat; pocket spring interior cushion. Covered in Tibor or Whitehead fabrics. Designer: A. J. Milne, MSIA. Makers: E. Horace Holme Ltd (GB)

Red beech chair with plaited rattan back: seat covered in a black-and-yellow check fabric. Designer: S. I. R. Bertil Fridhagen. Makers: A/B Svenska Möbelfabrikerna (SWEDEN)

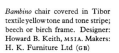

Bambino chair covered in Tibor textile yellow tone and tone stripe; beech or birch frame. Designer: Howard B. Keith, MSIA. Makers: H. K. Furniture Ltd (GB)

Armchair in Yugoslavian beech. Tapestry covered coil-sprung seat and rubberized hair back. Designer and maker: Roger Harcourt, High Wycombe College of Further Education (GB)

The *Milford* fireside chair from the *Ardale* range combines a polished sycamore frame with deep sprung upholstery and foam-rubber fillings, covered in attractive woollen tapestries. Designer: Laurence A. Reason. Makers: A. Reason & Sons Ltd (GB)

LEFT: Chair on birch frame finished mahogany, black, light grey and other colours. 'No-sag' sprung seat and back, seat padded foam rubber. Designer: Bengt Ruda. Makers: A/B Nordiska Kompaniet (SWEDEN)

Armchair in beech with yew arms, upholstered in grey moquette with Latex foam cushion seat on tension springs. Designer and maker: Peter Hayward, of the High Wycombe College of Further Education (GB)

RIGHT: Dining chair of natural red beech. Seat covered linen with a hand-printed leaf design in black on brown ground by Britt - Marie Arppe. Designer: Lea Nevalinna. Makers: TE-MA (FINLAND)

LEFT: Birch armchair with seat and back covered in a grey-green handwoven fabric. Designer: Stig Sallamaa. Makers: O/Y Stockmann AB (FINLAND)

RIGHT: Stacking armchair with red beech frame; seat and back covered with a black close-weave fabric over foam rubber. Designer: Axel Larsson. Maker: A/B Svenska Möbelfabrikerna Bodafors (SWEDEN)

Danish interior in which period and modern furniture are successfully blended. Table and chairs are in Royal Danish beech, with flattened arm rests and table top in walnut or mahogany finishes. Designed and made by: France & Daverkosen (DENMARK)

Waxed white ash writing bureau on black steel legs. It is equipped with plenty of cupboard, drawer and shelf space, and the writing surface to the fall is faced with black linoleum. Designed and made by René Jean Caillette (FRANCE)

Writing desk and chair in ash and walnut; the drawer fronts are shaped to form full-width handles. An enlarged drawing makes a decorative background panel. Designed by Geneviève Pons for 'La Maîtrise', Galeries Lafayette (FRANCE)

Teak study or dining table on brass legs, top surfaced with black Formica. Blue webbing is used for the seat and back of the matching teak chairs. Draperies are champagne with blue, yellow and brown motifs. Designer: A. A. Patijn. Makers: Meubelfabriek Zijlstra (HOLLAND)

Writing desk in natural acajou on copper-finished metal demountable base. Space for a typewriter is neatly provided by lowering the drawer unit. Chairs are upholstered in washable *Acella* plastic. The settee converts to a bed, to which the small circular table visible beneath the desk forms the headpiece. Designer: Gautier-Delaye. Makers: Vergnères Fils (FRANCE)

Polished beech sectional settee, and armchair, tension-sprung seat and back and spring-filled tapestry cushions. Designer: R. A. Long. Table by A. J. Milne, MSIA, *Skittles* rug by Ronald Grierson. For: Heal's of London (GB)

Beech settee with teak-stained legs, upholstered in hairlock and covered in a black, grey and white striped woollen fabric with ends in a darker colour. Designers: Ejner Larsen and A. Bender Madsen. Makers: Fritz Hansens Eftfl (DENMARK)

Settee in grey 'astrakan'-type fabric, buttoned in black. Cushions an arms covered in Tibor deep-textured Berkeley fabric in lemon yellow Overall size 8 feet 6 inches by 2 feet 2 inches. Designed by Kelvin McAvo for Liberty & Company Ltd (GB)

Rocking chair on wrought-iron frame lacquered black. The continuou back, seat and leg-rest is in natural rattan. Designer: Dirk va Sliedregt. Makers: Gebr. Jonkers (HOLLAND)

Settee-bed in agba and beech with back-rest and part of side rails covered in woven cane. Tweed in a yellow and natural mixture covers the hair mattress, which rests on rubber webbing. The standard lamp is in mahogany and brass. Designer: Geoffrey Dunn. Makers: Dunn's of Bromley (GB)

Settee with square ends upholstered in Tranås wool and rayon fabrics in a two-tone colour scheme. *Svedje* wool and hair carpet on pure linen warp. *Sorrento* hand-printed rayon draperies are designed by Robert Pippal. Makers: Tabergs Yllefabriks AB (SWEDEN)

Curved bench seat on fumed oak supports, upholstered in a rust-and-white hand-woven fabric. Natural dried leaves mounted on Oregon pine and covered with glass make a decorative top to the low coffee table. Designer and maker: Jean Royère (FRANCE)

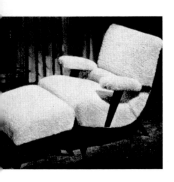

LEFT: Lounge chair, shaped to the contour of the body, and foot rest on hardwood frames finished in suede or black. *No-sag* springs; white tufted looptwist fabric covering over rubberised hair. Designers and makers: Selig of Leominster (USA)

Matching settee and chair upholstered in contrasting wool fabrics—exterior yellow, interior and foam rubber cushions in black, green and yellow stripes. Legs of polished beech, stained black. Designer: Svante Skogh, Arch. SIR. Makers: Ernst Hjertquist (SWEDEN)

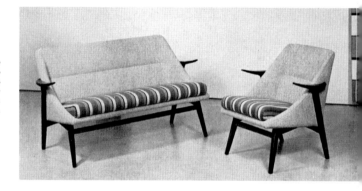

Settee and chair in polished beech, finished jacaranda. Hair padding, plain green wool fabric covering, with foam rubber cushions in contrasting green and brown stripes. Designer: Svante Skogh, Arch. SIR. Makers: Ernst Hjertquist (SWEDEN)

Three pieces in natural cherrywood upholstered in foam rubber over springs. Coverings are in De Ploeg *Dixie* wool fabrics in black/white (settee) and black/yellow for the chair. Designer: Th. Ruth. Makers: Wagemans & van Tuinen, NV, (HOLLAND)

Small settee on birch legs stained black, upholstered in fabrics to individual choice over deep foam rubber cushioning and *No-sag* springs. Designer: Bengt Ruda. Makers: AB Nordiska Kompaniet (SWEDEN)

Armless curved floating-seat sofa made in lengths from 7 to 12 feet on frame of walnut. Padded seat and back are covered in cotton, jute, rayon, bouclé or nylon metal texture fabrics designed by Hugo Dreyfuss. Designer: Vladimir Kagan. Makers: Kagan-Dreyfuss Inc. (USA)

Settee or day-bed unit in light oak or other woods with interior sprung cushions covered in a variety of texture fabrics designed by Hugo Dreyfuss. Designer: Vladimir Kagan. Makers: Kagan-Dreyfuss Inc. (USA)

BELOW: 'Knock-down' settee in Danish beech, a companion piece to the chair illustrated in our last volume. Seat of foam rubber on flat helical springs, free swinging back. Designer: Sigvard Bernadotte. Makers: France & Daverkosen (DENMARK) for John Stuart Inc. (USA)

Straight back settee on beech frame with shaped back and long seat cushions upholstered in a speckled wool fabric. Designers: Peter Hvidt and O. Mølgaard Nielsen. Makers: France & Daverkosen (DENMARK)

ABOVE: *Contour* lounge chair on walnut legs, with deep foam rubber upholstery covered in a black-and-white chenille texture fabric designed by Hugo Dreyfuss. Designer: Vladimir Kagan. Makers: Kagan-Dreyfuss Inc. (USA).

Oronsay. Beech frame upholstered rubberised hair; tension sprung seat and back, Latex foam cushion. It is upholstered in wool fabrics in a two-tone colour scheme. Designer: Ronald A. Long. Makers: R. S. Stevens Ltd (GB)

Beech armchair, legs stained teak; hairlock upholstery with wool fabric covering and contrasting cushion. Designers: Ejner Larsen and A. Bender Madsen. Makers: Fritz Hansens Eftfl (DENMARK)

Lightweight armchair in English beech; tension sprung seat and back and Latex foam cushion covered in grey/off-white tapestry with cherry pipings. Designer: F. G. Clark. Makers: George Clark (Bristol) Ltd (GB)

ABOVE: Beech armchair with walnut armrests and leg tips. Tension sprung seat, upholstered in yellow/black panama-weave wool over foam rubber. Designers: Poul Elnegaard (chair), Aagaard Andersen (fabric). Makers: Unika-Væv (DENMARK)

OPPOSITE: Light armchair on ash frame with bucket seat upholstered in a dark wool fabric. Designer: Pierre Guariche (FRANCE)

Texaloom cane chair in pale grey with foam rubber loose cushion covered in black/white *Helico* texturedrape designed by Tibor Reich, FSIA (GB)

Chair upholstered in grey wool fabric over hair with loose sprung cushion in contrasting stripes of yellow, grey and dark brown; legs and arm tips of teak. Designer: Kurt Olsen. Makers: A. Andersen & Bohm (DENMARK)

OPPOSITE: *Scania.* Beech frame, dark green wool upholstery, foam rubber cushions. Striped seat cushion rests on tension sprung base. Designer: Alf Svensson. Makers: Madrass-Fabriken Dux A B (SWEDEN)

Matching stool and chair in fumed oak upholstered in a grey woollen fabric. The chair has a detachable head-rest (not shown) and foam rubber padded seat. Designer: Hans J. Wegner. Makers: A. P. Stolen (DENMARK)

Easy chair with Latex foam padded armrests and cushioning, and tension-sprung seat and back. Medium oak or beech frame with walnut veneer. Designed and made by Greaves & Thomas Ltd (GB)

Wicker armchair on steel frame, lacquered black. Designed by H. Baliero for OAM (ARGENTINA)

Easy chair in fumed oak, oil finished, with loose foam rubber back and seat cushions on *Telax*-rubber bands. Designer: Poul M. Volther. Makers: Fælles-foreningen for Danmarks Brugsforeninger Møbler (DENMARK)

Bentwood dining chair in oak. The padded seat and back are covered in brown-and-white checked wool. Designer: D. S. Vorster. Makers: D. S. Vorster & Co. (Pty) Ltd (S. AFRICA)

Cherrywood dining chair with armrests carved to give a firm hand grip. Upholstered in blue wool over foam rubber. Designer: A. A. Patijn. Makers: Meubelfabriek Zijlstra (HOLLAND)

Steel-framed armchair, enamelled black with white plastic feet. Seat and back are of bent plywood, padded with foam rubber and covered in striped linen. Designer: W. H. Gispen. Makers: Kembo fabrieken (HOLLAND)

BELOW: Low armchair in walnut, upholstered in moquette in red, grey, mustard, black, green or fawn. Designer: Neil Morris. Makers: Morris of Glasgow (GB)

Adam. Low armchair in oak or beech. The hairlock-padded cushions are cover-ed in wool fabrics in a variety of colours. Designer: Kurt Østervig. Makers: Jason Furniture Factories (DENMARK)

Shelved-back armchair upholstered in black-and-yellow wool fabric; legs and armtips are of teak. Designer: Kurt Olsen. Makers: A. Andersen & Bohm (DENMARK)

Chair designed for tropical use constructed entirely of bent cane with soft cane bindings. Designed and made by Jean Royère in collaboration with Paul Gauberti (FRANCE)

Walnut armchair, upholstered in a printed linen fabric over foam rubber upholstery. Designer: T. H. Robsjohn-Gibbings. Makers: The Widdicomb Furniture Company (USA)

Low chair in acajou with sprung seat and back upholstered in grey handwoven fabric. From the *Formule* range of sectional furniture designed by H. Kempkes Jr. Makers: Kempkes' Meubelfabrieken, NV (HOLLAND)

LEFT: Armchair in walnut or teak with loose foam rubber cushions covered in a green close-weave wool fabric. Designer: Karl Erik Ekselius. Makers: A/B J.O. Carlsson (SWEDEN)

RIGHT: Walnut *Contour* chair, natural finish, upholstered hair and foam rubber covered in natural-and-black linen mixture weave by Hugo Dreyfuss. Chair designed by Vladimir Kagan. Makers: Kagan-Dreyfuss Inc. (USA)

Armchair of polished birch stained black, with pivoting or fixed back, deep foam rubber cushioning and *No-sag* springs in the seat. Designer: Bengt Ruda. Makers: A/B Nordiska Kompaniet (SWEDEN)

RIGHT: *Bock* chair on beech frame with birch legs stained black. Black saddle-girth and cotton-covered rubber cushion. Designer: Yngve Ekström Makers: ESE-Möbler (SWEDEN)

Kurt. Natural oak, upholstered *Epeda* springs and hairlock under Unica Væv fabrics. Designer: Kurt Østervig. Makers: Jason Furniture Factories (DENMARK)

Chrome plated steel base with horizontal 'cartridge' foam-rubber upholstery covered in fabrics to individual choice. Designer: George Nelson. Makers: Herman Miller Furniture Company (USA)

Walnut frame upholstered in a printed linen fabric over foam rubber. Designer: T. H. Robsjohn-Gibbings. Makers: The Widdicomb Furniture Company (USA)

Beech frame, stained black, with white plastic corded seat and back. Designer: Bertil Fridhagen. Makers: A B Svenska Möbelfabrikerna, Bodafors (SWEDEN)

Fibreglass plastic seat, black wrought-iron frame on hardwood rocker base, honey tone finish. Designer: Lawrence Peabody. Makers: Selig of Leominster (USA)

White beech frame, walnut faced beech back; seat covered Tibor fabrics. Designers: Meredew Design Group. Makers: D. Meredew Ltd (GB)

Fumed oak frame, hairlock seat, grey-brown wool fabric corver. Designer: Hans J. Wegner. Makers: Carl Hansen & Son Møbelfabrik (DENMARK)

Walnut, oak or mahogany frame; moquette upholstery over foam rubber. Designer: Neil Morris. Makers: Morris of Glasgow (GB)

Waxed Japanese ash frame, laminated bamboo seat. Designed by Isamu Kenmochi and Akira Shinjo, Industrial Arts Institute, Tokyo (JAPAN)

Lazy Bowl garden chair on gold anodized aluminium frame. The detachable rattan cradle seat is on nylon bearings and automatically adjusts to the sitter's weight. Designer: James C. Witty. Makers: The Troy Sunshade Co. (USA)

Occasional chair in natural beech with *Telax*-rubber banded seat and foam rubber cushions covered in fabrics to individual choice. Designer: Poul M. Volther. Makers: Fællesforeningen for Danmarks Brugsforeninger Møbler (DENMARK)

Reclining chair in moulded plywood, cellulose finished, with mahogany legs and frame. Designed and made by Martin Grierson (GB)

Wrought-iron garden chair lacquered orange, with white knobs; the seat is in perforated tôle. Designed and made by Jean Royère (FRANCE)

Occasional chair of English walnut, with woven piping cord seat. Designed and made by J. Y. Johnstone at the Royal College of Art (GB)

Forté laminated chair, walnut, mahogany, elm or oak veneer. Latex foam cushion. Designers and makers: E. Khan & Co. Ltd (Tecta Division) (GB)

Folding chair on black-lacquered tubular steel frame. The detachable canvas seat and back is made in several colours. Designer: Olof Pira. Makers: AB Nordisk Kompaniet (SWEDEN)

Birch dining chair with bent plywood seat and back rest covered in grey-green checked linen over foam rubber. Designer. W. H. Gispen. Maker: Kembo fabrieken (HOLLAND)

Stackable three-legged dining chair in beech or smoked oak with teak seat. Designer: Hans J. Wegner (DENMARK). For Woolland Bros. Ltd (GB)

Button-back wing settee and chair with flattened arm rests. The matching trolley has a fitted tray top. Designed and made by I. H. Hunt & Co. (Yatton) Ltd (GB)

Living-room with floor of *Accotile* cork. Makers: Armstrong Cork Co. Ltd. (GB). Upholstered chairs designed by Howard Keith; beech ebonised stacking chairs and natural beech table with black Warerite top by Robin Day. Draperies at left are *Macrahanish* hand-printed cotton designed by Robert Stewart; at right *Philodendron* hand-printed linen by Helen Close. For Liberty & Co. Ltd (GB)

Settee, table and chair of Honduras mahogany with loose sprung cushions upholstered in yellow wool fabric, with yellow-and-white striped seat and back facings. Curtains are off-white, carpet silver-grey. The light fitting is brass. Designer: A. A. Patijn. Makers: Meubelfabriek Zijlstra (HOLLAND)

BELOW: Swedish rocker, scrubbed pine; mahogany table wax finished; Isokon long chair in walnut and birch, upholstered Latex foam and lemon yellow tweed. Wall fitments of pine, natural waxed outside, cellulosed inside, on steel rod supports with turned beech finials. Designer Dennis Young ARCA, MSIA. Table and fittings made by Design London Ltd (GB) (*Photo: A. Lammer*)

Chairs in deep texture fabrics *Henley* white, and *Hong Kong* flame with grey-and-white motifs. Curtain *Cymbeline* in persimmon shot Lurex gold thread. Designer: Tibor Reich, FSIA. Makers: Tibor Ltd. Table by S. Hille & Co. Ltd. Chairs by H. K. Furniture Ltd (GB)

Dux chairs upholstered in Tranås wool and rayon fabrics. *Svedje* wool and hair carpet on pure linen warp. Makers: Tabergs Yllefabriks AB (SWEDEN)

Oiled teak table on black enamelled steel base. Designer: Pian Haggstrom. *Sab* teak chair, designed by Carin Bryggman; white wool seat cover handwoven by O/Y Metsovaara A/B. *Figaro* settee (see page 40). For TE-MA (FINLAND)

Bleached maple desk with natural ash top and sides, and maple chair upholstered in red leather. Polished brass pendant. Designer: Tommi Parzinger. Makers: Parzinger Originals Inc. (USA)

The copper-finished steel demountable framework of this dining group enables it to be easily packed. Table top and sideboard are in natural acajou; finger-holds are incorporated in the main body of the sideboard front, giving a smooth finish. Chairs are upholstered in washable *Acella* plastic. Designer: Gautier-Delaye. Makers: Vergnères Fils (FRANCE)

Four-foot sideboard in solid agba with walnut veneer on sliding doors; drop-leaf table, and slatted back chairs with tapestry seats. Designer: Herbert E. Gibbs. Makers: Herbert E. Gibbs Ltd (GB)

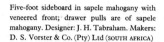

Five-foot sideboard in sapele mahogany with veneered front; drawer pulls are of sapele mahogany. Designer: J. H. Tabraham. Makers: D. S. Vorster & Co. (Pty) Ltd (SOUTH AFRICA)

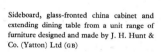

Sideboard, glass-fronted china cabinet and extending dining table from a unit range of furniture designed and made by J. H. Hunt & Co. (Yatton) Ltd (GB)

Beech dining group. The sideboard has an ash-lined fall front and the cupboard below is fitted with three shelves and a cutlery drawer. Exterior is veneered teak to match the shaped table top. The beech chairs have tapestry-covered stuffed seats and backs. Window draperies are *Coppice*, a cotton print designed by Mary White. Furniture designed by A. J. Milne, MSIA, for Heal's of London (GB)

Dining-room furnished in white birch with upholstery of *Sweet Corn*, *Mesh* or *Safari* Tibor fabrics. The table is extendible and on top of the sideboard is a small movable glass-fronted bookcase. Designers: Meredew Design Group. Makers: D. Meredew Ltd (GB)

Dining area in a Paris flat with *Securit* glass dividing wall. *Kimono* chairs and table base of wrought-iron stove-enamelled black, give added brilliance to the high gloss finish of the limewood top. Perforated tôle chair backs and black-and-yellow *Satellite* globes. Designer: Mathieu Matégot. Makers: Société Matégot (FRANCE)

Freba sideboard, comprising two cabinets with sliding doors of fibre and glass and a drawer unit, supported on steel tripod legs. Made in various woods, length 9 feet. Designer: Alfred Altherr, Arch. BSA. Makers: K. H. Frei (SWITZERLAND) *(Photo: Hans Finsler)*

Hand-made beech furniture with teak veneers. Chairs are upholstered in various fabrics over foam rubber. Designed by Nigel Walters, MSIA for Heal's of London (GB).

BELOW: Light oak bridge table with transparent glass surface; chair seats upholstered in plain green cotton. Designed and made by Jean Royère (FRANCE)

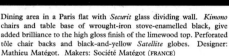

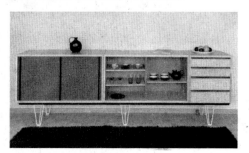

Solid hardwood sideboard on sycamore base, door panels veneered walnut, incised decoration. Designed and made by Bath Cabinet Makers Ltd (GB). (*Photo: Goran Billing*). FAR RIGHT: Cocktail cabinet with hand-decorated tiled drop front by Boris Chatman. Designed by Daisy Stricker for Rena Rosenthal Inc. (USA). BELOW: Windsor *Bergère* suite in beech, natural waxed finish, and elm and beech occasional table. The chair has an extra deep seat fitted with foam rubber cushion, with a feather-down filled back cushion. The tension sprung settee is similarly upholstered. Coverings are in a selected range of contemporary fabrics. Designer: L. R. Ercolani. Makers, Furniture Industries Ltd (GB)

View across the dining-room into the kitchen in the designer's own house in Tokyo. There are no dividing walls; instead the rooms can be closed off or thrown open to one another by means of sliding partitions running on grooved tracks inset in the flooring. Furniture & furnishings designed by Hiroshi Ohchi and made by the Fuse Manufacturing Co. Architect: Nobutoshi Satoh (JAPAN)

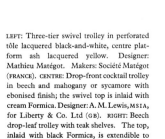

LEFT: Three-tier swivel trolley in perforated tôle lacquered black-and-white, centre platform ash lacquered yellow. Designer: Mathieu Matégot. Makers: Société Matégot (FRANCE). CENTRE: Drop-front cocktail trolley in beech and mahogany or sycamore with ebonised finish; the swivel top is inlaid with cream Formica. Designer: A. M. Lewis, MSIA, for Liberty & Co. Ltd (GB). RIGHT: Beech drop-leaf trolley with teak shelves. The top, inlaid with black Formica, is extendible to 3 feet. Designer: Yngve Ekström. Makers, Källemo Möbelfabrik AB (SWEDEN)

Occasional table on black wrought-iron legs with marble top and wicker magazine shelf. Designer: Maurizio Tempestini. Makers: John B. Salterini Co. Inc. (USA) Window draperies are *Electra*, a denim fabric on which the design is 'engraved' by a new printing process; a choice of six colours is available. Designers and makers, Titus Blatter & Co. (USA)

Limewood table on wrought-iron legs stove-enamelled black. The highly polished top contrasts with the black matt Formica surface of the drawer shelf *Kimono* chair on wrought-iron frame with tôle back and rattan seat. The wall mirror is also framed in rattan. Designer: Mathieu Matégot. Makers: Société Matégot (FRANCE)

Teak or mahogany small table, 22 inches high, with extending hinged top. The two leaves fold over one another, measuring 26 × 20½ inches when closed and 26 × 41 inches fully extended. Designers: Sven Engström and Gunnar Myrstrand. Makers: A/B Skaraborgs Möbelindustri (SWEDEN)

Glass-topped black wrought-iron table and chairs from the *Riviera* collection. The slip seats to the chairs are covered in sailcloth dyed a light orange, styled melon. Designer: Maurizio Tempestini. Makers: John B. Salterini Co. Inc. (USA)

Gate-leg table. The legs slide in radial grooves and are braced for strength and rigidity. Each pivots on a single radius arm about one of the four points in the central unit, thus dispensing with the normal bars and pivots at base. Designed and made by J. Y Johnstone, Des. RCA, at the Royal College of Art (GB)

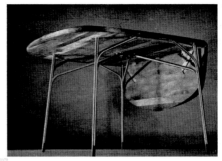

Oval drop-leaf table in birch, oak, walnut, mahogany, korina or cherrywood. Four legs swing out to support the extended leaves, which increase the width from 1 foot 6 inches to 3 feet 6 inches; length 5 feet 6 inches. Designer: Vladimir Kagan Makers: Kagan-Dreyfuss Inc. (USA)

Two-tier coffee table with a top of unusual design 2 feet 5 inches long. This and the shelf are veneered with oak, mahogany or stripey walnut in natural finishes. Designer: Ewart Myer. Makers: Horatio Myer & Co. Ltd (GB)

TOP: Occasional table in Australian walnut with underhung drawer. The top is 3 feet 4 inches long, the stretchers forming a magazine rack. Designed and made by James Herbert. ABOVE: Dining table in oak inlaid Indian laurel, with Indian laurel feet. The top is 4 feet long, extending by tambour action to 6 feet. Designed and made by J. R. Varrall. Both are students at the L.C.C. Technical College for the Furnishing Trades (GB)

While allowing for considerable freedom in the expression of details and refinements, the trend of modern furnishing is towards a certain discipline both of shape and in the manner of siting. A process of tidying up, which started in the kitchen, is now finding its way around the house. It is partly an æsthetic exercise in spatial geometry, but it is also (and more important from the practical point of view) the result of endeavouring to make homes easier to run and more convenient to live in.

Because the practical and æsthetic aims are therefore of a positive and purposeful nature, the keynote of what is still clumsily referred to as ' contemporary design' is a solid one that should ensure more than an ephemeral existence if logically pursued.

Furniture is the functional basis of domestic comfort within the shelter, heat and light-providing architectural framework. Its design is as much a science as an art and if the purity and simplicity of form emerging from proper scientific study exhibits a tendency toward starkness, any such starkness is better countered in the less functional aspects of furnishing, manifest in wallpapers, textile patterns, carpets and other items giving freer rein to expression in colour and pattern, than by injudicious departure from well-tried forms.

The rooms and furniture illustrated in this section show many interpretations within this broad theme and are loosely classified according to types of room and varieties of furniture within recognised categories. The representation is typical of modern thought and reveals the current trends of the world's leading designers.

Living-room furnished in natural mahogany, the bedroom in ash and light blue Formica, with a white cord dividing screen. A sense of unity is achieved by the use of black for the panel above the bed, the cushion-to the long bench, and Formica facings to cabinet. Armchairs have deep Latex foam cushioning and are upholstered in dark and light shades of blue and green; dining chairs are in red. The glass-topped small metal table stands on a golden yellow rug. Furniture made by Garfagni and Castellaneta. Bedroom mural in tones of grey by R. Fumeron. Interior designed by Ramos (FRANCE)

Bookcase faced with teak; small palette table and writing desk in natural mahogany finish. The deep sprung settee and chair are upholstered in a tapestry weave. In the inner room, the dining group is veneered in mahogany and rosewood. Interior furnished by Harrods of London (GB)

A basic two-colour scheme relieved by touches of yellow. Wallpaper from the Crown range of the Wall Paper Manufacturers Ltd; its simplicity heightens the effect of the dark toned furnishing. Coffee table and mahogany sideboard are designed by Terence Conran. Interior furnished by Peter Jones Ltd (GB)

Cocktail cabinet (replacing original doorway) inset in a slatted mahogany living-room wall. Photostat enlargement of a Steinberg drawing mounted on the door makes a decorative panel when it is closed. The bench seat is in birch. Designer: Ian Bradbery, MSIA. Makers: Modular Displays Ltd (GB)

ABOVE: Furniture in black and green *Beka* lacquer finish, desk interior sycamore. The typewriter folds back inside; raised writing shelf is in green glass. Walls are light grey, with yellow-green panel over desk; carpet grey-green; armchairs upholstered in yellow. Tile hearth, chimney encased in tôle frame. Interior designed and executed by Raphaël (FRANCE)

Open plan interior with dividing walls in a herring-bone plastic wallpaper, and in dark wood panelling. Bleached walnut, teak and lacquer furniture; carpet beige. Built-in television set, radio and tape recorder in wall fitment at left of desk
Designed by Paul László and executed by László Inc. (USA)

BELOW: Bleached walnut combination unit incorporating fitted bar, radio and recording equipment, writing desk and book storage; built-in lighting in canopy and bar make it entirely self-contained. Designer: Hans N. Wormann. Makers: F. Bauerschmidt & Son (USA)

ABOVE: Walnut shelf unit on brass supports nailed into brick wall. Beneath is a custom made walnut cabinet, and at right a unit housing radio, amplifier and record player in the top half with storage space below; top is a burl walnut. Designed and made by William Pahlmann Associates Inc. (USA)

ABOVE: Gramophone and record cabinet, 3 feet wide, in Heart Rimu wood mounted on black iron base. The roll-back top gives easy access to the record player. Designer: John Crichton (NEW ZEALAND). RIGHT: Wall unit incorporating a built-in television, radio and tape recorder. When not in use it is completely hidden behind folding doors
Designer: Paul László. Made by László Inc. (USA).

Bar in walnut, 4 feet 4 inches high, fitted with refrigerator and interior lighting. The fall is surfaced with black arborite stain resistant plastic. Matching stool has a green leather-covered seat. Designer: Josef Frank. Makers: Svenskt Tenn AB (SWEDEN)

Beech sideboard, mansonia veneer, with routed front and three drawers. One-third fitted shelf enclosed by door, two-thirds by fall front. Height 4 feet. Designed by H. E. Long, MSIA. For Heal's of London (GB)

BELOW: A colourful floor laid with *Accoflex* vinyl asbestos marbled and plain black tiles; many designs and colours are available. Makers: Armstrong Cork Co. Ltd. The coffee tables on polished steel frames with slate/mahogany tops and brass fittings are designed and made by Michael Wickham. Chairs are by Buoyant Upholstery Co. Ltd (GB) *(Photo: Michael Wickham)*

Hardwood desk veneered in rosewood and mahogany with ample
storage space beneath the raised top. It is also available in walnut.
Designer: Christopher Heal, FSIA. Makers: Heal's of London (GB)

ABOVE: Bureau made in nutwood or cherrywood with
maple surface to writing shelf. Pearwood chair upholstered in yellow plastic. Designers and makers:
Möbelfabrik Gebrüder Rohrer GmbH (GERMANY)

Scored brick fireplace framed
within black wrought-iron screen,
with hook-on shelves for plants
or books. Slung seat and back to
chair and settee are in a black
plastic fabric. Designer and maker:
Jean Royère (FRANCE)

Knock-down desk and chair in
natural teak. Designer: C. Braakman. Makers: NV Utrechtsche
Machinale Stoel-en Meubelfabriek UMS (HOLLAND)

ABOVE: Oak bureau on black wrought-iron frame,
natural parchment surface to fall. Wrought-iron
chair upholstered in black-and-white cotton check.
Desk designed by Jean Royère; chair by Jean-Paul
Gauberti (FRANCE)

BELOW: Mahogany and redbeech desk/table with hinged top. The small matching cabinet underneath is on castors and can be slid out. Designer: Axel Larsson. Makers: AB Svenska Möbelfabrikerna Bodafors (SWEDEN)

Continuous wall unit in smoked oak and pine. The same woods are used for extending table and divan, which has interior sprung back rest and seat upholstered in Unika-væv fabrics in plain grey and *Icicle* grey, white and black. Designer and maker: Knud Juul-Hansen (DENMARK)

BELOW: Drawing table for home use on white-lacquered steel frame, 2 feet 8 inches high. Fitted with two drawers and a side tray, and concealed lighting in the lid. Designer and maker: Jacques Dumond (FRANCE)

Writing desk on white-enamelled steel frame, rosewood top, with micarta box for papers. Charles Eames steel wire chair upholstered in Naugahyde. Desk designed by George Nelson. For Herman Miller Furniture Co. (USA)

ABOVE: Cherrywood writing desk, matt finish, with black plastic surface to pull-out writing shelf. The sides are extended to form a bookshelf; front sliding panels are in walnut. Designers and makers: Möbelfabrik Wilhelm Renz KG (GERMANY)

BELOW: Storage unit in African walnut on black angle iron frame. Top cabinet has sliding glass doors; lower doors are faced with washable eighteenth-century photostated engravings. Designer: Terence Conran. Makers: Conran Furniture (GB)

ABOVE: Custom-designed walnut bar and sideboard unit on polished brass legs, with marble plant shelf. The dining table is by the Herman Miller Furniture Company, and the chairs by Knoll Associates. Yellow carpet over white rubber flooring. Interior designed by architect Felix Augenfeld (USA) (*Photo: Alexandre Georges*)

RIGHT: A setting illustrating the advantages of an overall planned scheme in furniture design. All the pieces shown are from the G-Plan range in a light oak finish; the chairs are upholstered in wool fabric shot with Lurex metallic thread. Designers and makers: E. Gomme Ltd (GB) (*Photo: Anthony Denney, Vogue Studios*)

BELOW: Waxed elm dining group from the Windsor range. Seats of chair and the two 'love seats' are especially shaped for comfort; the curved back and rails are in beech. Designer: L. R. Ercolani. Makers: Furniture Industries Ltd (GB)

BELOW: Cooker-trolley in walnut, linseed finish, fitted with double-plate electric cooker and compartments for utensils and ingredients. Designers: Kim Hoffmann and Stephen Heidrich (USA)

LEFT: *Pavone* moulded foam rubber seat cushion and Hairlok preformed back upholstered in a two-tone colour scheme. A matching settee is also made. Designer: Howard B. Keith, MSIA. Makers: H.K. Furniture Ltd (GB)

RIGHT: *Formell* in beech; elm, mahogany, walnut, jacaranda or teak finish. Upholstered *Dux* springs and foam rubber with wool fabric cover. Designer: Alf Svensson. Makers: Ljungs Industrier AB (SWEDEN)

BELOW: *Palmir* tension sprung chair with moulded Hairlok back; Lintafoam cushion. A matching settee is also made; both are available in a wide range of covering fabrics. Designer: Howard B. Keith, MSIA. Makers: H.K. Furniture Ltd (GB)

ABOVE: Armchair with firm rubber-slatted seat on ebonised cherrywood legs. Yellow/black striped tweed cover over foam rubber padding. Designers and makers: Wörrlein Werkstätten (GERMANY)

ABOVE: Natural cherrywood armchair from the *Casala* range. Foam rubber padding with black/white wool fabric cover. Designer: D. Hinz. Makers: Carl Sasse KG (GERMANY)

LEFT: Moulded plywood chair on steel legs enamelled black. Seat padded foam rubber, back rubberised hair, upholstered mohair wool tweed. Ten different colours are available. Designer: Earle A. Morrison. Makers: Robin Bush Associates Ltd (CANADA)

RIGHT: *Sark* on hardwood frame upholstered rubberised hair. Cover is in natural and black *Stratford* deep texture Tibor fabric. Latex foam cushion. Designer: Ronald E. Long, MSIA. Makers: R. S. Stevens Ltd (GB)

BELOW: *Congo* in cherrywood, sprung seat and foam rubber padded back. Upholstered in De Ploeg *Gent* moss-textured wool fabrics in natural and black. Designer: Th. Ruth. Makers: Wagemans & van Tuinen NV (HOLLAND)

BELOW: *Balmoral* on hardwood frame. Rubberised hair upholstery with deep texture fabric cover in contrasting colours. Latex foam cushion. Designer: Ronald E. Long, MSIA. Makers: R. S. Stevens Ltd (GB)

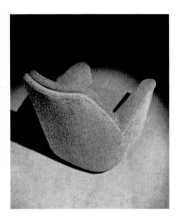

ABOVE: Wing chair on beech frame, natural finish; tension sprung seat and back, Latex foam cushion. Inside covered tomato tapestry, outside black mohair. Designer: F. G. Clark. Makers: George Clark (Bristol) Ltd (GB)

LEFT: Beech frame, dark mahogany finish; bucket seat and foam rubber loose cushions upholstered in wool fabric. Designer: Svante Skogh, SIR. Makers: A/B Hjertquist & Co. (SWEDEN)

RIGHT: *Dormouse* on welded steel frame, vertical coil springing. Upholstered in rubberised hair and plastic foam with grey and white wool tweed cover. Designer: Ernest Race, RDI, FSIA. Makers: Ernest Race Ltd (GB)

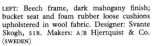

White walls and ceiling and mahogany linings to doors and windows give light and warmth to this dining-room in a converted basement flat. A birch-slatted wall conceals the original fireplace; the old recesses hold (*Right*) a storage fitment framed in mahogany and (*Left*) a sideboard backed by a photographic texture panel. Chairs and sideboard are by Hille of London. Lino-topped dining table, edged birch, with matt black metal tube legs and chrome metal cross brace designed by Ian Bradbery and Derek Newton; bent brass chrome-plated electric fire reflector by Anthony Mann, MSIA. Interior designed by Ian Bradbery, MSIA. Executed by Modular Displays Ltd (GB)

RIGHT: *Chatsworth* solid beech trolley, medium or natural finish; trays are surfaced with washable Vynide or with selected oak veneers. Makers: Compactom Ltd (GB)

FAR RIGHT: Polished brass tea wagon, shelves of heat-resistant black Arborite. Designer: Josef Frank. Makers: Svenskt Tenn AB (SWEDEN)

Laurel dining group, chairs upholstered natural *Stratford* texture fabric; draperies Olive-shot-Lurex *Berkeley* and black and white *Helico*; deep cherry 'Marble' Banbury carpet. Tigoware ceramics and fabrics designed by Tibor Reich, FSIA. Furniture made by W. G. Evans & Sons Ltd; fabrics by Tibor Ltd; Tigoware by Joseph Bourne & Son Ltd (GB)
(Photo: Studio Kordes)

RIGHT: Laundry-kitchen panelled in fir plywood, grey washable finish. Ceiling of painted fir beams with exposed hemlock plank floor above. Ceramic plaques by Hugh Jones, bowl by Claude Vermette. Designer: Philip F. Goodfellow, MRAIC (CANADA)

BELOW *Left:* Cherrywood trolley; top tray revolves and is surfaced with stain-resistant red plastic. Designers and makers: Möbelfabrik Wilhelm Renz KG (GERMANY). *Right:* Red and white kitchen. Working surfaces in dark green plastic, doors faced Tavanit plastic. Black-and-white *Cerabati* tiled floor. Designed and executed by Janette Laverrière (FRANCE)

RIGHT: *Bambino* child's chair on ebonised birch frame; foam rubber padded seat and back covered in light grey knubby wool fabric. Designer: Ilmari Lappalainen. Makers: Askon Tehtaat O/Y (FINLAND)

BELOW: *Alderney* on beech frame. Upholstere rubberised hair and covered in a wide range fabrics in contrasting colours. Designer: Ronal E. Long, MSIA. Makers: R. S. Stevens Ltd (G1

ABOVE: Moulded chair on ebonised beech legs. Upholstered in turquoise blue wool fabric with cushion in grey. Designer: Alf Nilsson. Makers: AB Knolls Eftr (SWEDEN). BELOW: *La Martingala* Metallic tube frame, upholstered foam rubber on resilient webbing. Removable cotton, wool, or lastex cover. Designer: M. Zanuso. Makers: Ar-flex S.pA (ITALY)

LEFT: Fumed oak dining chair, oil finish. Foa rubber padded seat with wool fabric cove Designer: Paul M. Volther. Makers: Fælle foreningen for Danmarks Brugsforeninge Møbler (DENMARK). RIGHT: Laminated bee chair, lacquered black, on nickel finished ste rod frame, rubber feet. Also made in teak c rosewood. Designer: Arne Jacobsen. Make Fritz Hansens Eft. A/S (DENMARK)

RIGHT: *Stroma* on hardwood frame. Rubberised hair upholstery with deep texture fabric cover in contrasting colours; Latex foam cushions. A matching settee is also made. Designer: Ronald E. Long, MSIA. Makers: R. S. Stevens Ltd (GB)

ABOVE: Slung seat on walnut, ash or mahogar legs; laminated arms. Upholstered firm elast slats and foam rubber with custom-made wo or cotton covering. Brass fittings. Designe G. F. Frattini. Makers: Figli di Amedeo Cassir (ITALY)

LEFT, Walnut, ash or mahogany sided chair; upholstered elastic slats and foam rubber. Designer: G. F. Frattini. Makers: Figli di Amedeo Cassina (ITALY). RIGHT: Redbeech chair, foam rubber pad, turquoise wool cover. Designer: B. Fridhagen. Makers: AB Svenska Möbelfabrikerna Bodafors (SWEDEN)

ABOVE: Redbeech chair with shaped arm rests. Slung seat upholstered foam rubber and black tweed. Designer: Axel Larsson. Makers: AB Svenska Möbelfabrikerna Bodafors (SWEDEN). RIGHT: Beech chair; sprung seat; covered plain red and red/white wool fabric. Designer: G. Eberle. Makers: Gebrüder Thonet AG (GERMANY). BELOW: *Albaro* Plywood seat on metal tubular frame, foam rubber cushion. Designer: G. Pulitzer. Makers: Ar-flex S.PA (ITALY)

LEFT: Cherrywood armchair with grey-and-white tapestry cover. Designer: A. A. Patijn. Makers: Meubelfabriek Zijlstra (HOLLAND). RIGHT: Desk chair in oiled teak. Upholstered black wool fabric over foam rubber. Designer: Kurt Olsen. Makers: A. Andersen & Bohm (DENMARK)

ABOVE: Beech stools, upholstered foam rubber and covered in a wide range of fabrics. Designer: Howard B. Keith, MSIA. Makers: H. K. Furniture Ltd (GB)

RIGHT: *Thema* beech frame chairs. Seat cushions and backs padded foam rubber with red check wool fabric covers. Designer: Yngve Ekström. Makers: ESE Möbler AB (SWEDEN)

ABOVE: Stool with shaped seat, padded foam rubber, on black-lacquered cherrywood legs. Designer: Christav Paleske. Makers: Wörrlein Werkstätten (GERMANY)

RIGHT: *Magistrate* stool on beech legs, polished natural, walnut or mahogany finish; top upholstered foam rubber. Designer: Howard B. Keith, MSIA. For Heal's of London (GB)

LEFT: Light beech *Casala* stool. Seat upholstered black and yellow wool fabric. Designer: D. Hinz. Makers: Carl Sasse KG (GERMANY)

RIGHT: Beech *Vanson* dining chair. Seat upholstered in Latex foam, back in rubberised hair, covered in a pale sage green Sanderson fabric. Designer: Peter Hayward, MSIA. Makers: W. G. Evans & Sons Ltd (GB) (*Photo: C.o.I.D.*)

RIGHT: *Columbus* beech frame; moulded seat upholstered wool fabric and foam rubber padding. Designer: Hartmut Lohmeyer (GERMANY) Makers: Ljungs Industrier A/B (SWEDEN)

BELOW: Easy chair with pre-formed aluminium seat on steel legs; upholstered foam rubber. Designer: James A. Howell (USA). Makers: Galleria Mobili d'Arte (ITALY)

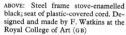

ABOVE: Steel frame stove-enamelled black; seat of plastic-covered cord. Designed and made by F. Watkins at the Royal College of Art (GB)

BELOW: Dining chair on steel legs with laminated plywood back. Foam rubber seat cushion is covered in black/white plastic, the back in black plastic. Designer: E. Harlis. Makers: Gebrüder Thonet AG (GERMANY)

ABOVE: *Java* chair on black iron frame designed to fit woven cane bucket seat. Designer: John Crichton. Frame made by Steelex (NEW ZEALAND)

Moesch high-backed woven cane armchair on black iron frame. Makers: Rohrmöbelfabrik W. Jenny AG (SWITZERLAND)

ABOVE: Beech dining chairs, plywood backs, from the *Casala* range. The foam rubber seat cushions are faced with Acella washable plastic. Designer: D. Hinz. Makers: Carl Sasse KG (GERMANY)

Waxed elm glass-fronted bookcase; interior lined felt and fitted with *Securit* glass shelves. Armchair on black-lacquered metal frame is upholstered in bright red wool fabric over Latex foam. Carpet is grey, rug burnt Sienna. Furniture designed and made by René Jean Caillette (FRANCE)

ABOVE: Knock-down bookshelves in red beech and mahogany. Designer: Carl-Axel Acking. Makers. AB Svenska Möbelfabrikerna Bodafors (SWEDEN)

ABOVE: Bookcase in black bean and ebonised sycamore, with adjustable shelves. Length 5 feet. Designer: Eric G. Clements, Des. RCA, MSIA. Maker: H. A. Lock (GB) (*Courtesy: Miss A. Jones*)

LEFT: Unit cupboard in mahogany and redbeech. Designer: Axel Larsson. Makers: AB Svenska Möbelfabrikerna Bodafors (SWEDEN)

RIGHT AND BELOW: Mahogany display/cocktail cabinet designed as a dividing unit, with Vynide-covered fall and sliding doors to cocktail side. End supports inlaid Indian laurel. Designed and made by James Herbert at the L.C.C. Technical College for the Furnishing Trades (GB)

Sycamore cabinet, ebony handle and feet; sliding glass front panels. Designed and made by Jarvis Lebetkin at the L.C.C. Technical College for the Furnishing Trades (GB)

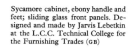

ABOVE: *Kontrast* cabinet in matt-polished teak, display shelves enclosed within sliding glass doors. Designer: Yngve Ekström. Makers: Källemo Möbelfabrik A B (SWEDEN). LEFT: Bookshelf and cupboard combination in cherrywood, 4 feet 4 inches high, with black backing to shelves. Designers and makers: Möbelfabrik Wilhelm Renz K G (GERMANY)

Mahogany desk with armour-plated glass top; supports and drawer handles are in polished brass. Designed by Cherna Schotz. The chair, upholstered in velvet over Latex foam, with brass-turned legs is an Italian design by Carlo Pagani. For Peter Jones, London (GB) (*Photo: John Lewis & Co. Ltd*)

ABOVE: Bridge table in nutwood, with chairs in smoked oak. Designed and made by Knud Juul-Hansen (DENMARK)

Table for use between two armchairs forming quarter-circle seating. Stove-enamelled base enclosed in polished brass band, Micarta top edged brass. Designers: Kim Hoffmann and Stephen Heidrich. Makers: Ironmasters (USA)

Small maple table on brass-tipped legs, with lacquered top. Designers and makers: A. Hainke, GmbH (GERMANY)

ABOVE: Ash coffee table and chair; Tavanit plastic top to table, chair upholstered bright green cotton fabric. From a range designed and made by Janette Laverrière (FRANCE)

LEFT: Card table in teak designed by Finn Juhl. Made by Niels Vodder (DENMARK)

FAR LEFT: Dining table on waxed elm base, elliptical smoked glass top, 5 feet 7 inches in length. Designed and made by René Jean Caillette (FRANCE). LEFT: Teakwood dining table designed by K. E. Ekselius. Made by AB J. O. Carlsson (SWEDEN)

BELOW: Small cherrywood table and (*right*) dining table in beech with top surfaced in ivory Resopal plastic, cherrywood edge. Designers and makers: Wörrlein Werkstätten (GERMANY)

ABOVE: Knock-down coffee table in oiled teak. Length 4 feet 11 inches. Designer: Kurt Olsen. Makers: A. Andersen & Bohm (DENMARK)

Dining table on cast-iron pedestal base enamelled black or white; the top is extendible and is made in walnut, oak, rosewood or Micarta. Chairs are in birch with walnut back, or the reverse. Designer: George Nelson. Makers: Herman Miller Furniture Co. (USA)

BELOW: Beech occasional table, 4 feet 2½ inches long. Top edged cherrywood with black Resopal plastic surface; also made with ivory surface. Designer: Satink. Makers: Wörrlein Werkstätten (GERMANY)

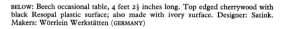

Small table on splayed legs carved in solid walnut. Designer: Josef Frank. Makers: Svenskt Tenn AB (SWEDEN)

ABOVE: Cabinets made in elm or birch with sliding doors, recessed drawer fronts, and striped glass sliding panel to display section. Designer: Ilmari Lappalainen. Makers: Asko O/Y(FINLAND)

LEFT: A space-saving fitted wall niche with built-in lighting strip. The shelves are glass, record player and record storage unit are lacquered white, and below is a green felt-lined bar with sliding oak doors. Furniture and upholstery are in black and white, carpet red. Interior designed and executed by Jacques Dumond (FRANCE)

BELOW: Occasional table in solid teak with top edged in brass. Designer Vladimir Kagan AID. Makers: Kagan-Dreyfuss Inc. (USA)

Cherrywood sewing table on black-stained supporting frame. Designer: Satink. Makers: Wörrlein Werkstätten (GERMANY)

ᴀʙᴏᴠᴇ: Living-room with combined table, bookshelf and screen unit in ash. End supports are black metal, and the table is surfaced in white Formica. The black-lacquered metal chairs are Danish, designed by Arne Jacobsen. Interior designed by Jul De Roover. Unit made by L. Ruttiens-Lierre (BELGIUM)

Television/writing/storage fitment composed of *Vanson* units in mahogany and rosewood (alternative finish mahogany or walnut) mounted on plastic covered steel legs with adjustable feet in brass or plastic; top cases have sliding doors in clear or figured glass. The television set is a Pye model designed by Robin Day, ꜰsɪᴀ. The units and chair (made in mahogany or walnut) are designed by Peter Hayward, ᴍsɪᴀ. Makers: W. G. Evans Ltd (ɢʙ)

LEFT: Bleached walnut writing desk. The 7-foot top is faced with beige leather and the 3-foot extension shelf in white micarta. The underframe is in solid brass, dull chrome finish; the drawer handles are Plexiglass. Designed by Paul László AID. Makers: László, Inc. (USA)

White oak sideboard with drop front wine cupboard and sliding glass doors to china cabinet, which is fitted with a half shelf. From the 'Golden Key' range of furniture designed and made by Palatial Ltd (GB)

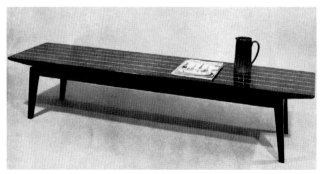

ABOVE: Pine sideboard, 5 feet long, lipped on front edge with teak; drawer fronts and finger grips are also teak, and the doors are sand-blasted pine. Designed and made by J. R. Houghton, at the Royal College of Art (GB)

Cocktail table in oak, afrormosia, mahogany or walnut. The inlaid top is 6 feet long. Designer: Sigrün Bülow-Hübe. Makers: Ak Works (CANADA)

Room divider on white-painted tubular steel frame. The bottom shelf is in solid mahogany. with upper shelf, cabinet and drawers in hardwood faced with Formica or Warerite. Designed and made by Kandya Ltd (GB)

ABOVE: Cocktail cabinet in bleached walnut, interior polished black, with top of flap surfaced in silver-grey Formica. Drawer fronts are veneered cherrywood with sycamore inlay. Designer: F. M. Gross, FSIA, FRSA. Makers: Beck & Pollitzer (Contracts) Ltd (GB)

BELOW: Hilleplan 'Junior' desk with mahogany pedestal cabinet, front veneered ash or rosewood; also available with fitted drawers. The desk top is surfaced in black or grey linoleum. Designed by Robin Day, ARCA, FSIA. For Hille of London Ltd (GB)

Hand-made side table with top in plastic laminate, inlaid skiver centre and brass edge; ebonised underframe and legs, with brass stretchers and toes. The drawer fronts are painted white. Designed by H. Stephenson, MSIA. For Heal's of London (GB)

Occasional table on hand-carved polished walnut base, with thick, brilliant crystal top measuring 2 feet 4 inches across. Designers and makers: Fontana Arte (ITALY)

ABOVE: Walnut drop leaf table with 'ke ina' butterfly inlay. The top 6½ feet lo and over 3 feet at widest point when fu open. Designer: Tommi Parzing Makers: Parzinger Originals Inc. (USA

LEFT: Plastic-topped table and chairs steel legs; the chairs are in differe colours. Designer: W. Frey, SWB. Make Stella-Werke AG (SWITZERLAND)

Occasional table, with incorporated ma zine rack, in walnut, oil finish. Design Vladimir Kagan, AID. Makers: Kaga Dreyfuss Inc. (USA)

ABOVE: Small mahogany table; the top is inlaid with maple. Designed and made by Oskar Riedel (AUSTRIA)

ABOVE: Oak settee with shelf unit in teak. Upholstery *No-sag* springs, light grey wool fabric cover, black cushions. Designer: Hans Olsen. Makers: Hovedstadens Møbel- og Madrasfabrik (DENMARK). LEFT: Convertible settee in cherrywood; the arm rest swings down level with the base to form a bed. Back cushions upholstered coconut fibre, seat cushions feathers and foam rubber. Designers and makers: Wörrlein Werkstätten (GERMANY)

ABOVE: Occasional table in striped walnut or natural oak veneers. The flap ends are supported on automatic self-locking steel brackets. Designer: D. W. Munckton. Makers: Yatton Furniture Ltd (GB)

White glaze on matt black tiled top with edge of ebonised wood; polished brass legs. Designer: Brian Hubbard. Makers: Chelsea Pottery (GB)

ABOVE: *Vanson* unit assembled as a sideboard, using a cupboard, wine cabinet and display cases in mahogany and rosewood mounted on plastic covered steel legs with adjustable feet in brass or plastic; alternative finishes are mahogany or walnut. Designer: Peter Hayward, MSIA. Makers: W. G. Evans & Sons Ltd (GB)

The 'Penguin' wall bookshelf in na oak, for small format books, or ments. Designer: Frank Height, RCA, MSIA. Makers: Beaver & T Ltd (GB)

LEFT: Wall unit with shelves and cat in maple. The left-hand ca designed to hold records or folio b has sliding doors in red or other colours; the cabinet on the right pull-down writing shelf. Des Alfred Altherr, SWB. Makers: F Frei and Richard Münch (SWITZER)

Wall cabinet in mahogany with doors and drawers veneered in ash; the slatted rack below is in cherrywood. Interior trays are faced with plastic, handles brass. Designed and made by Roger Fitton, at the High Wycombe College of Further Education (GB)

Sectional wall magazine racks (1, 2 or 3 sections) of half-inch lacquered cane hung on simple plaster hooks or brass wood screws. Designers and makers: Standish-Taylor (Designs) Ltd (GB)

Interior furnished in natural and lacquered teak, with beech occasional chair. Dining table and chairs are designed by Erik Fryklund. Makers: A B Hagafors Stolfabrik; nesting tables *Kombinett* by Alf Svensson. Makers: Tingströms Möbelfabriks A B; chair with loose cushions *USA 143*, by Folke Ohlsson. Makers: Ljungs Industri AB; settee *College* designed and made by Erik Berglund, Uno Swalén, Eilas; *Trio* cabinet with sliding doors and centre drawer section by A B Hugo Troeds Industrier (SWEDEN) (*Courtesy: 'FORM' Magazine*)

Telephone table in laminated beech. Designed by Kristian Vedel. Makers: Torben Ørskov & Co. (DENMARK)

Breakfast table and stools on white-enamelled metal legs, brass tipped. The table top is black micarta; seat cushions upholstered in yellow and white striped linen over foam rubber. The small six-fold Chinese screen is in gold, white and black. Designer: Tommi Parzinger. Makers: Parzinger Originals Inc. (USA)

BELOW: Twin occasional tables with slatted oak tops mounted on black iron underframe. Designer: John Crichton. Maker: J. Shaw (NEW ZEALAND)

LEFT: Pull-out dining table on steel base, with hardwood top surfaced in linoleum. Designed by Fred Ruf, SWB. The plywood chairs on lacquered metal legs are by Hans Bellmann, SWB. Makers: Wohnbedarf AG (SWITZERLAND)

Drop-flap dining table with top faced grey-and-white check Formica or Warerite, and matching chairs; contrasting gay colours are used for the fronts, tops and shelves of the cabinet and white metal-frame room divider. Designers and makers: Kandya Ltd (GB)

RIGHT: Mahogany sideboard with sliding doors; interior fitted two drawers and shelf. Designer: Robert Heritage, Des.RCA, MSIA. Makers: G. W. Evans Ltd (GB). BELOW RIGHT: Occasional table in afrormosia, oil finish. The brass-tipped legs are ebonised black. Designed and made by A. Younger Ltd (GB). BELOW: Dining group in ash, with chair seats and backs in nylon cane. The table top folds over, and the articulated metal base enables it to serve also as a console. Designer and maker: Maxime Old (FRANCE)

LEFT: Chest of drawers, writing table, cabinets and bookshelf designed as unit pieces for combined or separate arrangement. They are made in oil-finished teak with edges and legs in oak. The chair is in oak. Designer: Svante Skogh. Makers: AB Seffle Möbelfabrik (SWEDEN)

BELOW: An attractive colour scheme, with chairs upholstered in *Shaftesbury* deep-texture turquoise fabric; curtains in *Cymbeline* texture drape interwoven with Lurex. The fabrics and 'marble' carpet are designed by Tibor Reich, FSIA. Fabrics made by Tibor Ltd, and carpet by Ian C. Steele & Co. Ltd. The television set is a Pye model; furniture by H. K. Furniture Co. Ltd (GB)

BELOW: Living-room furnished in acajou, with desk top surfaced in black Formica; the bookshelves slot into the end supports and can be varied in height. A light grey 'marbled' linoleum covers the floor. Designer: Jul De Roover. Furniture made by De Bruyn Frères (BELGIUM)

ABOVE: Eight-drawer double chest on dark mahogany base. It is lacquered in custom colours—here shown in white with gold bronze hardware. Designer: Tommi Parzinger. Makers: Parzinger Originals Inc. (USA)

ABOVE: Cocktail cabinet on ebonised underframe fitted with a plant shelf and built-in fluorescent lighting. The front can be a frame for embroidery, painting, or other work of art. Designer: Ernst Pollak, MSIA. For Heal's of London (GB)

Cabinet in ash, natural gloss finish, supported on black-enamelled iron legs. The sliding doors are lacquered grey. Designed and made by Jacques Dumond (FRANCE)

ABOVE: Cherrywood frame with boomerang-shaped rosewood stretchers. Designed and made by J. A. Scott, student at the Royal College of Art (GB)

Interwoven wicker chair, polished hardwood frame. Designed and made by Władysław Wołkowski (POLAND)

TOP: Easy chair in oak, afrormosia, mahogany or walnut; coloured webbing. Designer: Reinhold Koller. Makers: Aka Works (CANADA). ABOVE: Rubber-banded oak folding chair, rubbed oil finish; brass fittings. Designed and made by John Ravillious, student at the High Wycombe College of Further Education (GB)

BELOW: Folding chair on black-lacquered iron frame; plaited rattan seat and back with armrests of oiled teak. Designer: Arne Nilsson. Makers: Hans-Agne Jakobsson AB (SWEDEN)

LEFT: Plaited soft wicker chair on hardwood base. RIGHT: Bent cane corded chair. Both are designed and made by Władysław Wołkowski (POLAND)

ABOVE LEFT: Bucket chair on nickel-finished steel rod base; upholstered foam rubber with wool fabric cover. Designers: Nanna and Jørgen Ditzel. Makers: Fritz Hansens Eft A/S (DENMARK). RIGHT: Garden chair in nut brown plasticised cane with natural cane bindings. Designed and made by Janine Abraham (FRANCE)

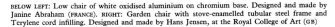

BELOW LEFT: Low chair of white oxidised aluminium on chromium base. Designed and made by Janine Abraham (FRANCE). RIGHT: Garden chair with stove-enamelled tubular steel frame and Terylene cord infilling. Designed and made by Hans Jensen, at the Royal College of Art (GB)

ABOVE: Cocktail stool on black metal base, tipped rubber. Steel-rimmed preformed seat upholstered foam rubber with green wool fabric cover. Designer: Italo Meroni. Made by Giulio Meroni (ITALY)

LEFT: Dressing-table stool in rosewood, with seat of saddle-stitched cowhide. Designed and made by J. R. Houghton, student at the Royal College of Art (GB). RIGHT: Moulded fibre-glass chair in a wide range of pigmented colours on stove-enamelled tubular steel legs; loose foam-rubber cushion. Designer: Aidron Duckworth. Makers: Kandya Ltd (GB)

BELOW: Birch armchair with sprung seat and deep foam-rubber cushioning; upholstered green wool fabric. Designer: Olof Ottelin. Makers: O/Y Stockmann AB (FINLAND)

ABOVE *Left:* Padded chair on birch frame, loose foam-rubber cushion, wool fabric cover. Designer: Olof Ottelin. Makers: O/Y Stockmann AB (FINLAND); *Right: Sitwell-sofa* of upholstered 'Stracolite' on steel legs. Designer: Hans Bellmann, SWB. Makers: Strässle Söhne & Company (SWITZERLAND). BELOW *Left:* Covered hardwood chair, latex foam cushions; underframe ebonised beech. Designers: Students Bernard Gay and B. A. North, L.C.C. College for the Furnishing Trades (GB); *Right: Maori* hardwood frame, latex seat cushion on Rotex rubber webbing; back upholstered rubberised hair, large range of covering fabrics. Designer: Ronald E. Long, MSIA. Makers: R. S. Stevens Ltd (GB)

LEFT: Birch low chair with loose foam-rubber cushions covered in wool fabric. Designer: Olli Borg. Makers: Asko O/Y (FINLAND)

RIGHT: *Sunburst* in beech, with a wide fan back of tapering ginger-finished spokes, sprung seat. The loose foam-rubber cushions are covered in Danish wool fabrics. Designed by Paul M. Volther (DENMARK), for Berge-Norman Inc. (USA)

RIGHT: White beech stacking chair with padded seat; the back panel is in a natural or coloured finish. Designers and makers: Kandya Ltd (GB)

ABOVE: Beech armchair lacquered black, with brass-tipped legs; leather-banded seat and back. The loose foam-rubber cushions are covered in ribbed wool fabric. Designer: Jos. De Mey. Makers: 'Luxus' (BELGIUM)

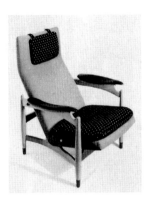

Beech armchair with teak arm-rests and feet. Upholstered grey-green wool fabric over Moltoprène on *No-sag* springs, with foam cushions in black-and-gold. Designer: Jos. De Mey. Makers: Van Den Berghe-Pauvers (BELGIUM)

RIGHT: Garden chair on steel frame lacquered black with laminated seat in ash or teak. Designers: Nanna and Jørgen Ditzel. Makers: Møbelfabriken Kolds Savværk A/S (DENMARK)

ABOVE: Yew frame with preformed seat and back in ash. The latex foam seat and back cushions are covered in forest-green tapestry. Designed and made by David Davenport, student at the High Wycombe College of Further Education (GB)

Chair in beech, natural finish. The loose foam-rubber cushions covered in deep texture wool fabric are supported on rubber webbing. Designed and made by John Strange, at the High Wycombe College of Further Education (GB)

Beech and walnut frame, back of preformed ash ply. Frame seat with rubber webbing supporting latex cushions covered in black moquette. Designed and made by Colin Gibson, High Wycombe College of Further Education (GB)

LEFT: Matching chair and stool in teak, padded foam rubber, with wool fabric cover. Designers: Nanna and Jørgen Ditzel. Makers: Søren Willadsens Møbelfabrik (DENMARK)

RIGHT: Square-built armchair upholstered in textured cotton over foam rubber on rubber webbing; ebonised beech legs. Designed by Edson Crafts, James A. and Marie Howell. Makers: Selig Manufacturing Co. (USA)

BELOW: Tubular steel frame, tipped rubber; deep-textured wool fabric cover over foam rubber. Designer: Christa von Paleske. Makers: Wörrle: Werkstätten (GERMANY).

ABOVE LEFT: Armchair on black-lacquered steel base, upholstered in thick ribbed black-and-white wool fabric over foam rubber. Designer: Olli Borg. Makers: Asko O/Y (FINLAND). RIGHT: Model for wood frame construction on waxed beech legs; upholstery Aeropreen foam plastic on Pirelli rubber webbing, with removable cushions. Designed and made by Martin Grierson, LSIA. BELOW: Sculptured chair and ottoman on ebonised beech legs, with deep foam-rubber cushioning on springs; grey textured wool fabric cover. Designed by Edson Crafts, James A. and Marie Howell. Makers: Selig Manufacturing Co. (USA)

ABOVE: Beech tension-sprung tub chair with latex foam cushion and interior upholstered in off-white tweed, exterior in black mohair. Designer: F. G. Clark Makers: George Clark (Bristol) L. (GB)

OVE: Laminated beech chair on ack iron legs. Upholstered foam bber and De Ploeg *Rapallo* and *yoto* wool fabrics. Designer: Th. uth. Makers: Wagemans & Van uinen NV (HOLLAND)

ABOVE: High-backed armchair on splayed aluminium legs painted white, tips brass. Cornflower blue textured fabric cover over foam rubber. Designer: Norman Fox MacGregor. Makers: Valley Upholstery Corporation (USA)

Easy chair on metal legs lacquered in graphite grey or white. *No-sag* springs in seat and back; seat and arms padded foam rubber, back padded fibre. Designer: Bengt Ruda. Makers: Nordiska Kompaniet A/B (SWEDEN)

LEFT: *Stafford* amply-proportioned dining chair on beech or mahogany legs, upholstered latex foam over Pirelli rubber webbing. Designer: Robin Day, ARCA, FSIA. Makers: Hille of London (GB)

BELOW: *Braemar* on hardwood frame. Rubberised hair upholstery, with deep texture fabric cover in contrasting colours; latex foam seat cushion. Designer: Ronald E. Long. Makers: R. S. Stevens Ltd (GB)

OVE: Armchair on ebonised eech legs; upholstered foam rub-er over rubber webbing, with tton covering fabric. Designed Edson Crafts, James A. and arie Howell. Makers: Selig anufacturing Co. (USA)

GHT: *Acantha* on hardwood frame, ith rubberised hair upholstery d deep texture fabric cover; tex foam seat cushion. Designer: onald E. Long, MSIA. Makers: . S. Stevens Ltd (GB)

LEFT: Oak frame; seat and back upholstered in wool fabric over foam rubber. Designer: Ejvind A. Johansson. Makers: Fællesforeningen for Danmarks Brugsforeninger (DENMARK). RIGHT: Ring frame of laminated ash, or walnut/mahogany, natural finish, with suspended foam-rubber cushioned seat; stove-enamelled rubber-tipped iron base. Designer: Parisi. Makers: Figli di Amedeo Cassina (ITALY)

ABOVE: Desk or dining chair with solid mahogany arms and legs. The latex padded seat is upholstered in black and white textured moquette. Designer: Ronald E. Long, MSIA. Makers: R. S. Stevens Ltd (GB)

LEFT: Beech frame, natural oak or walnut finish. Upholstered in tapestry or uncut moquette; tension sprung seat with latex cushion, sprung and padded back. Designers and makers: Yatton Furniture Ltd (GB)

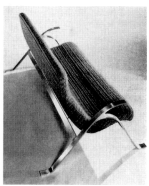
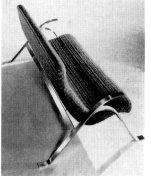

ABOVE: Stainless steel frame; seat upholstered in deep texture *Luxuratex*, designed by Hugo Dreyfuss, over hair and foam rubber. Sofa designed by Vladimir Kagan, AID. Makers: Kagan-Dreyfuss Inc. (USA)

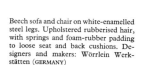

Beech sofa and chair on white-enamelled steel legs. Upholstered rubberised hair, with springs and foam-rubber padding to loose seat and back cushions. Designers and makers: Wörrlein Werkstätten (GERMANY)

Easy chair on copper-plated rolled-steel frame, with walnut or birch turnings banded in copper or brass. Reversible foam-padded cushions. Designer: Robert Kaiser. Makers: Primavera (CANADA)

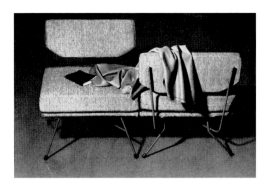

Elettra chair-settee combination on lacquered tubular metal frame with rubber-tipped ends. The foam-rubber sprung cushions have detachable covers. Designers: Belgiojoso-Peressutti-Rogers. Makers: Ar-flex (ITALY)

Maori settee on ebonised beech legs. Back upholstered rubberised hair; seat, 'Rotex' rubber webbing, with latex cushions in contrasting colours. Designer: Ronald E. Long, MSIA. Makers: R. S. Stevens Ltd (GB)

ABOVE: Chaise longue on ebonised laminated plywood (or natural beech) frame; upholstered latex foam on Pirelli webbing with cotton/rayon deep-texture cover. Designer: A. J. Milne, FSIA. For Heal's of London (GB). LEFT: Sectional settee designed as a room divider with built-in walnut bookshelves to right arm; sprung seat and deep air-foam upholstery under strié fabric cover. Designer: Norman Fox MacGregor. Makers: Valley Upholstery Corporation (USA). BELOW: Mahogany frame; seat and back padded foam rubber on *No-sag* springs, steel-blue wool cover. Designer: Jos. de Mey. Makers: Van Den Berghe-Pauvers (BELGIUM)

ABOVE: Dining chairs in natural or ebonised beech, or smoked oak; laminated seat and back. Designer: Ejvind A. Johansson. Makers: F. D. B. Møbler (DENMARK)

ABOVE: Teak armchair upholstered in black ox-hide. Designed by A. Bender-Madsen and Ejner Larsen. Made by L. Pontoppidan (DENMARK)

ABOVE: Laminated beech-frame bedroom chair with 'coat-hanger' back; foam rubber-padded seat, handwoven wool fabric cover. Designed and made by Sven Staaf and Lars Olson, SIR (SWEDEN)

ABOVE: Broad frame natural oak chair with padded seat upholstered in black leather. Designer: Hans J. Wegner. Made by Johannes Hansen (DENMARK)

ABOVE: *Windsor* armchair in natural beech, wax finish; latex foam cushion with detachable cover. Designer: L. R Ercolani. Makers: Furniture Industries Ltd (GB)

RIGHT: White hardwood rocking chair with padded seat cushion and head-rest. Designed by Karl-Axel Adolfson. For Gösta Westerberg Möbel AB (SWEDEN). FAR RIGHT: Moulded fibreglass seat on polished steel tapered legs. Available in yellow, black, turquoise, or deep blue, with wool-covered foam rubber cushion. Designed and made by Kay Kørbing (DENMARK)

ABOVE: Red beech frame, teak armrests, mahogany, jacaranda or ebonised finish; *No-sag* springs in seat and back. Designer: Bengt Ruda. Makers: AB Nordiska Kompaniet (SWEDEN)

ABOVE: Oregon pine frame with corduroy kapok-stuffed cushions on rubber webbing. Designed and made by John Tucker, High Wycombe College of Further Education (GB)

ABOVE: Steam-bent ash frame, loose foam rubber cushion on tension springs. Designed and made by John and James Herbert and E. Rodker, L.C.C. Technical College for the Furnishing Trades (GB)

ABOVE: Walnut, saddle, or nubian finish hardwood frame with 'spear-head' armrests of African inspiration. Cane back, foam rubber seat cushion with zippered cover. Made in Denmark for Selig of Leominster (USA)

ABOVE: *Kendal* in solid walnut, hand-sprung seat, and padded back with rubberised-hair filling; wool tapestry cover. Designer: Laurence A. Reason. Makers: A. Reason & Sons Ltd (GB)

RIGHT: High-back sewing chair in white beech. Upholstered foam rubber on Pirelli webbing with wool fabric covering; the head cushion is adjustable. Designed and made by D. Merew Ltd (GB). FAR RIGHT: Oiled walnut frame with hand-woven wool fabric covers on loose foam rubber cushions. Designer: Reinhold Koller. Made by Aka Works (CANADA)

LEFT: Girl's study/bedroom in a lively and fresh-looking colour scheme. It i furnished with 'poly-Z' link-units i walnut, built up as a continuous wa fitting with matching chair. The inlai linoleum floor covering is both practica and decorative. Interior designed an executed by A. A. Patijn (HOLLAND)

BELOW: Writing table in figured teak framing in ash; drawer fronts faced i Formica with brass pulls. Designed an made by Roger Fitton, High Wycomb College of Further Education (GB)

Triva work- or dining table in teak or jacaranda on square section metal legs lacquered graphite grey. The three-drawer pedestal is detachable and can be placed inside of outside the legs to the right or left. Designer: Erik Herløv, MAA. Made by AB Nordiska Kompaniet (SWEDEN)

ABOVE: Secretaire in teak, designed and made by Gösta Westerberg Möbel AB (SWEDEN). The oak chairs with woven fibre seats are designed by Hans J. Wegner. Makers: Carl Hansen & Son (DENMARK)

ABOVE: Teak writing table with top extensions on ball bearings; the drawers are detachable, and can also be placed at right. Designers: Tove and Edv. Kindt-Larsen. Made by Gustav Bertelsen & Co. (DENMARK)

ABOVE: Writing table in English walnut and amboyna, inlaid with ebony; top cabinet fitted with a tambour shutter and pull-out top. Designed and made by Barry Warner, Leicester College of Art (GB)

ABOVE: Drop-leaf writing desk in rosewood with oiled teak veneer; underframe and spindle-back chair in nubian (as shown), or in walnut or saddle finish. With leaf extended, the top measures 5 feet 8 inches. Made in Denmark. For Selig of Leominster (USA)

RIGHT: Corner of study, with writing desk, wall cabinet and chair in figured oak. Designed and made by Wor·de·Klee, Inc. (USA)

ABOVE: *Contour* two-seater, upholstered in white cowhide, with connecting shelf and base in walnut, oil finish. Designer: Vladimir Kagan, AID. Made by Kagan-Dreyfuss Inc. (USA)

ABOVE: Rosewood armchair with loose seat and back cushions of foam rubber covered in wool tapestry. Designed and made by O. Tybulewicz at the Royal College of Art (GB)

ABOVE: Occasional chair upholstered in powder blue silk; the frame is mahogany with an 'antique white' finish. Designer: Harvey Probber. Made by Harvey Probber, Inc. (USA)

ABOVE: *Kirby* dining chair. Hardwood frame, upholstered wool tapestry over plastic foam on Pirelli webbing. Designer: Laurence A. Reason. Makers: A. Reason & Sons Ltd (GB)

ABOVE: *Menton* on yew underframe. Sprung pre-formed seat with wool fabric upholstery over 'Parkertex' foam, padded back and loose seat cushion. Designed and made by Parker-Knoll Ltd (GB)

Oak settle designed to seat three for television viewing. The curved back, padded with rubberised hair, and loose Dunlopillo seat cushion are covered in Tibor *Tiara* fabric. Designed and made by Edward Baly (GB)

ABOVE: Chaise-longue in pecan wood, warm emberglow finish, with coil-sprung seat and foam rubber cushions; fitted muslin cover. Designed and made by Tomlinson (USA)

ABOVE: *Triton* tension-sprung beech frame arm-chair, natural or ebonised finish, or in walnut or mahogany. Fitted with loose seat cushion in Lintafoam rubber and upholstered in a wide range of covering fabrics over Lintafelt padding. Designer: Howard B. Keith, MSIA. Made by H. K. Furniture Ltd (GB)

ABOVE: Solid teak frame easy chair with tip-back adjusting to the sitter's weight. Designed and made by Advance Design, Inc. (USA)

ABOVE: Foam rubber on pre-formed shape, covered handwoven wool fabric; beech legs. Designed by Hiort af Ornäs (FINLAND). For Gösta Westerberg Möbel AB (SWEDEN)

ABOVE: Low armchair from a suite in a two-tone deep texture wool fabric over rubber webbing and deep plastic foam padding, with foam rubber seat cushion dove-tailed into the back. The ebonised beech legs are fitted with brass ferrules. Designed by A. J. Milne, FSIA. For Heal's of London (GB)

LEFT: Armchair with long Dunlopillo-cushioned seat; pale polished beech legs. Upholstered in black-and-white tweed, or in alternative colours; also made in hide. Designer: Michael Inchbald, MSIA, FRSA. Made by Michael Inchbald Ltd (GB)

ABOVE: Settee and chairs with pre-formed back and seat on ebonised beech legs. The seat is upholstered in De Ploeg grey/black *Chicago* fabric over 'Epeda' springs; the back in grey *Livorno* over foam rubber. Designer: Th. Ruth. Made by Wagemans & Van Tuinen, NV (HOLLAND)

ABOVE: Teak open-unit bookcase for 'Penguin' small format books, back faced in Formica in a variety of colours. Designed and made by Barry Warner, Leicester College of Art (GB)

ABOVE: Cane chairs on tubular iron legs, lacquered black, with seat cushions in latex foam; ash box-table on black iron legs mounted on castors houses radio, records and record player; the interior is lined in orange Feutrine, the top surfaced in white Formica. The dining table top, surfaced in grey Formica, extends to 5 feet 6 inches; its base, and that of the studio couch, is of square section iron, lacquered black. Interior designed and executed by Janine Abraham (FRANCE)

BELOW: Armchair, and teak-topped coffee table on steel underframe with teak feet; chair upholstered in blue wool fabric, handwoven by Doris Nielsen. Designer: Finn Juhl. Made by Niels Vodder (DENMARK)

Danish oiled-teak furniture in a setting reflecting the warm tones of the wood, and enlivened by brilliant touches of scarlet. The 'bumper' settees have loose, sprung seat and back cushions, and the armrests can be placed at either end; they are thus adaptable to a variety of seating arrangements. Interior designed and furnished by Harrods of London (GB)

ABOVE: Stretched perforated-metal armchair, lacquered black, on black iron frame; Dunlopillo seat and back cushions. Designed and made by Société Matégot (FRANCE)

BELOW: Black tubular-iron frame chair with slung seat in tan leather. Designed and made by Adams, s.r.l. (ARGENTINA)

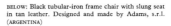

ABOVE: *H-W-H* chair of generous proportions. Wool fabric covering over preformed Latex foam padded seat and tapered cushion; chrome metal underframe. Designed by Robin Day, ARCA, FSIA. For Hille of London (GB)

ABOVE: Loveseat covered in close-woven finely texture fabric over foam-padded frame, with loose foam rubber sea cushion on flat springs; walnut base. Designers: James A and Marie Howell. Makers: Design Previews Inc. (USA)

FAR LEFT: Tubular steel frame wit free-swinging back and shaped tea armrests. Upholstered rough-textur wool fabric over Latex foam. De signed and made by A. A. Patij (HOLLAND). LEFT: Laminated as frame, cotton-covered metal sprin suspension, and loose Latex foa cushions with zippered covers. De signed by P. Guariche, M. Morti and J. A. Motte. Made by Et Steiner (FRANCE)

RIGHT: Laminated beech chair (legs executed in thirty-eight layers). Also made with solid teak seat and teak finish to legs. Designer: Arne Jacobsen, MAA. Made by Fritz Hansens Eft A/S (DENMARK)

BELOW: Laminated birch seat and back; solid birch underframe with walnut finish. Designed and made by M. Chomentowska, at the Warsaw Institute of Industrial Design (POLAND)

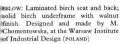

ABOVE: Teak frame armchair, woven wicker seat and back. Designed and made by Rastad og Relling (NORWAY)

BELOW: Rosewood dining chair, 'handle' back of preformed ply or framed up; beige hide upholstery over foam rubber. Designed and made by John Strange, High Wycombe College of Further Education (GB)

ABOVE: *Imperial Contemporary* chair in yellow birch; solid birch legs, moulded seat and back with walnut veneer, or other finish. Designer: Jan Kuypers, ACID. Made by the Imperial Furniture Mfg. Co. Ltd (CANADA)

ABOVE: Pearwood dining chair, bright black ebony veneer; seat cushion covered in grey fabric handwoven by Hélène Henry. Chair designed and made by Max Ingrand (FRANCE)

LEFT: Tubular-iron frame chair, stove-enamelled black, iron mesh seat and Latex foam cushions with removable linen covers. Designed and made by M. Baugniet (BELGIUM)

RIGHT: Coffee table in walnut, mahogany, or oak, oil finish. The tray leaf is faced with Formica material; with ends extended, top measures 6 feet 8 inches. Designer: K. Stonor Poulsen. Made by Scandia Furniture Reg'd (CANADA)

BELOW: Beech table and 'knock-down' chairs, transparent lacquer finish. The table top is in hardboard with Hornitex or Resopal surface; the chair seats, upholstered in Molto-pren with washable plastic covering, are easily removable for cleaning. Designed and made by Josef Theisen, OHG (GERMANY)

ABOVE: Oak frame settee with rubber-webbing seat and detachable metal legs; the Latex foam cushions are reversible. Designer: Herbert Yates. Made by Herbert Yates Group Ltd (GB)

LEFT: Armchair on oil finish walnut base; 'No-sag' springs and Latex foam upholstery with striped wool fabric cover in blues, greens, and purples. Designers: James A. & Marie Howell. Made by Design Previews Inc. (USA)

ABOVE: Oiled teak bar stool on sculptured legs; sprung cushion upholstered in black leather. Designer: Vladimir Kagan, AID. Made by Kagan-Dreyfuss, Inc. (USA)

ABOVE: Black-lacquered birch chair with reversible foam rubber cushions covered in plain wool fabric. Designer: Grunsven. Made by NV Ums-Pastoe (HOLLAND). BELOW: Convertible armchair/bed with fold-down back and slide-out base. Walnut finish birch frame, red/black wool repp covers over sprung cushions and base. Designed and made by M. Chomentowska, Warsaw Institute of Industrial Design (POLAND)

ABOVE: Folding chair in oak with canvas seat and adjustable leather straps. Designer: Professor Ole Wanscher. Hand-made by A. J. Iversen (DENMARK)

RIGHT: Teak cabinet with brass hinges, and matching five-drawer chest of the same height. Width of cabinet: 4 feet 6 inches. Designer: Børge Mogensen. Made by P. Lauritsen & Son (DENMARK)

ABOVE: *Cortina* Rio-jacaranda cabinet, plastic lacquer finish; base and front framing in dark-stained beech. Designer: Svante Skogh, SIR. Made by Seffle Möbelfabrik AB (SWEDEN)

ABOVE: Combination cabinets in teak and red beech from the *Librett* multiple-unit series. Designer: Bertil Fridhagen, SIR. Made by AB Svenska Möbelfabrikerna (SWEDEN)

LEFT: Sectional cupboard unit in oiled teak or black tubular metal frame, with sliding doors in white and black hardboard; teak desk and dining table. Designer: Lea Nevanlinna. The chairs in white-painted birch with padded seat and back covered in black wool fabric, are by Ilmar Tapiovaara. For TE-MA O/Y (FINLAND)

LEFT: Bookcase units in oak, mahogany, or walnut; dark, medium and natural finishes. Designer: Neil Morris. Made by Morris of Glasgow (GB)

ABOVE: Unit cabinet in oak; drawers, and doors of cupboard section faced in teak. Designer: Åage Herman Olsen. Made by Thysen Nielsen (DENMARK)

ABOVE: Bookcase in teak, part of a unit series. Designers: Peter Hvidt and O. Mølgaard Nielsen. Made by Søborg Møbelfabrik A/S (DENMARK)

ABOVE: Six-drawer cabinet in pine. Designed by T. Kempe. Made by Waggeryd AB. For Gösta Westerberg Möbel AB (SWEDEN)

LEFT: Teak combination unit with movable cabinets and shelves designed for variable arrangement. Made by AB Skaraborgs Möbelindustri (SWEDEN)

ABOVE: *Columna* laminated birch dining chairs, lacquered black or other colours; contrast upholstery over foam rubber. Designer: Ilmari Lappalainen. Made by Asko O/Y (FINLAND)

ABOVE: Two-height table, dining or low occasional; tops mahogany, walnut or teak veneers; legs and underframe rosewood or beech finish. Matching chairs upholstered in a wide variety of covering fabrics. Designed by Christopher Heal, FSIA. For Heal's of London (GB)

RIGHT: Walnut finish dining suite on black lacquered legs; chairs upholstered in Tibo *Henley* fabric. On the right a matching *Librenza* unit, and sprung settee and arm chair with Latex foam cushions. Designed and made by E. Gomme Ltd (GB)

ABOVE: Dining group in teak. The under leaf of the table pushes out on pivoting rods, extending the top to 7 feet 10 inches. Designers: Peter Hvidt and O. Mølgaard Nielsen. Made by Søborg Møbelfabrik (DENMARK)

RIGHT: Dining chair in mahogany or other hard wood, ebonised or natural finish. Webbed and sprung seat covered in a wide choice of fabrics, or upholstered in leather. Designed and made by Trollopes of London (GB)

RIGHT: Teak plant table with interchangeable decorated tile top and space for alternative types of plant container. Designed and made by Bernard North and Michael Butterworth, L.C.C. Technical College for the Furnishing Trades (GB)

LEFT: Birch table and laminated chairs, light and dark finish, on steel tube legs. Designer: Hans Bellman. Made by AG Möbelfabrik Horgen-Glarus (SWITZERLAND)

RIGHT: Nesting tables on beech legs, rosewood or ebony top with heat-resistant finish. Designed and made by Edward Baly (GB)

BELOW: Egg-shaped occasional table in oak, walnut or teak. Designed and made by D. Meredew Ltd (GB)

ABOVE: Prototype model of work- or dining table in ash, top stained black, with brass fittings. The legs are adjustable to five different heights, or fold flat for storage. Designed by Arne Karlsen (DENMARK)

ABOVE: Coffee table, grey and white tiled top set in a mahogany frame; black hardwood base. Designer: John Crichton. Made by R. H. Saunderson (NEW ZEALAND)

LEFT: Birch table, coloured linen undershelf. The height can be lowered by swinging the top over to the longer arm of the axis, with book shelf reversed to right. Designed and made by M. Chomentowska, Warsaw Institute of Industrial Design (POLAND)

ABOVE: Occasional table, tray top in oil-finished teak or American walnut on black-lacquered tapered legs. Designed by Fritz Hansens Eft. A/S. For Raymor (USA)

ABOVE: Pedestal tables, metal base, white, grey, or charcoal fused-on colour; white plastic laminate, walnut veneer, or marble top. Moulded plastic/fibreglass chair on cast aluminium base in correlated colours. Designed and made by Knoll Associates, Inc. (USA)

RIGHT: Glass-topped occasional table with woven cane shelf; carved base in teak, palissander, or other woods. Designed by Tove and Edv. Kindt-Larsen. Made by Gustav Bertelsen & Co. (DENMARK)

BELOW: Teak dining table, legs smoked oak; top extends to 3½ yards. Designer: Hans J. Wegner. Made by Andr. Tuck (DENMARK)

RIGHT: Glass-topped coffee table on walnut, birch, or mahogany legs; iron, brass, or copper stretchers. Designer: Robert Kaiser. Made by Primavera (CANADA). BELOW: Occasional table on carved peteribi base, double glass top. Designed and made by Adams, s.r.l. (ARGENTINA)

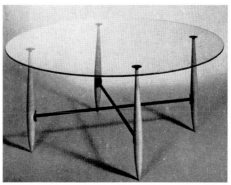

LEFT: Chest-of-drawers in cherry-wood. The pivoting brass bow handles are partially plastic covered and fit into a routed recess in the drawer fronts. Designed and made by M. S. Wason at the Royal College of Art (GB)

BELOW: Bedstead in smoked oak with boxed-in sprung mattress; rail ends. Designer Hans J. Wegner. Made by Ry Møbler (DENMARK)

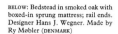
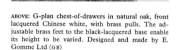

ABOVE: G-plan chest-of-drawers in natural oak, front lacquered Chinese white, with brass pulls. The adjustable brass feet to the black-lacquered base enable its height to be varied. Designed and made by E. Gomme Ltd (GB)

BELOW: Pedestal dressing table in mahogany; drawer fronts veneered fiddle ash with white china knobs. The right wing of the triple mirror is on a separate swivel for close make-up. Designed by Robert Heritage, MSIA. For Heal's of London (GB)

ABOVE: Poudreuse with twin adjustable mirrors and pivoting plastic-faced cosmetic trays. Hand-made in solid niove and olive ash veneers; satin brass metalwork. Designer: Nigel Walters, MSIA. For Heal's of London (GB)

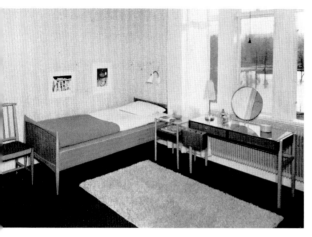

ABOVE: Combined dressing table and chest-of-drawers in teak and rosewood; brass pulls, interior lined sycamore; top fitted with movable trays and pull-out shelf. Designed and made by Barry Warner, Leicester College of Art (GB)

ABOVE: Red beech *Bodabed* with deep spring mattress, ends panelled in Galon vinyl plastic; teak and red beech glass-topped bedside table and dressing table with pivoting cosmetic compartment; red beech 'hanger-back' chair. Designer: Bertil Fridhagen, SIR. Makers: AB Svenska Möbelfabrikerna (SWEDEN)

ABOVE: Bedroom furnished in acajou sapele, bedhead in light grey leather and black Formica, with matching bedcover. End wall dark violet; beige linoleum and 'thumbletweed' light grey rugs cover the floor; armchair upholstered in yellow. Designer: Jos. de Mey. Furniture made by Van Den Berghe-Pauvers (BELGIUM)

ABOVE: Bed-sitting room with space-saving folding bed unit in pale green Japanese lacquer. It swings up to the level of the first bookshelf when closed, thus becoming part of the wall fitment. Bookshelves are in pearwood on brass rod supports. Designed and made by F. M. Gross, FSIA, FRSA (GB)

BELOW: Cabinet-made dining table and sideboard in solid mahogany, clear cellulose lacquer finish, dulled and waxed. The sideboard is 5 feet 9 inches wide and has end cupboards fitted with adjustable shelves. The doors are made of small matched V-jointed panels, flush-mounted with the drawer fronts. The middle rail forms both drawer pull and cupboard handle. Designed and made by Robin Nance (GB)

Dressing table and stool in sapele; the stool has a fitted foam rubber cushion. Designer: J. H. Tabraham. Made by D. S. Vorster & Co. (Pty) Ltd (SOUTH AFRICA)

Cabinets in teak solid and veneer, doors and drawers veneered Indian laurel. The end cabinet, fitted either as a bureau or for cocktails, has a fall-front veneered Prima Vera; top surfaces in heat-resistant clear lacquer finish; handles in stainless steel. Designer: W. H. Russell, FSIA. Makers: Gordon Russell Ltd (GB)

Hallway with curved sapele staircase rising between white-plastered and sapele-panelled walls; the treads are faced black lino and edged in aluminium. The light-beech chairs are upholstered in grey-green fabric over foam cushioning. Designer: Jos. De Mey. Executed by Van den Berghe-Pauvers (BELGIUM) ▶

Steel-tube light-weight settee and chair, upholstered in a wide range of covering fabrics over deep foam-rubber cushioning. The coffee table, designed in proportion, is on a Tee-section steel frame with laminated plastic, teak or walnut veneered top. Designer: Florence Knoll. Made by Knoll International Ltd (USA/GB)

Corner fireplace in multicolour brick with curved hearth and mantelshelf in *tête-de-nègre* and white brick. Designed and executed by Jean Royère and Yves de Parcevaux (FRANCE)

A restful sunroom with walls of treated Weltex wood and peacock-blue Japanese strawcloth; seagrass/rattan woven curtains; teak and cane furniture. Designer: John Crichton (NEW ZEALAND)

1 Lounge group in solid teak: table model No. 531, and chair No. 137 with foam padded seat and back rest upholstered in Thai silk; a wide range of covering fabrics is available. Designer: Finn Juhl, m.a.a. Makers: France & Son A/S (DENMARK)

2 Lounge group No. 115 from the *Artifort* range: foam-padded laminated shell on hardwood legs, with white cotton felt and metaflex spring-unit cushion, upholstered in *Rapallo* and *Stalakite* wool covering fabrics. Designer: Theo Ruth Makers: Wagemans & Van Tuinen NV (HOLLAND)

3 Built-in lounge bar in polished brass decorated
with panel prints of botanical subjects in
colours chosen to match the colour scheme of
the room. Interior designed and executed by
Ets. Vanderborght Freres SA (BELGIUM)

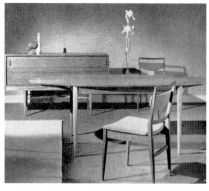

Dining group in mahogany with muninga veneers. The table top extends to 6 feet 8 inches, with the leaves folding back under the top when not in use. The sideboard has flush-closing sliding doors with brass handles; interior fitted two drawers in addition to storage space. Designer: Robert Heritage, MSIA. Made by Heal's of London (GB)

Living-room of a country house near Paris. White Comblanchien stone floor, walls cream-painted and multicolour brickwork. The curved settee and chair are upholstered in red plush velvet; wing chair in black; low tables are marble-topped on black wrought-iron base. The spiral stair is in white-lacquered metal with unpolished glass treads; window curtains white, patterned in tones of green.

Basement room in the same house, furnished for shooting parties. White ceramic-tile floor quartered in nigger-black; white chintz curtains with a two-tone green design by Paule Marrot; black wrought-iron table surfaced in red Formica. Chairs in yellow and in taupe ribbed velvet; carpet garnet-red. Architect: A. Bernard. Furniture and fittings by Jean Royère (FRANCE)

Living-room with dining corner. Low-slung foam-padded armchair on walnut frame; low walnut table with reversible top (one side faced black matt Formica); dining table in Mansonia walnut. Designer: Gianfranco Frattini. The ebony finish dining chairs are by Gio Ponti. Furniture made by Figli di Amedeo Cassina (ITALY)

Living room furnished in walnut with loose well-padded foam-rubber cushions to settee and armchairs; these are fitted with removable covers. The low coffee table has a glass under shelf for magazines. Designer: A. A. Patijn. Furniture made by Meubelfabriek Zijlstra (HOLLAND)

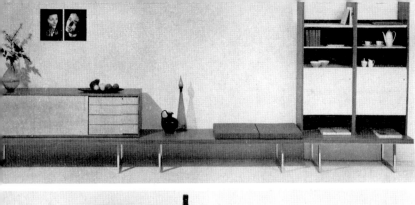

Group of bench units in nutwood on chrome steel base, with ash-fronted matching chest and bookshelves. Designed and made by Wörrlein Werkstätten (GERMANY)

Low table, 3 feet 4 inches square in teak, rosewood or ash with ebony dowels; hassocks upholstered in nylon foam with removable cotton covers. Designed for TV or informal entertaining by Axel Thygesen. Made by Interna (DENMARK)

Living room furnished in oak: the dining table and chairs are designed by Olavi Hänninen, sofa and glass-topped table by Hiort af Ornäs (FINLAND); the lounge chair and stool are by Yngve Ekström of Sweden. The wall cabinets with plaited-cane fronts are designed by Evy Westerberg-Levander. For Gösta Westerberg AB (SWEDEN)

ABOVE: Wire and steel rod basket chairs, white or black finish; cushions in moulded rubberised hair and foam plastic. Designed by Braakman & Dekker. Made by NV Ums-Pastoe (HOLLAND)

◄ College chair on black metal frame with woven cane elliptical seat and back. Designed by Frank Watkins. Made by Finmar Ltd (GB)

Cabinet made chair in teak; nylon cord seat, back, and armrests. Designed by H. Vestergaard Jensen. Made by Peder Pedersen (DENMARK)

Mademoiselle chair in birch, natural or ▶
black finish. Designer: Ilmari Tapiovaara. Makers: Asko O Y (FINLAND)

ABOVE: Chair in ash or teak w
foam rubber triangular seat cush
Designer: Hans Olsen. Makers:
Birksholm (DENMARK)

Chair in ash with laminated back
and leather-covered seat. Designer:
Vilhelm Wohlert. Makers: Arne
Poulsen (DENMARK)

◀ *The Egg* pre-formed fibre-glass s
upholstered in Dunlopillo; s
chrome metal swivel base. Desig
Arne Jacobsen. Made by F
Hansens Eft. (DENMARK) for F
mar Ltd (GB)

RIGHT: Beech armchair upholstered in latex foam and plastic foam. Designed and made by Brian Dollemore, High Wycombe College of Further Education (GB)

FAR RIGHT: Beech chair with moulded seat and back rest. Designed and made by Zdzisław Wróblewski, Warsaw Institute of Industrial Design (POLAND)

RIGHT: Steel-tube chair, upholstered in dark grey and yellow wool fabrics over foam rubber. Designed by R. & E. Goovaerts-Kruithof. Made by S. A. Gobert (BELGIUM)

FAR RIGHT: Armchair in beech, legs tipped teak; preformed seat, upholstered foam rubber and wool covering fabric, with loose foam cushion. Designer: Björn Engö. Made by Möre Stolfabrik A/S (NORWAY)

RIGHT: Side chair, angle-section steel frame, foam rubber seat and back cushions. Designer: C. S. Noxon. Made by Metalsmiths Co. Ltd (CANADA)

FAR RIGHT: Chair made in birch or teak, clear resin finish; with moulded plywood back; hairlock seat cushion. Designed by members of the Tokyo Industrial Arts Institute (JAPAN)

Reversible chair, iron-tube and wire frame construction; upholstered in hand-woven fabric over foam rubber. Designer: Martin Eisler. Makers: Forma (ITALY/BRAZIL)

Tube-iron and wire frame easy chair with carved wood arm-rests; upholstered in hand-woven fabrics over foam rubber. Designer: Carlo Hauner. Makers: Forma (ITALY/BRAZIL)

Side chair, steel-tube frame, upholstered foam rubber and tweed covering fabric; an alternative model has arm-rests in cherry-wood. Designed and made by Wörrlein-Werkstätten (GERMANY)

257

1

Side chair. Fibreglass shell, upholstered Dunlopillo; metal underframe, finished eggshell black or satin chrome. Made by Conran & Company Ltd (GB)

2

Armchair in teak with laminated arm rests; foam-padded seat and back. Designer: Finn Juhl, m.a.a. Made by Bovirke (DENMARK)

1 *Tuan* beech frame settee; back upholstered preformed rubberised hair on springs, seat tension-sprung with foam rubber cushions. Available in a wide range of covering fabrics and in three sizes. Designer: Howard B. Keith. Makers: H. K. Furniture Ltd (GB)

2 Six-foot wide ash frame settee; upholstered foam rubber with 'no-sag' springs in back, and hair and coil-sprung seat; satin aluminium dual base with stainless steel adjustable glide feet. Designer: Ward Bennett. Makers: Lehigh Furniture Corporation (USA)

3 G-plan three-seater setee on black-lacquered legs with brass feet. Hardwood shell upholstered in wool fabric over foam rubber; foam rubber sprung seat cushion, and fitted elbow rests. Made by E. Gomme Ltd (GB)

3

Cane frame chair with woven cane base and deep seat; foam rubber cushion. Designed by Erik Andersen and Palle Petersen. Made by Bovirke (DENMARK)

BELOW: *Liege* cherrywood daybed, reversible cushions upholstered foam rubber on feather base with yellow, blue and red wool fabric covers. Made by Wörrlein Werkstätten (GERMANY)

Large Eve foam padded plastic shell chair on red-beech legs; 'no-sag' springs in seat. Designer: Kerstin Hörlin-Holmqvist. Makers: AB Nordiska Kompaniet (SWEDEN)

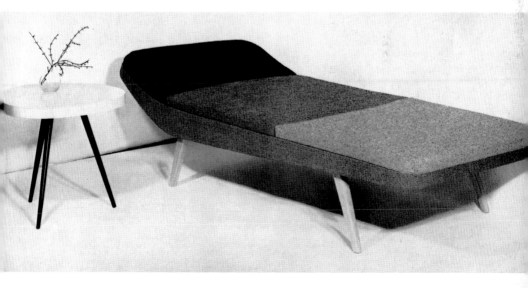

◄ *Tutbury* armchair on beech frame, natural finish, or in light or dark walnut, or mahogany; tension-sprung seat and foam cushion upholstered in moquette or tapestry fabrics. Makers Parker-Knoll Ltd (GB)

Chair in teak with stitched leather slung seat and foam-padded seat and back cushions. Designer: Björn Engö. Makers: Möre Stolfabrik A/S (NORWAY)

Divanette with hardwood frame back cushions and seat, upholstered metaflex spring-unit, white cottonfelt and foam rubber with De Ploeg *Bolivia* covering fabrics; oval chrome metal tube legs with plastic caps. Designed by Theo Ruth and Kho Liang Ie; the latter also designed the glass-topped black-lacquered metal table. Made by Wagemans & van Tuinen NV (HOLLAND)

RIGHT: Flat-steel frame chair, upholstered in wool fabric over deep foam rubber cushioning. Designer: W. H. Gispen. Made by Kembo Meubelfabrieken NV (HOLLAND)

BOTTOM RIGHT: Teak chair with woven cane seat and back. Designed by Peter Hvidt and O. Mølgaard-Nielsen, m.a.a. Makers: Søborg Møbelfabrik A/S (DENMARK)

Milano foam-padded shell on stained beech legs. Back upholstered Dux spring unit and cotton felt; coil-spring seat, and foam cushion with zippered cover. Designer: Alf Svensson. Makers: Ljungs Industrier AB (SWEDEN)

ABOVE: Woven bamboo screen on black iron frame 2 feet 5 inches high. Designed and made by Mosuke Yoshitake (JAPAN)

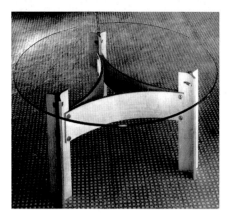

Glass-topped occasional table on laminated wood base. Designed and made by Gautier-Delaye (FRANCE)

Cocktail/coffee table in walnut, medium or dark finish, or in oiled teak; the pull-out shelves are surfaced in green and ivory Resopal. Designed and made by Wilhelm Renz KG (GERMANY)

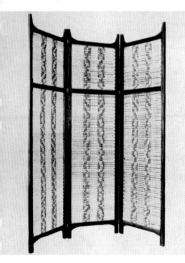

Hinged screen on oiled walnut frame, 6 feet 6 inches high; handwoven panels in natural bamboo, and orange, blue and tan yarns. Designed and made by James and Marie Howell (USA)

Hanging screen composed of traditional forms in 6-mm acrylic plastic, and 2-mm polished brass and black iron, with engraved decoration. Designed and made by Yasuhiro Hiramatsu (JAPAN)

Knock-down coffee table in Burma teak, oiled finish. Designed and made by Wilhelm Renz KG (GERMANY)

BELOW: Teak occasional table; the top is reversible and faced with plastic on one side. Designer: C. Braakman. Makers N.V. Ums-Pastoe (HOLLAND)

ABOVE: Occasional table on black-lacquered sculptured hardwood base; plate glass top. Designer: Jos. De Mey. Makers: 'Luxus' (BELGIUM)

Occasional table with saddle-stitched coachhide top 36 inches long; underframe polished brass. Designed by J. Jaraczewska and E. Ihnatowicz. Makers: W. J. Mars & Co. Ltd (GB)

◄ Teak frame coffee table with mosaic-inlaid top, 5 feet long, or with solid teak or ceramic tile top; the legs and trim are in brass or aluminium. Designed and made by the Aka Furniture Co. Ltd (CANADA)

ABOVE: Occasional table, slatted sapele top on metal tube base lacquered grey. Designed and made by Eric Lemesre (BELGIUM)

ABOVE: Laminated birch table on black iron legs. Designer: Tapio Wirkkala. Makers: Asko O/Y (FINLAND)

Coffee table in Burma teak with yellow laminated-plastic elliptical top. Designed and made by Barry Warner, Leicester College of Art (GB)

Knock-down occasional table in 'keyaki' wood with clear lacquer finish; the legs are affixed to the top with forked bolts in a dull black finish. Designed by members of the Tokyo Industrial Arts Institute. Made by Fuji Jidosha Co. Ltd (JAPAN)

ABOVE: Lamp table in black iron, containing a perforated metal drum fitted with a coral fibreglass diffuser decorated with a pressed butterfly and leaves; plate glass top. Designer: John Crichton. Makers: P. Pausma (NEW ZEALAND)

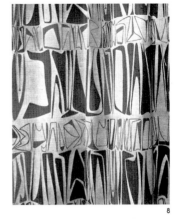

6

7

8

9

6. *Jamaica*. Spun rayon and cotton in red and grey; mulberry and tan; or green and orange. Designed and produced by Ben Rose Handprinted Textiles.

7. 50-in. hand-print on rayon and cotton dobby satin produced by W. Foxton Ltd. Colours: green and gold; red and fawn; brown and gold; and rust and green all with touches of nigger brown on cream ground.

8. *Cuneiforms*. 64-in. loomed haircloth in orange and brown designed by Ruth Adler and hand-printed by Edward C. Schnee.

10

9. Printed linen available in black or red; earthenware dove made by Gustavsbergs Fabriker A B; and vase in clear and white crystal made at Paolo Venini's Glassworks, Murano.

10. Printed linen in red or dark green.

All designed by Tyra Lundgren for A B Nordiska Kompaniet.

1. Background: 50-in. embroidered satin available in brown or green satin with white chain stitch, and in white satin with green or red stitching. Foreground: 48-in. candlewick, natural ground with the candlewick design in a choice of two, three and four colour schemes. Both are *Rosebank* fabrics produced by Turnbull & Stockdale Ltd.

2. *Astral*. Cotton, rayon and mohair hand-printed casement fabric designed by Mrs. John S. Bolley and made by Goodall Fabrics Inc.

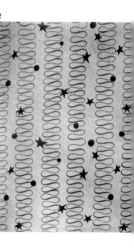

6. *Eroica*. 50-in. acetate and gimp cotton brocade in a range of eleven two-colour or tone-on-tone effects. Designed by Frank R. Gibson, MSIA, and produced by Morton Sundour Fabrics Ltd.

7. *Allegro*. 50-in. screen print on heavy cotton, available in three colour schemes, designed by Humphrey Spender, MSIA, and produced by Edinburgh Weavers.

3

4

3. *Buttons and Bows*. 50-in. *Ever-glaze* chintz designed by Duncan Grant and produced by George Henderson Textiles Ltd. Colours: apple green and blue with maroon stripe; pink and blue with indigo stripe; orange and blue with green stripe; and grey and yellow with cerise stripe.

4. *Horsemen*. Beige linen with motif in pale blue, dark blue and terra-cotta, designed by Noreen Bennett, ARCA, for L. D. Ziegler.

5. *Oats*. 36-in. printed rayon or 50-in. linen, white ground with motif in colour to suit individual requirements, designed and printed by Winning Read.

5

6

7

1

1

1. *Hunter.* Hand-printed cotton and mohair fabric with a linen-like texture in beige, grey, flamingo and blue, designed by Ivan Bartlett and produced by Goodall Fabrics Inc.
2. 51-in. cotton or spun rayon crêpe in six colours on a white or cream ground, designed by Märta Maria Dahlén and produced by Molnlycke Vafveri A B.
3. *Maya Fresco.* Hand-printed cotton and mohair fabric, in light blue, spruce, gold, tan and grey. Designed by Jean and Hellen Gazagnaire and produced by Goodall Fabrics Inc.

2

5

4

4. *Texas.* 50-in. printed linen cloth designed by Marjorie Young and produced by Donald Bros Ltd. A choice of five attractive colour schemes on a white background.
5. 50-in. printed linen in green, brown and red on white ground, designed by Josef Frank and produced by Svenskt Tenn.

6. *Print and Imprint.* Hand-print on Angora satin, in grey, bright navy, lilac, ruby and dark brown, designed by Ivan Bartlett and produced by Goodall Fabrics Inc.
7. *Birds in Trees.* Spun rayon designed by Mary Oliver and screen-printed in four colours by Silfa Fabriksaktiebolag.
8. *Arcady.* 50-in. screen-print on heavy cotton designed by Hans Tisdall and produced by Edinburgh Weavers. Bright chintz colours on white or pale pink, and in soft shades of blue or green on white.

9. *Daphne.* 50-in. printed rayon, cotton satin or permanent glaze chintz, available in pink, peach, pale lime, sea-green, blue or beige. Designed by Frank R. Gibson, MSIA, and produced by Morton Sundour Fabrics Ltd.
10. *Trees.* Hand-screened spun rayon designed by Edward J. Wormley and produced by Schiffer Prints Division of the Mil-Art Company Ltd. Colours: celadon green and bark brown on grey; light and bark brown on sand; blue-green and moss-green on natural.

1. *Egyptian Fantasy*. Designer: Peter Shuttleworth. Producers: The Wall Paper Manufacturers Ltd. Decorations in pink, green, grey, maize and terra-cotta on white or black ground.

3. *Sea Horses*. Designer: Bruce Hollingsworth. Producers: John Line & Sons Ltd. Available on white or blue ground.

2. *Cheerio*. Designer: Lawrence Gussin. Producers: Wall Trends Inc. Handprinted in chartreuse, white and black on Chinese red. Available also on *Stylon* wall canvas.

5. Designer: R. H. Callwood. Producers: The Wall Paper Manufacturers Ltd. Blue-grey, green or white grounds with flowers and leaves in grey, turquoise, red, yellow, green and white.

4. Producers: Arthur Sanderson & Sons Ltd. Off-white design on blue, oyster, green and apricot satinette grounds.

6

6. *Swedish Homecrafts*. Designer : Marianne Fisker. Producer : Ernst Dahl. Background green with decorations in white and yellow.

7

8

7. Designer: Margaret Simeon. Producers: Lightbown Aspinall branch of The Wall Paper Manufacturers Ltd. Motif in white on pale grey ground.

8. *Blue Oranges*. Designer: Mellville Cross. Producers: Inez Croom Inc. Hand-printed by silk screen in green, blue or white.

9. Designer: Philip Pompa. Producers: John Line & Sons Ltd. Available in a range of colourings.

9

Birds in the Reeds. Hand-printed linen and cotton mixture in grey and green; beige and green; blue and brown; brown and yellow; beige and grey; or yellow and grey. Designer: Kristin Ingelög. Makers: Mölnlycke Väfveri AB (SWEDEN).

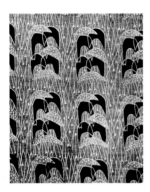

Wig-line-theme. Warp of cotton, weft of spun rayon, in green, brown and grey, or grey-green, yellow and red. Designer: Carl-Arne Breger. Makers: Mölnlycke Väfveri AB (SWEDEN).

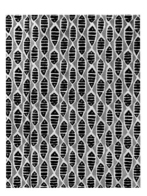

The Runestones. Linen with the motif in brown or grey. Designer: Dagmar Halle Makers: Saléns (SWEDEN).

BELOW: *Ellesmere* (left). 50-inch screen printed linen, also in sky-blue/sag green; crimson/stone; pale blue/navy Designer: Eryl Rice. *Astrid* (background 50-inch screen-printed linen, also i ground shades of yellow, blue, green mushroom, elephant and chestnut. De signer: Marian Mahler. Both made b Donald Bros Ltd. Pottery cockere designed and made by Dorothy Brendon From Annette Handcrafts of Britain (GB)

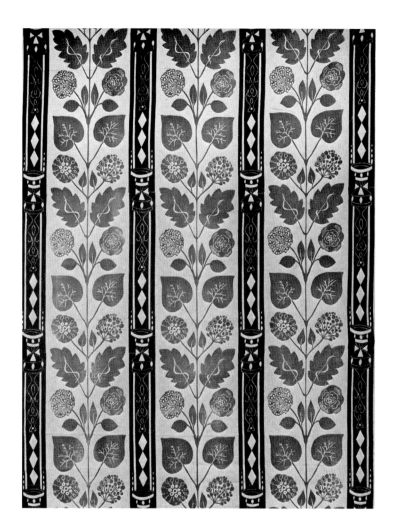

RIGHT: *Orlando*. 50-inch rayon satin in lime green and grey. Designer and printer: Winning Read (GB).

BELOW: 48-inch Jacquard woven heavy long staple spun rayon, Grafton furnishing fabric, white abstract figures on lime green ground or in other colours to order. Designer: Jacqueline Groag, MSIA. Makers: Calico Printers Association Ltd (GB).

Thistles. Warp of cotton, weft of spun rayon, in green, yellow and white, and other colour schemes. Designer: Else Marie Thorkildsen (SWEDEN).

Indian Summer. White cotton with design in blue, carmine and yellow-green. Designer: Dagmar Haller. Maker: Eric Ewers (SWEDEN).

Vibrations. 48-inch satinweave in mulberry and bronze-green, raspberry and jade blue, or stone grey and rock tan. Designers and makers: Ben Rose Hand-printed Textiles (USA).

LEFT: *Si and No* (Typewriter characters). All-cotton warp sateen in chartreuse and brown on white; copper and brown on beige; two-tone grey on natural; and green and slate on natural. Designer: Bernard Rudofsky. Makers: Schiffer Prints Division of Mil-Art Co Inc (USA).

RIGHT: *Overture.* Hand-printed on angora satin in yellow, green and blue; dark and medium green; tan and brown; brown and avocado; green and purple; red and grey. Designer: Dorothy Clark. Producers: Goodall Fabrics Inc (USA).

White rayon with design in yellow, orange, blue, grey and black. Designed and printed by J. Craig (GB).

LEFT: *Wireworks*. Bleached pure linen hand-printed in one colour to order. Designer: Ruth Adler. Makers: Adler-Schnee Associates (USA).

By the Horn. Linen and cotton mixture in green, grey, yellow and brown on white, or green, blue, grey and yellow on paler yellow ground. Designer: Timo Sarpaneva. Makers: Mölnlycke Väfveri AB (SWEDEN).

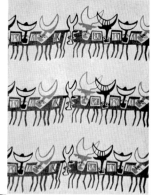

Fruit Delight. 48-inch linen hand-printed in five different colour schemes on a natural ground. Designer: Robert A. Stewart. Makers: Liberty & Co Ltd (GB).

LEFT: *Sticks and Stones*. Bleached pure linen hand-printed in two colours to order. Designer: Ruth Adler. Makers: Adler-Schnee Associates (USA).

Arches. Handprint on linen and cotton mixture in grey, brown and yellow, or red, blue and grey. Designers: Lars-Erik Falk. Makers: Mölnlycke Väfveri AB (SWEDEN).

BELOW: 48-inch Coconada cloth with wool content jacquard cross stripe, available in four different colour combinations. Design based on Windsor Castle with Elizabethan flowers and figures. Producers: W. Foxton Ltd (GB)

BELOW: 48-inch two-colour screenprint on fibro basket-weave cloth, available in cherry and stone or forest and gold. Designer: Roger Nicholson. Makers: David Whitehead Ltd (GB)

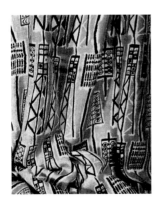

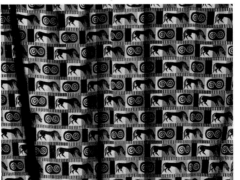

ABOVE: Curtains of 48-inch machine print on spun rayon, available in chocolate, blue, olive gold; olive, salmon, beige; or cerise, indigo, grey. Designer: Marion Mahler. Makers: David Whitehead Ltd (GB)

LEFT: *Altamira.* 50-inch screen print in five colourings on crêpe cotton. Designer: Christine Clegg. Makers: Edinburgh Weavers (GB)

BELOW: Background: 50-inch fabric, cotton warp and wool weft, in eight different colours. Makers: Old Bleach Furnishing Fabrics (N. Ireland). Foreground: 48-inch screen-printed cotton, dark eggshell green with the motif in black and white. Designer: Terence Conran. Makers: David Whitehead Ltd (GB)

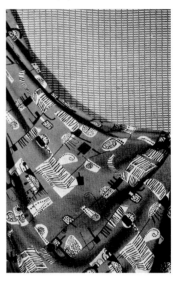

White cotton printed with yellow stripe and dark grey motif. Designer and printer: Robin Thomas. Producers: Mill House Fabric Printers (Penzance) Ltd (GB)

ABOVE: 50-inch cotton twill or linen in colours shown and in blue-green, yellow and black on natural ground. A *Rose-bank* fabric. Makers: Turnbull & Stockdale Ltd (GB)

48-inch machine-print on spun rayon, available in forest, black, turquoise and citron; gun-metal, flame, gold and black; brown, black, gold and lime; or madder, black, turquoise and lime. Designer: Jacqueline Groag MSIA. Makers: David Whitehead Ltd (GB)

The Siamese Ballet. Hand-screened fabric in grey and red, black and turquoise, brown and orange, or green and black, all on natural ground. Designer: Edward Daly Brown. Makers: Schiffer Prints Division, Mil-Art Co. Inc (USA)

RIGHT: 48-inch textured cotton screen-print. Designer: Terence Conran. Makers: David Whitehead Ltd. Extreme right: *Foreshore.* 50-inch printed cotton. Designer: Lucienne Day ARCA. Makers: Edinburgh Weavers. Earthenware dish by Joan Motley (GB)

BELOW (Left): *Acres.* 50-inch screen-print on crêpe cotton in five colourings. Designer: Lucienne Day ARCA. Makers: Edinburgh Weavers. Centre: 50-inch screen-print in black and rust on fawn tinted cotton sateen. Designer: Barbara Pile. Makers: David Whitehead Ltd. Right: 48-inch screen-print in black on four contrasting grounds or in red on white. Designer: Terence Conran. Makers: David Whitehead Ltd (GB)

Trapez. 50-inch linen or cotton satin in white and four contrasting colours. Designer: Arne Jacobsen. Makers: Graucol Textiles (DENMARK)

Pygmalion. 50-inch screen-printed chintz available in any colours to special order. Designer: Hilda Durkin. Makers: Warner & Sons Ltd (GB)

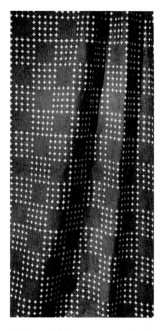

Woodcuts. 50-inch screen-printed linen in five separate colour schemes. Designer: Sylvia Priestley. Makers: Liberty & Co. Ltd (GB)

BELOW: *All Square.* 50-inch heavy white cotton block-printed in grey-blue, chestnut, mustard and black. Designed and printed by Ronald Grierson MSIA (GB)

Suan-Pan. 51-inch handprint on cotton in six colours. Designer: Bent Karlby. Makers: Frederik Fiedler A/S (DENMARK)

BELOW: *Mosaic.* Handprint in two colours on bleached linen. Designer: Bent Karlby. Makers: Frederik Fiedler A/S (DENMARK)

Collier. 50-inch linen or cotton satin with white diamonds on grounds of coal black, dark petrol, dark brown or dark grey. Designer: Arne Jacobsen. Makers: Graucob Textiles (DENMARK)

BELOW: *Chanticleer.* 36-inch sateen nursery print in scarlet, ochre and prune on pale grey. Designer and printer: Meriel Tower (GB)

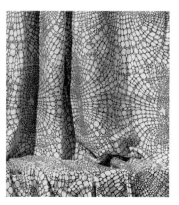

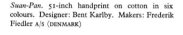

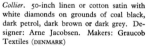

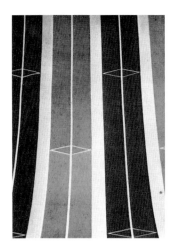

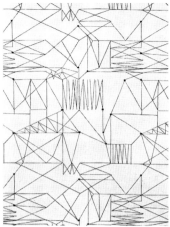

BELOW: *Polynesia* hand-printed design in deep purple on 36-inch fine mountain grey linen. Designed and printed by Diana Bloomfield (GB)

Termidor cotton velour in black, three shades of yellow, and white. Designer: Astrid Sampe. Makers: A/B Nordiska Kompaniet (SWEDEN)

Graphica 48-inch printed cotton with design in black on white, yellow, orange or khaki grounds. Designer: Lucienne Day, ARCA. For Heal's of London (GB)

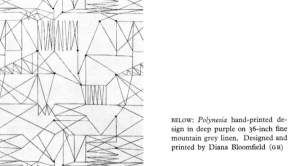

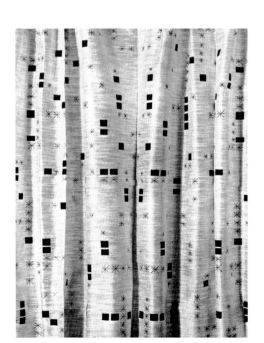

Central Park South. 50-inch white raysilk with silk-screen printed design in colours to special order. Designer: Ruth Adler. Makers: Adler-Schnee Associates (USA)

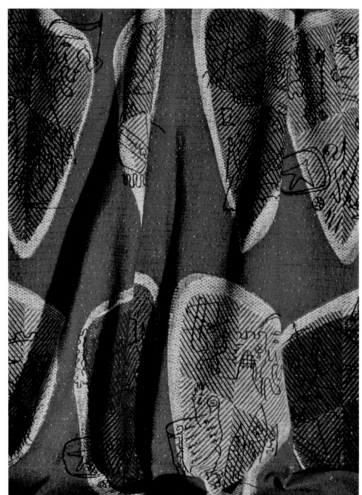

Honeycomb screen-printed design in avocado, mustard or mocha on 50-inch basket weave linen. Designer: Ethel Dean. Makers: Schiffer Prints Division, Mil-Art Co. Inc. (USA)

History of Shapes. Historical tapestry specially designed for Imperial Chemical Industries Ltd, . . . typical shapes throughout the ages from the first axe to the space ship. The tapestry is unique as it has been hand Jacquard woven and hand-screen printed, the fabric being constructed from pure silk and Ardil (protein fibre), and interwoven with non-tarnishing metallic threads. Although the fabric has all the deep texture qualities it is quite light and it has a soft and gentle drape. The repeat is 50 inches. Designer: Tibor Reich, FSIA. Makers: Tibor Ltd (GB)

BELOW: 50-inch screen prints on rough textured cotton. *Masts* (*Left*) designed by Hans Tisdall and (*Right*) *Banderole* designed by Humphrey Spender. Makers: Edinburgh Weavers (GB)

BELOW (*Left*): 48-inch printed cotton in mauve/grey/green; brown/pink/mushroom; green/blue/grey; orange/yellow, blue; grey/brown/lime. Designer: Mary White. (*Right*): *Trio.* 48-inch roller printed cotton. The design in black-and-white on chartreuse, orange, grey, green and yellow grounds. Designer: Lucienne Day, ARCA. For Heal's of London (GB)

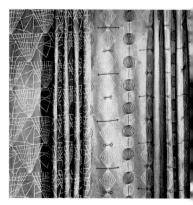

ABOVE (*Left*): *Delta.* 48-inch printed cotton, the design in white on grey, red, lime or green grounds. Designer: Walter Kramer. (*Right*): *Spinners.* 48-inch printed cotton with design in white and black on terra-cotta, olive-green, red, grey and chartreuse grounds. Designer: Mary Warren. For Heal's of London (GB)

ABOVE (*Left*): 48-inch spun rayon. Also available in
lavender, fawn and green. (*Right*): 48-inch spun
rayon with design as shown or in green/yellow/grey
and lime green/turquoise/mushroom on off-white
ground. Designer: Marion Mahler. Makers: David
Whitehead Ltd (GB)

BELOW (*Left*): *Rush and Reed* and (*Right*): *Manx*.
50-inch rayon, cotton and linen in colourings to
special order. Designer: Karen Bulow. Makers:
Canadian Homespuns Reg'd (CANADA)

ABOVE (*Left*): *Dandelion Clocks*. 48-inch printed rayon with
design in black on yellow, grey, turquoise and cerise grounds.
(*Right*): *Rig*. 48-inch printed cotton in brown/turquoise;
grey/red; mushroom/olive; forest green/lime. Designer:
Lucienne Day, ARCA. For Heal's of London (GB)

RIGHT: *Spiney Pines*. Hand-screen print on 50-inch cotton Dreamspun; coral, lemon, and other grounds. Repeat 29 inches. Designed by Ruth Adler for Adler-Schnee Associates (USA). BELOW: Cotton screen-print in mustard, white, black, turquoise on grey-green, and other colourings. Designer: Jacqueline Groag, FSIA. Makers: Haworth's Fabrics Ltd (GB)

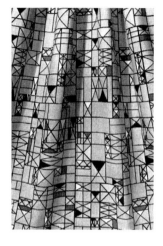

RIGHT: 50-inch Rosebank cotton print. Designer: Irene Browning. Makers: Turnbull & Stockdale Ltd (GB). FAR RIGHT: 48-inch thick cotton screen-print, as shown, and in scarlet/grey and pink/grey. Designer: Margaret Simeon. Makers: Sixten & Cassey Ltd (GB).

BELOW: 50-inch textured cotton screen-print in red, green and black on a grey rope ground. Designer: Philip Stockford, FRSA. Makers: Turnbull & Stockdale Ltd (GB). BELOW, RIGHT: *Strings and Things*. Screen-print on cotton Dreamspun or nubbin fabrics. Chartreuse, orange, and other grounds. Designed by Ruth Adler for Adler-Schnee Associates (USA)

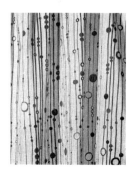

TOP AND BOTTOM: 48-inch all-cotton machine-printed jacquard texture fabrics; each is available in five different colour combinations. Designer: J. Hill. Makers: Tootal Broadhurst Lee Co. Ltd (GB). FORE-GROUND: *Helico* texturedrape, a 48-inch upholstery fabric with cotton mercerized warp and textured gimp weft. Designer: Tibor Reich, FSIA. Makers: Tibor Ltd (GB)

Village Church. 48-inch printed cotton or satin, with design in black on yellow or white; or white line on orange, khaki, blueberry or sea-green grounds. Designer: Hilda Durkin. For Heal's of London (GB)

48-inch machine-printed rayon fabrics. That shown at left is also available in tomato red, pale green, tan and wine; the other in vermilion, light green and burgundy. Both are designed by Marion Mahler for D. Whitehead Ltd (GB)

Autumn 48-inch cotton printed in five colours on a plain ground; six colour combinations are available. Designer: Frits Wichard. Makers: De Ploeg, Bergeyk (HOLLAND)

Guêpe (Wasp). 52-inch cotton flock-print in two colours. Designed by Kunstgewerbe-schule, Zürich. Made by Wohntextil AG (SWITZERLAND)
(Photo: Hans Finsler)

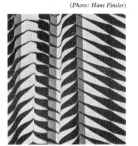

Nature Abstraite. 52-inch cotton-sateen with design printed in blue on grey, red, green and yellow grounds. Designed by Kunstgewerbe-schule, Zürich. Made by Wohntextil AG (SWITZERLAND).
(Photo: Hans Finsler)

Keyhole. 48-inch Studio-loom fabric with hand-screen printed design in blue/dove-grey/gunmetal on grey; orange/tan/grey on yellow. Repeat 12½ inch. Designers and makers: Ben Rose (USA)

Zotis. One colour design on plain satin ground, in crimson and ivory or deep blue and mushroom. Designed and printed by Winning Read (GB)

LEFT: *Cosmos.* Pale grey hand-printed Splendoline fabric. Circles in elephant-grey, golden yellow and white; dots in bright green-blue and terra-cotta. Designer: Gudrun Orrghen-Lundgren. Makers: A/B Olssons Textilfabriker (SWEDEN)

BELOW: *Kaleidoscope.* 48-inch Fortisan poplin or chintz multicolour print on light grey ground. Repeat 24-inch. Designer: Alexander Girard, AIA. For Herman Miller Furniture Co. (USA)

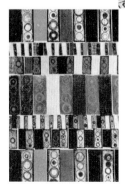

48-inch heavy spun rayon with machine-printed design in green, gold or blue pre-dominating colours. Designer: Jacqueline Groag, FSIA. Makers: D. Whitehead Ltd (GB)

Scherzot. Splendoline fabric hand-printed in three colours. The leaves are in bright and medium grey, with markings and irregular lines leading into the leaves in dark grey. Designer: Gudrun Orrghen-Lundgren. Makers: A/B Olssons Textilfabriker (SWEDEN)

Fruit Cup. 50-inch cotton screen-printed to order in the customer's own choice of colours. Designers: Libert Dessins (FRANCE). For Warner & Sons Ltd (GB)

Colonnade. 50-inch screen print on heavy cotton crepe, in red, rust, green or mauve colourings. Repeat 19½ inches. Designer: Hilda Durkin. Makers: Edinburgh Weavers (GB)

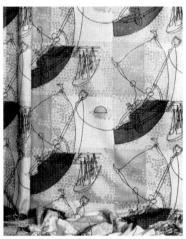

Arab Dhow. 50-inch screen print on heavy cotton crepe in gold plum and sage: sky blue, primrose and leaf green; grey, blue and yellow; blue, grey, red and gold. Repeat 26½ inches. Designer: Hilda Durkin. Makers: Edinburgh Weavers (GB)

Scrub Oak. 48-inch screen-printed cotton, ratiné linen, or antique satin, produced in a choice of twenty-six colour combinations. Designer: John Brook. Makers: J. & J. Brook Associates (CANADA)

Since furnishing textiles are not subjected to the same kind of use as wearable fabrics, there is a difference in scope for design, weave and material which strongly favours the furnishing textile designer. His latitude is such that he can, if he wishes, look upon his medium as a painter does his canvas, but, in addition to its being a vehicle for applied design, there are inherent potentialities of texture and weave as pattern sources in the material itself.

The vocabulary with which designers are thus provided, although extended from time to time by the introduction of new techniques and synthetic yarns, has been available for a very long time. Courage in exploiting its possibilities, however, has not always been in evidence and is in fact inclined to fluctuate. At the present time it is particularly encouraging to observe that some of the more conservative textile firms have begun to allow a lighter and more adventurous note to pervade their work. The decorative and yielding qualities of their furnishing fabrics counter the hard geometry of a modern interior.

This section is not intended as a summary of total output, but as being representative of the forward trends in design that are likely to have an influence on future production, or that have themselves grown from similar influences in the past. It demonstrates that there exists a wholesome and enterprising regard for the decorative potentialities of the modern idiom.

TOP: 48-inch roller-printed cotton fabrics in colours shown and in three other combinations. Designers and makers: Tootal Broadhurst Lee Co. Ltd (GB)

CENTRE (left): Screen-print on 36-inch textured cotton. Designed and hand-printed by Alison Hurd (GB). (Right) 48-inch textured gimp weave interwoven with gold Lurex. Also available in yellow, bright red, kingfisher blue and other colours, all with gold Lurex and black. Designers and makers: W. Foxton Ltd (GB)

BOTTOM (left): 50-inch spun rayon, as shown, and in other colourings. Designer: Robert Shaw. Makers: The Old Bleach Linen Co. Ltd (NORTHERN IRELAND). (Right) 48-inch vat printed cotton; also made in other colour combinations on fawn and turquoise blue grounds. Designers and makers: W. Foxton Ltd (GB)

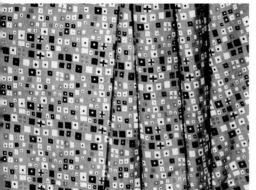

ABOVE: 48-inch cotton print in black/white and alpine rose on grey; also available in white/blue/turquoise on vermilion ground, and other colourings. Designed by Jacqueline Groag, FSIA. For John Lewis & Co. Ltd (GB)

ABOVE RIGHT: *Trapeze* handprint on linen, batiste, or fibreglass fabrics 48-inches wide. Colours are gunmetal/dove; mustard/persimmon; chamois/ochre; bitter green/emerald, all on white ground with black horizontal line overprint. Designers and makers: Laverne Inc. (USA)

RIGHT: *Construction* two-colour print on 50-inch bleached linen in custom colours. Designed by Ruth Adler. Made by Adler-Schnee Associates (USA)

BELOW: *Daystar* handprint on batiste, linen, cotton, or fibreglass fabrics 48-inches wide. In silver and aqua, sandalwood and brown, red and black, all on white ground. Designers and makers: Laverne Inc. (USA)

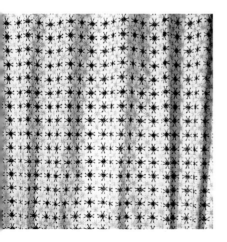

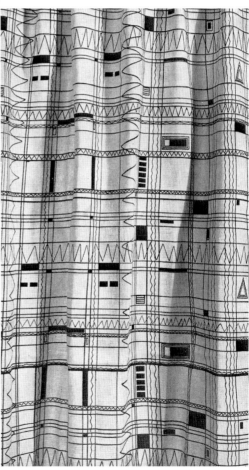

BACKGROUND: 50-inch Rosebank machine-print on crêpe cotton. It is available in five different colour combinations. Designer: W. Hertzberger. Makers: Turnbull & Stockdale Ltd (GB). FOREGROUND: 50-inch spun rayon woven fabric, as shown, and in other colourings. Designer: Robert Shaw. Makers: The Old Bleach Linen Co. Ltd (NORTHERN IRELAND)

ABOVE: Carmyle Wilton wool carpeting, 27 inches wide, on jute and cotton base; multi-colour pattern on charcoal or wine ground. Makers: James Templeton & Co. Ltd (GB)

BELOW: *Surte* handwoven Gobelin tapestry in grey, black, and dark red. 7 × 5 feet. Designer: Ann-Mari Forsberg. Made by Märta Määs-Fjetterström AB (SWEDEN)

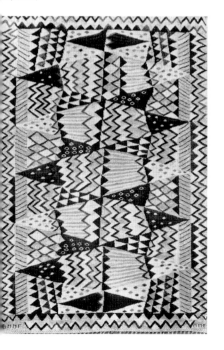

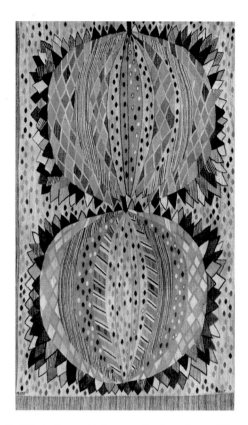

ABOVE: *The Melon* handwoven Gobelin tapestry in yellow and green. 6 feet 7½ inches × 4 feet 2½ inches. Designer: Ann-Mari Forsberg. Made by Märta Määs-Fjetterström AB (SWEDEN)

BELOW: *Wild Ducks* handwoven linen tapestry in natural, black-and-white. Designed and made by Dora Jung (FINLAND)

BELOW: Roller printed cotton rep. Alternate leaves in shaded grey tones and in deep turquoise, with dividing lines in two grey tones. Designer: Gudrun Orrghen-Lundgren. Makers: Borås Wäfveri A/B (SWEDEN)

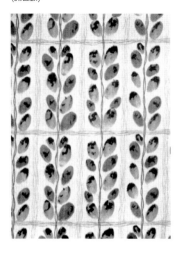

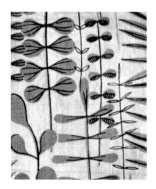

ABOVE: *Astrid* 50-inch hand-screen printed cotton on grey, orange, green, sapphire, or wine grounds. Repeat 24 inches. Designer: J. Johnson. Makers: Morton Sundour Fabrics Ltd (GB)

RIGHT AND FAR RIGHT: *Foliation* two-colour hand-print, and *Blockweave* four-colour hand-print on 48-inch linen, cotton and rayon, or cotton sheer fabrics in a choice of thirty standard colours. Designer: Micheline Knaff. Makers: J. & J. Brook Ltd (CANADA)

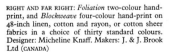

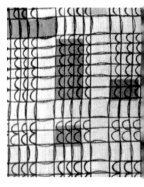

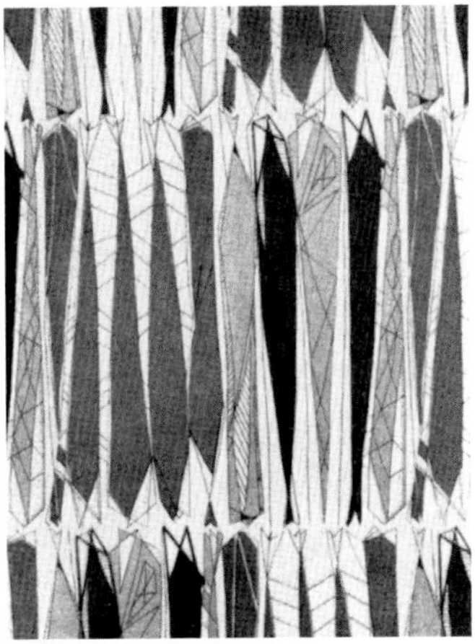

LEFT: *Stim* hand-print on quality Splendolin fabric. Abstract fish shapes grouped alternately in green-blue, and medium blue/yellow green colourings with veining and outlines in black. Designer: Gudrun Orrghen-Lundgren (SWEDEN). Makers: Sandvika Vaeveri A/S (NORWAY)

LOW: *Clarrisa* four-colour hand-print on quality tton. White bleached ground, large squares in rk grey screen, rectangles deep blue, smaller uares almond green, leaves plum colour with the nge reprint in deep blue. The pattern is im-ovised, the lines uneven and irregular to give it e. Designed and printed by Gudrun Orrghen-undgren (SWEDEN)

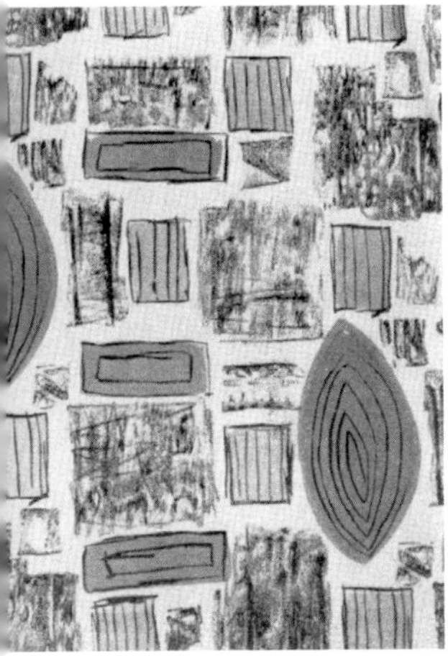

BELOW: 48-inch roller print on textured cotton. It is also available in five other colour combinations on grey, red, yellow, buff, and black grounds. Designers and makers: David Whitehead Ltd (GB)

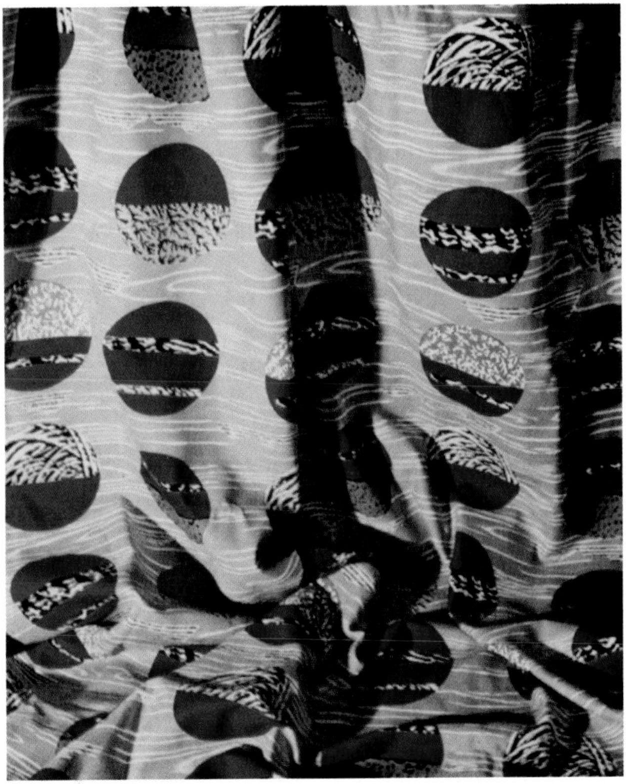

ELOW: *Tattoo* 50-inch hand-printed linen in ey/blue, tan/orange; or in plain orange or blue. esigner: Astrid Sampe. Makers: A/B Nordiska ompaniet Textile Workshop (SWEDEN)

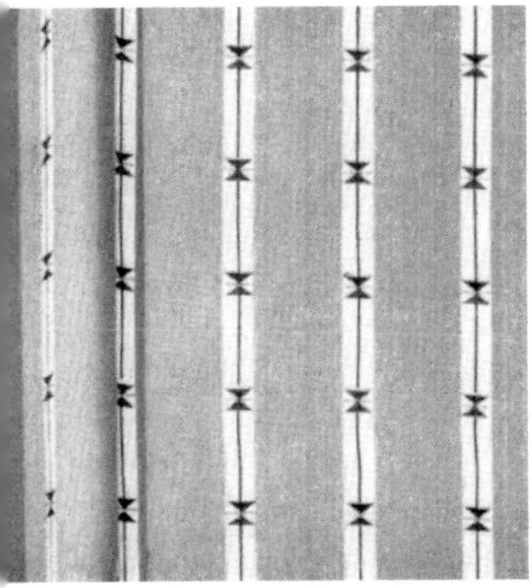

LEFT: *Bric-a-Brac* hand-screen print on 48-inch textured cotton. Other grounds are grey, blue, lilac, topaz, jade green. Designer: Walter Krauer. Makers: Morton Sundour Fabrics Ltd (GB).
RIGHT: *Cryptography* hand-print on heavy quality all cotton Arc-en-Ciel fabric, 52 inches wide. Designer: Sergio d'Angelo Reggiori. Makers: Manifattura JSA (ITALY)

BELOW: Blended textile/wallpaper designs: (*Left*) *Venezia* cotton mural drape of shaded diamonds on bands of grey, black and brick. Designed by Tibor Reich, FSIA. Made by Tibor Ltd (GB); (*right*) *Intaglio*, a Palladio wallpaper of shadowed stippled squares in blue with lilac on white. Designed by Roger Nicholson. Made by The Wall Paper Manufacturers Ltd (GB) (*Photo: Copyright Manchester Cotton Board*)

BELOW: 48-inch textured cotton with stylised flower print in cornflower blue, yellow, red, black and green on white plaques against grey ground and in other colourings. Designer: Elsie Smith. Makers: Turnbull & Stockdale Ltd (GB)

ABOVE: *Corinne* 50-inch textured cotton print in lemon/grey/black/white on red ground; and in four other colour combinations. Designers and makers: Morton Sundour Fabrics Ltd (GB)

ABOVE: *Sicilian Lion* large-scale Palladio wallpaper in gold on white or black ground. Designer: Roger Nicholson. Makers: The Wall Paper Manufacturers Ltd (GB). In the foreground are hand-printed cotton fabrics *Saraband* designed by Robert McGowan for Edinburgh Weavers and *Cassata*, a huge-scale fruit print designed by Betty Middleton-Stanford for Liberty & Co. Ltd (GB) *(Photo: Copyright Manchester Cotton Board)*

LEFT: *Sticks* hand-print on heavy quality all-cotton Flamenco fabric, 52 inches wide. Designer: Gio Ponti. Makers: Manifattura JSA (ITALY). The enamel plate and bowl shown with it are designed and made by Edward Winter (USA) *(Bowl by courtesy S. W. Vickery, Esq.)*

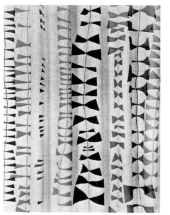

ABOVE: Linen upholstery weave in black and white, 48 inches wide. Designed and made by Ets. Marchant & Stichelmans SA (BELGIUM)

ABOVE LEFT: *Summer Meadow* screen-print on 48-inch satin rayon, with patented crease-resistant finish. Four different colour combinations are available. Designed and made by Tootal Broadhurst Lee Co. Ltd (GB). ABOVE RIGHT: *Lotus* five-colour print on textured cotton, 48 inches wide. Other ground colours are moss green, light blue, and light and dark grey. Designed and made by Morton Sundour Fabrics Ltd (GB)

RIGHT: *Kite Tails* four-colour print in charcoal, orange, fuschia, and ochre on heavy cream linen, 50 inches wide. Also printed on Fortisan silk; colour choice may be custom ordered. Designer: Gere Kavanaugh. Made by Isabel Scott Fabrics Corp. (USA)

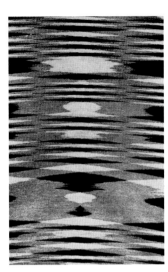

ABOVE LEFT: *Icicle* upholstery fabric, dip-yarn two-colour weave in yellow, orange, red, purple, blue, turquoise, green, all with black. Designed and made by Unika-Væv (DENMARK). ABOVE RIGHT: 36-inch cotton or flax fabric block-printed in Veronese green, cobalt, and black on white ground. Designed for nursery use by D. Dybowska. Printed at the Warsaw Institute of Industrial Design (POLAND)

ABOVE LEFT: *Sunflower* black block print on spectrum yellow silk, 48 inches wide. Horizontal repeat, 16 inches. RIGHT: *Fishtail* dark red, pale blue, and black screen-print on white linen, 48 inches wide; horizontal repeat 16 inches. Both fabrics are designed and printed by Kathleen Le Mare of London Textile Group (GB)

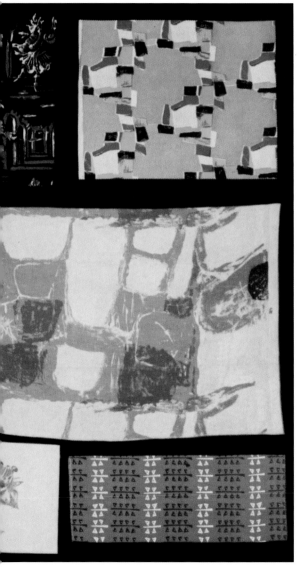

1 *Californian Poppy* screen-print on fine cotton 48 inches wide; repeat 24 inches. Also with blue or pink flowers, and on black, red, fawn, or grey/blue grounds. Made by David Whitehead Fabrics Ltd (GB)

2 *Rosa* screen-print on fine cotton, 50 inches wide. Designed by Marina Hoffer, MSIA. Made by Warner & Sons Ltd (GB)

3 *Ballet Nègre* screen-printed rayon-satin, 48 inches wide; available in three colourways. Designed by Desville of Paris. Made by Tootal Broadhurst Lee Co. (GB)

4 Screen-printed fine waffle-textured cotton, 48 inches wide; available in six colourways. Made by David Whitehead Fabrics Ltd (GB)

5 *Tropical Leaves* screen-printed cotton satin, 48 inches wide; available in five colourways. Designed by Helen Dalby. Made by Morton Sundour Fabrics Ltd (GB)

6 *Matador* screen-print on cotton satin, 48 inches wide; pattern repeat 19¼ inches. Designed by Anthony Harrison. Made by Edinburgh Weavers (GB)

7 *Skara Brae* screen-print on heavy cotton-tweed curtain fabric; pattern repeat 21¼ inches. Designed by William Scott. Made by Edinburgh Weavers (GB)

8 Non-shrink, non-stretch glass fibre curtain fabric, 46 inches wide, with a stained-glass effect screen-printed design. Made by Vetrona Fabrics Ltd (GB)

9 *Kensington* screen-printed Everglaze chintz, 50 inches wide; in seven colourways. Made by Donald Brothers Ltd (GB)

10 *Dogstooth* machine-print on textured cotton, 50 inches wide. Designed by Ronnie Thomas. Made by Turnbull & Stockdale Ltd (GB)

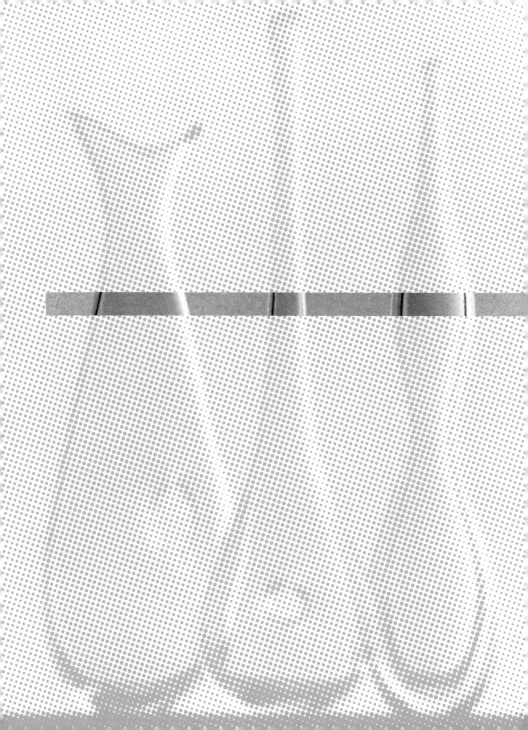

glass | Glas | Verrerie

Ash bowl in amber glass
designed by Lucrecia Moyano
and made by Rigolleau Crystal Works SA

Hand-made oval vase (a unique
piece) of clear lead crystal,
inner wall fused
with crackled metal oxide,
designed by A. D. Copier and
made by N. V. Nederlandsche Glasfabriek Leerdam.

BELOW and OPPOSITE: Glassware designed by Mrs Gunnel Nyman and made by Notsjo Glasbruk A B: clear-glass cream jug and sugar bowl, vase with an outer section of clear glass and an inner section of either clear, yellow or lilac glass. EXTREME RIGHT: Vase of clear glass. All with mouche

Double-walled glass bowls designed by Hugo Gehlin and made by Gullaskrufs Glassworks. (The space between the two thicknesses of glass produces an interesting result.)
LEFT: *Selena* bowl with Moonstone lustre
designed by Sven Palmquist and made by A B Orrefors Glasbruk.

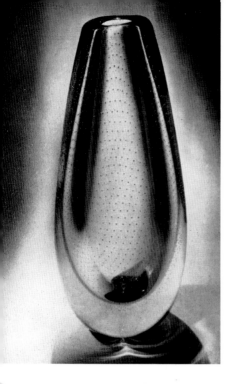

ABOVE: Vase in clear glass with smoke stripes,
designed by Mrs Gunnel Nyman and made by Notsjo Glasbruk AB.
LEFT: Coloured cut glass vase and vase with inlaid thread,
designed by Elis Bergh and made by Kosta Glasbruk.

LEFT: Vases and bowl of thin lead crystal designed by Nils Landberg and made by AB Orrefors Glasbruk.
BELOW: Coloured decorative glassware in Ariel technique designed by Edvin Ohrström and made by AB Orrefors Glasbruk.
The design on the plate is in light blue on a clear crystal ground.

BELOW: Clear lead-crystal goblet
engraved with ibex
designed by A. D. Copier
and made by N. V. Nederlandsche
Glasfabriek Leerdam.

BELOW, CENTRE:
The *Ariel* vase, designed by Don Wier
and made by Steuben Glass Inc.,
in clear hand-fashioned crystal
with laid-on decoration.
The Shakespearean theme
was engraved by copper wheel.

BELOW, RIGHT: Cut crystal oval bowl
and matching candlesticks—
the latter have removable lids
which enable them to be used also
for fruit or flowers—designed by
G. L. de Snellman-Jaderholm
and made by Riihimaki Glassworks.

eft: Crystal bubble-glass bowl. Centre and right: Vase and bowl in soda glass,
ll designed by Per Lütken and made by Holmegaards Glassworks A/S.
oth bowls are of white glass: vase is of coloured glass with clear glass 'knobs'.
IGHT, TOP: Bowl of clear crystal with applied prunt decoration:
iameter 3¾ in. Hand-fashioned by Steuben Glass Inc. and designed in their Design Department.
ENTRE: Centrepiece in bubble glass, designed by Lucrecia Moyano
nd made by Rigolleau Crystal Works SA
OTTOM: Undecorated glassware designed by Simon Gate and Edward Hald
nd made by A B Orrefors Glasbruk.

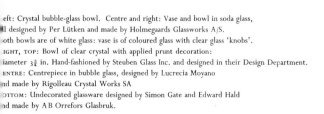

1. Slanting ashtray in heavy crystal, diameter 6½ in., designed and made by Steuben Glass.
2. 10-in. lead crystal fruit dish, decorated with lightly cut lines forming an effective background to the heavily cut star motif, designed by Irene Stevens, ARCA, and made by Thomas Webb & Corbett Ltd.
3. Engraved crystal bowl designed by Åse Voss Schrader and made by Studio Schrader.
4. Heavy crystal engraved vase designed by Herman Bongard and made by Hadelands Glasverk.

5

6

7

5. Heavy crystal vase made by Hadelands Glasverk.

6. Cut glass crystal bowl designed by Arttu Brummer and made by Riihimaki Glassworks.

7. Clear oven-proof glass mixing bowl with ringed fluting which acts both as measuring gradation and decoration, designed and made by The British Heat Resisting Glass Co. Ltd.

8. Engraved crystal vase designed by Åse Voss Schrader and made by Studio Schrader.

9. Vase and bowls in Graal technique, sepia and clear crystal, designed by Edward Hald and made by A B Orrefors Glasbruk.

9

8

1. Cut glass wine glasses and decanter made by
   Hadelands Glasverk.
2. Lead crystal water set with decorative claw
   handle on jug, available in flint, amber, sapphire and sea green. Designed by W. J.
   Wilson, MSIA, and made by James Powell
   & Sons (Whitefriars) Ltd.

3. Emerald green bubble glass water jug and tumbler, sherry decanter and
   glass, designed by G. L. de Snellman-Jaderholm and made by Riihimaki
   Glassworks.
4. Lamp-blown decanter and liqueur glass with opaque white embedded stripes
   designed by Fritz Lampl and made by Orplid Glass Ltd.

5. Lead crystal sherry decanter and glass with deeply cut rings designed by Irene Stevens, A R C A, and made by Thomas Webb & Corbett Ltd.

6. Perfume bottle and two vases designed by Edvin Ohrström and made by Sandviks Glasbruk.

7. Hand-blown whisky and cocktail glasses of clear soda glass with applied spiral decoration designed by Per Lütken and made by Holmegaards Glasværk A/S.

8. Glassware designed by Sven Palmqvist and made by A B Orrefors Glasbruk.
   LEFT: Ravenna bowl, dark blue with brown and red decoration. RIGHT: Small Kraka bowl in light opal blue with 'net' design. BACKGROUND: Moonstone-coloured Selena vase.

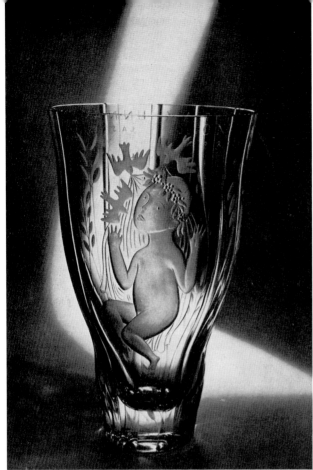

1

1. Clear oven-proof glass gravy boat and platte traditional early Georgian design interprete a modern material, designed and made by British Heat Resisting Glass Co. Ltd.

2. Engraved white crystal vase designed by Helena Tynell and made by Riihimaki Glassworks.
3. Hand-fashioned flat-sided clear crystal fish, height 3 in., designed and made by Steuben Glass.

3

Engraved English flint crystal tankard,
designed by J. Granville Barker, A R C A,
and made especially for Liberty & Co. Ltd.

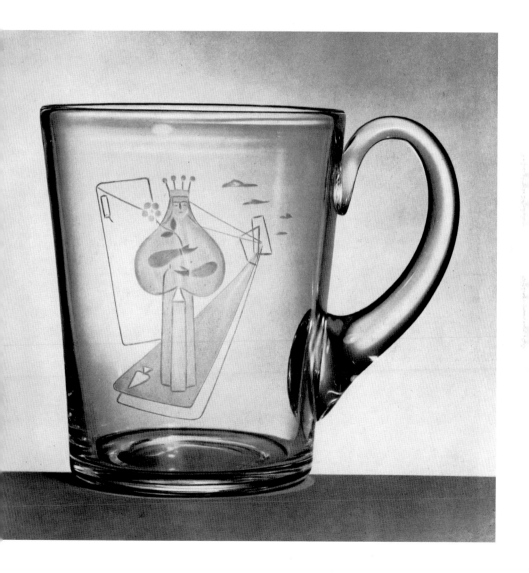

Lead crystal glass water set available in flint and amber, or flint with a ruby foot. Designer: W. J. Wilson, MSIA. Makers: James Powell & Sons (Whitefriars) Ltd (GB).

ABOVE: *Northern Lights*. *Ariel* vase in sombre purple, the design formed by the introduction of air into the wall of the glass. Designer: Edvin Öhrström. Makers: AB Orrefors Glasbruk (SWEDEN).

Glass fountain with symbolic figures, part seal, part bird, rising above the bowl on a wave-decorated pedestal. Designers and makers: Steuben Glass (USA).

Neckan's Dance. *Ariel* vase in clear crystal, the design formed by the introduction of air into the wall of the glass. Designer: Edvin Öhrström. Makers: AB Orrefors Glasbruk (SWEDEN).

RIGHT: Ruby red crystal vase and turquoise blue plate. Designer: Vicke Lindstrand. Makers: AB Kosta Glasbruk (SWEDEN).

ABOVE: *The Princess on the Pea* (motif based on Hans Christian Andersen's fairy tale). Copper wheel engraving. Designer: Ingeborg Lundin. Makers: AB Orrefors Glasbruk (SWEDEN).

LEFT: *White threads.* Crystal bowl and vase with white glass threads. Designer: Vicke Lindstrand. Makers: AB Kosta Glasbruk (SWEDEN).

BELOW: *Boot* design tumblers with silk-screened decoration based on raffia or fibre boots. Designers and makers: Corning Glass Works (USA).

ear crystal punch, flower or
uit bowl with glasses to match.
esigners and makers: Tiffin
assmasters (U.S. Glass Co)
SA).

OPPOSITE: *Ravenna* bowls. Designer: Sven Palmqvist. Makers: AB Orrefors Glasbruk (SWEDEN).

ABOVE: *Autumn*. Crystal vase with multi-coloured decoration. ABOVE RIGHT: *Abstracts*. Clear crystal with black, blue and green inner decoration. RIGHT: *Coral*. Crystal with white inner decoration. All designed by Vicke Lindstrand. Makers: AB Kosta Glasbruk (SWEDEN).

Crystal bowl with polychrome decoration on the inside. Designer: Vicke Lindstrand. Makers: AB Kosta Glasbruk (SWEDEN)

Cased crystal bowl with moon-coloured decoration, and bottle-shaped vase with dark blue inner decoration. Designer: Vicke Lindstrand. Makers: AB Kosta Glasbruk (SWEDEN)

LEFT: Glass decorated in intaglio technique. Designer: Monica Bratt. Makers: Reijmyre Glasbruk for AB Nordiska Kompaniet (SWEDEN)

BELOW: Engraved crystal vase. Designer: Ingeborg Lundin. Makers: AB Orrefors Glasbruk (SWEDEN)

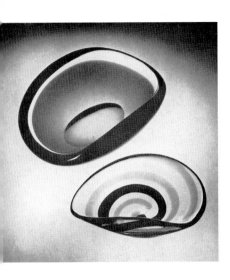

Crystal bowls with coloured decoration, one with ruby lining, the other with bands of blue, green and black. Designer: Vicke Lindstrand. Makers: AB Kosta Glasbruk (SWEDEN)

ABOVE: Clear crystal fruit bowl. Designer: Per Lütken. Makers: Holmegaards Glasværk A/S (DENMARK)

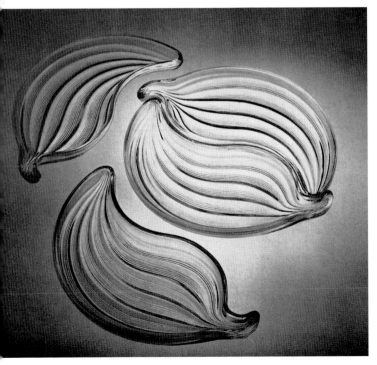

Hors d'oeuvres dishes, usable singly or interlocked. Designer: Nils Landberg. Makers: AB Orrefors Glasbruk (SWEDEN)

Unica pieces, clear crystal with opalescent treatment in blue and white. Designer: F. Meydam. Makers: NV Nederlandsche Glasfabriek 'Leerdam' (HOLLAND)

ABOVE: Crystal bowl in the *Graal* technique. Designer: Edward Hald. Makers: AB Orrefors Glasbruk
(SWEDEN)

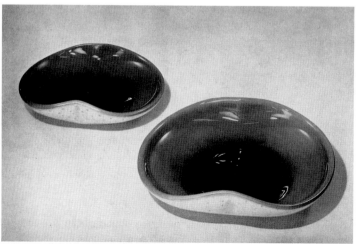

Glass bowls lined with jade, orchid or grey with bubbles in the white crystal underside. Makers: Erickson Glass Works (USA)

Clear crystal vase, cut and polished. Designer: F. Meydam. Makers: NV Nederlandsche Glasfabriek 'Leerdam' (HOLLAND)

ABOVE: Bowls of white crystal. Designer: Tapio Wirkkala. Makers: Karhula-Iittala Glassworks (FINLAND)

Bowl of clear red crystal with bubble decoration. Designer: Lucrecia Moyano. Makers: Cristalerias Rigolleau SA
(ARGENTINA)

RIGHT: Vase and ashtrays in clear crystal. Designer: Per Lütken. Makers: Holmegaards Glasværk A/S (DENMARK)

ABOVE: Thick crystal vase with opal-coloured decoration applied on the inside. Designer: Vicke Lindstrand. Makers: AB Kosta Glasbruk (SWEDEN)

Unica bowl, clear crystal with white opal and light blue decoration, mounted on a wooden base. Designer: A. D. Copier. Makers: NV Nederlandsche Glasfabriek 'Leerdam' (HOLLAND)

BELOW: Crystal bowl with opal-coloured coil motif. Designer: Lucrecia Moyano. Makers: Cristalerias Rigolleau SA (ARGENTINA)

ABOVE: Clear crystal bowl decorated with free-drawn black lines and bubbles. Designer: Lucrecia Moyano. Makers: Cristalerias Rigolleau SA (ARGENTINA)

ABOVE: *Unica* bowl of clear crystal with opalescent treatment in blue. Designer: A. D. Copier. Makers: NV Nederlandsche Glasfabriek 'Leerdam' (HOLLAND)

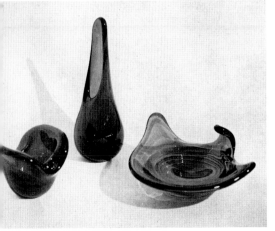

Blue soda-glass vases and bowl. Designer: Per Lütken. Makers: Holmegaards Glasværk A/S (DENMARK)

Engraved clear crystal vase. Designer: John Selbing.
Makers: AB Orrefors Glasbruk (SWEDEN)

Blown crystal vases and scent bottles. Designer: Fritz
Lampl. Makers: Orplid Glass Ltd (GB)

RIGHT: Clear crystal trinket jar. Designed and made by
Tiffin Glassmasters (USA)

Hand-made crystal vase with colour incorporated in the body of the glass. Designer: Vicke Lindstrand. Makers: Kosta Glasbruk AB (SWEDEN)

LEFT: Cut-glass crystal flower vase. Designer: Jyunshiro Satoh. Makers: Kagami Crystal Glassworks (JAPAN)

The shape of glass is revealed in its high-lights as much as by its contours. Piercing the mass of the lower body creates new highlights which add interest to the shape and further emphasize its intrinsically liquid quality

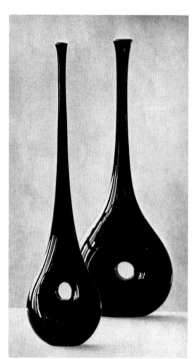

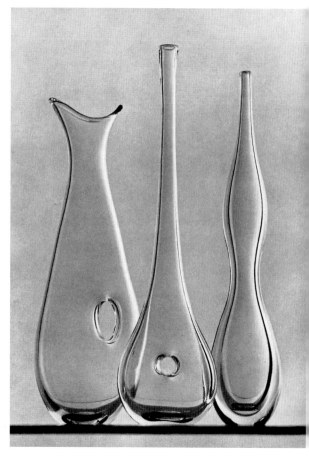

Vase Forms in black and clear glass. Designer: Vicke Lindstrand. Makers: AB Kosta Glasbruk (SWEDEN)

ABOVE: Engraved vase in clear crystal. Designer: Nils Landberg. Makers: AB Orrefors Glasbruk (SWEDEN). RIGHT: Crystal engraved liqueur bottle. Designer: Edward Hald. Makers: AB Orrefors Glasbruk (SWEDEN)

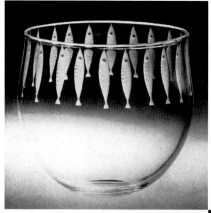

Engraved clear crystal bowl. Designer: Ingeborg Lundin. Makers: AB Orrefors Glasbruk (SWEDEN)

BELOW: Crystal flower vase engraved with figures of saints. Designer: Vicke Lindstrand. Makers: AB Kosta Glasbruk (SWEDEN)

Engraved clear crystal vase. Designer: Sven Palmqvist. Makers: AB Orrefors Glasbruk (SWEDEN)

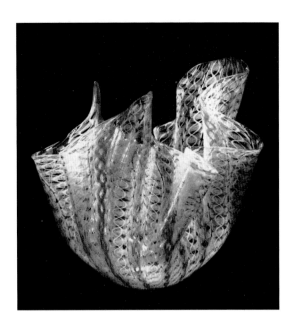

ABOVE: Cut crystal bowl. Designer: Tapio Wirkkala. Makers: Iittala Glassworks (FIN-LAND). RIGHT: Glass bowl in pastel colours, the shape derived from a floating lace handkerchief. From Liberty & Co. Ltd. Designer and maker: Paolo Venini of Murano (ITALY)

Clear crystal bowl engraved with a 'splash' motif ascending from the base. Designer: Edvin Öhrström. Makers: AB Orrefors Glasbruk (SWEDEN)

Ariel blown glass vases, two with exterior decoration of air-filled clear crystal streaks. The tallest is 13 inches high. Designer: Edvin Öhrström. Makers: AB Orrefors Glasbruk (SWEDEN)

Engraved crystal vase, 12 inches high, and sherry and hock glasses with air-filled twisted stems. Designers and makers Stuart & Sons Ltd (GB)

Wood Anemone. Blown clear crystal shallow plate, 13½ inches diameter, engraved by copper wheel with a design specially created by wood engraver Reynolds Stone for Steuben Glass (USA)

Tulip Bowl. Shallow, three-sided bowl of clear crystal sheared to a curving line around the rim and engraved with a tulip. Width 11½ inches. Designer: Don Wier. Makers: Steuben Glass (USA)

Clear crystal vase, 12 inches high, with *Snake and Frogs* engraving designed by John Nash, RA, for Steuben Glass (USA)

Clear crystal carafe and drinking glasses with engraved linear design. The carafe measures 4 inches at the base and, with a glass on top, is 12 inches high. Designer: Edvin Öhrström. Makers: AB Orrefors Glasbruk (SWEDEN)

Engraved vase of clear crystal, 11¾ inches high. Designer: Nils Landberg. Makers: AB Orrefors Glasbruk (SWEDEN)

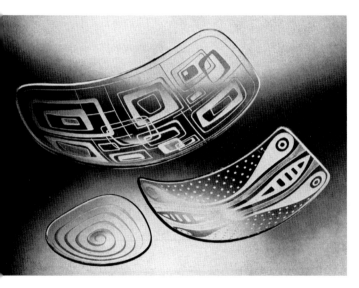

Clear crystal blown glass vase, 8¼ inches high, with engraved decoration. Designer: Bengt Orup. Makers: AB Johansfors Glasbruk (SWEDEN)

Clear crystal blown glass dishes with engraved decoration. The largest is 11 inches by 4 inches, the smallest 2½ inches in diameter. Designer: Nils Landberg. Makers: AB Orrefors Glasbruk (SWEDEN)

Clear crystal blown glass vase 10¾ inches high, and dish with engraved linear design. Designer: Nils Landberg. Makers: AB Orrefors Glasbruk (SWEDEN)

Crystal vase, about 12 inches high, and bowls in the *Graal* technique. Designer: Edward Hald. Makers: AB Orrefors Glasbruk (SWEDEN)

LEFT: Steel-grey crystal vase, 6 inches high, on clear crystal base. Designer: Edvin Öhrström. RIGHT: Clear crystal bowl, engraved decoration giving an under-water effect of floating shapes; diameter 7 inches. Designer: Ingeborg Lundin. Makers: AB Orrefors Glasbruk (SWEDEN)

iligran glass. Vase, 6 inches high; bowls 4¾ and 3¼ inches high; and ornamental dish. Designer: Nanny Still. Makers: Riihimaki Glassworks (FINLAND). BELOW: Hand blown clear crystal vases and bowl. The taller vase is 12½ inches high, the bowl 8¼ inches wide on a 3-inch base. Designer Nils Landberg. Makers: A B Orrefors Glasbruk (SWEDEN)

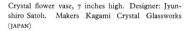

Clear crystal vase and bowl with spun thread decoration in black, white and red. Height of vase 10¾ inches, diameter of bowl 6 inches. Designer: Vicke Lindstrand. Makers: A B Kosta Glasbruk (SWEDEN)

Crystal flower vase, 7 inches high. Designer: Jyunshiro Satoh. Makers Kagami Crystal Glassworks (JAPAN)

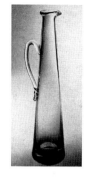

Oil, vinegar and mustard bottles in coloured or clear crystal glass. Designer: R. Stennett-Willson, MSIA. Made for J. Wuidart & Co. Ltd (GB). RIGHT: Blown glass flower jug, 9¾ inches high. Designer: Arthur Percy. Makers: Gullaskrufs Glasbruks AB (SWEDEN)

Cut crystal decanter and wine glasses. Designer: Jyunshiro Satoh. Makers: Kagami Crystal Glassworks (JAPAN). RIGHT: Blown glass vase, 14½ inches high, with applied swirl decoration. Designer: Hugo Gehlin. Makers: Gullaskrufs Glasbruks AB (SWEDEN)

Cut crystal bottle and tumbler. Height of bottle (without stopper) 10½ inches. Designer: Bengt Orup. Makers: AB Johansfors Glasbruk (SWEDEN). FAR RIGHT: Clear crystal jugs and bowls. The jugs range from 3-pint to ½-pint capacity; the larger bowl is 5¾ inches in diameter. Designer: Ingeborg Lundin. Makers: AB Orrefors Glasbruk (SWEDEN)

Cone-shaped decanter with a wide, steady base and diagonally cut teardrop stopper. Capacity 36 fluid ounces. Designers and makers: Steuben Glass (USA). FAR RIGHT: Heavy crystal jug and vase. Designer: Timo Sarpaneva. Makers: Karhula-Iittala Glassworks (FINLAND)

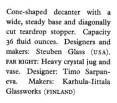

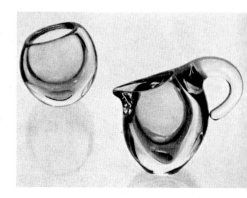

Glasses from the *Frances* wine service made in clear crystal and in two colours. Designer: R. Stennett-Willson, MSIA. Made for J. Wuidart & Co. Ltd (GB)

ABOVE: Engraved clear crystal wine glasses from the *Chevalier* service. Designer: Bengt Orup. Makers AB Johansfors Glasbruk (SWEDEN). BELOW: Crystal champagne glass with engraved bamboo design. Designer: Jyunshiro Satoh. Makers: Kagami Crystal Glassworks (JAPAN)

Crystal wine glasses decorated gold or palladium. Designers and makers: Imperial Glass Corporation (USA)

Wicker-covered wine pitcher, and crystal glasses with ball and cone air cavity in base. Designer: Tapio Wirkkala. Makers: Karhula-Iittala Glassworks (FINLAND)

Blown crystal compote in cased charcoal glass. Base 8 inches high, bowl 8½ inches wide. Designer: Carl E. Erickson. Makers: Erickson Glassworks (USA)

White opaque crystal vases and bowl, black decoration. Designer: Paul Kedelv. Makers: AB Flygsfors Glasbruk (SWEDEN)

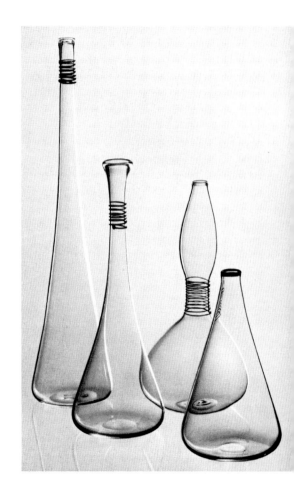

White crystal vase, 9 inches high, and etched bowl. Designer: Sven Palmqvist. Makers: AB Orrefors Glasbruk (SWEDEN)

Clear crystal vases decorated with spirals of black glass. Heights range from 8¼ inches to 18¼ inches. Designer: Nils Landberg. Makers: AB Orrefors Glasbruk (SWEDEN)

Vases in coloured crystal in sizes ranging from about 12 inches tall. Designer: Nils Landberg. Makers: A B Orrefors Glasbruk (SWEDEN)

Clear crystal vase, 11 inches high, with white thread decoration; it is also made with the thread design in black. Designer: Vicke Lindstrand. Makers: A B Kosta Glasbruk (SWEDEN)

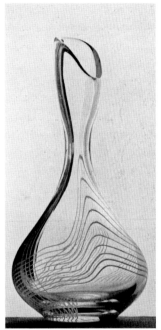

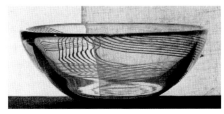

Clear crystal bowl, diameter 7¼ inches, also with black or white thread decoration. Designer: Vicke Lindstrand. Makers: A B Kosta Glasbruk (SWEDEN)

The treatment of glass assumes decorative qualities on account of shape, colour, opacity, texture, dimpling and bubbling, apart from whether or not it carries any applied surface cutting or etching. The growing tendency to appreciate glass as a fluid form, rather than as a mere vehicle for applied decoration, has resulted in many interesting technical developments which have sought to embody expressive design forms within the glass itself and to exploit the effects of internal refraction and surface reflection with great effect. The net result, as is well exemplified, has been to emphasise the natural beauty of the material, regardless of whether its raison d'être leans toward the purely decorative or the strictly functional.

When surface decoration is applied, as in the examples shown on these first pages, it has often been done in a manner which either brings life, and sometimes comedy, to a rather ordinary shape, or which lends emphasis and 'body' to a shape which stands to gain in quality from such treatment.

ABOVE: *Vegetal form* crystal sculpture about 7 inches high. Designer Bengt Orup. Makers: AB Johansfor Glasbruk (SWEDEN). LEFT: *Hello Cat* Engraved crystal plate, 11½ inches diameter. Shape designed by Helena Tynell; engraving by Th. Kappi Makers: Riihimaki Glassworks (FINLAND)

ABOVE: *Atlantis* Clear crystal vase, cut decoration fish on a background of black nets embodied in the glass. Designer: Vicke Lindstrand. Makers: AB Kosta Glasbruk (SWEDEN). RIGHT: Crystal flower bowl with a graduated bubble pattern, and ashtray with painted design in red and black. Designer: Lucrecia Moyano. Makers: Cristalerias Rigolleau (ARGENTINA). BELOW: Clear crystal bowls with engraved exterior decoration; 10½, 6½ and 4¼ inches in diameter. Designer: John-Orwar Lake. Makers: Ekenäs Glasbruk AB (SWEDEN)

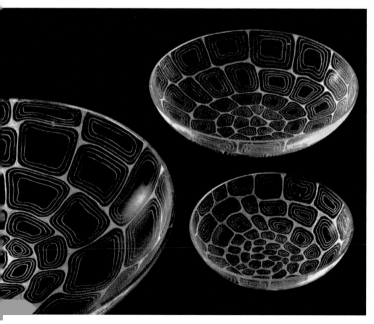

ABOVE: Crystal vase decorated in the *Ariel* technique. Designer: Edvin Öhström. Makers: AB Orrefors Glasbruk (SWEDEN)

Crystal vases in clear green, bluish and deep violet colourings. Designer: Kaj Franck. Makers: o/y Wärtsilä-concern AB Notsjö Glassworks (FINLAND)

ABOVE: White crystal vases, 7½ and 5¼ inches high. Designer: Sven Palmquist. Makers: AB Orrefors Glasbruk (SWEDEN)

BELOW: Light green glass flower vase. Designer: Jacob E. Bang. Makers: A/S Kastrup Glasværk (DENMARK)

ABOVE: Thin-walled 'muslin' glass vase and compote. Colours: champagne, lustre, or clear crystal. Designer: Liskova. Makers: Moser Glassworks (CZECHOSLOVAKIA)

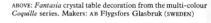

ABOVE: *Fantasia* crystal table decoration from the multi-colour *Coquille* series. Makers: AB Flygsfors Glasbruk (SWEDEN)

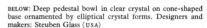

BELOW: Deep pedestal bowl in clear crystal on cone-shaped base ornamented by elliptical crystal forms. Designers and makers: Steuben Glass (USA)

ABOVE: Two-colour vases: blue/crystal, amethyst/crystal; yellow/white opalescent crystal. 6, 7, and 9 inches high, Designer: Arthur Percy. Makers: Gullaskrufs Glasbruks AB (SWEDEN)

BELOW: Matching vase and bowl of Venetian glass, in tones of lilac and green with concentric pattern in yellow. Designer: Flavio Poli. Makers: Seguso, s.r.l. (ITALY)

ABOVE: *Unica* crystal vases; orange, blue and yellow colourings. 10, 9½ and 14 inches high. Designer: F. Meydam. Makers: NV Koninklijke Nederlandsche Glasfabriek Leerdam (HOLLAND)

BELOW: Abstract form in high-polished crystal, Designer: Michel Daum. Makers: Daum Cristallerie de Nancy (FRANCE)

ABOVE: *Serica* vases, 5, 3 and 4½ inches high. Lined vase at left is in blue crystal; centre, clear with coloured opal; right, white opal with three coloured eyes. Designer: Iep Valkema. Makers: NV Koninklijke Nederlandsche Glasfabriek Leerdam (HOLLAND)

ABOVE: Vases and jug in ruby and clear crystal glass. Designed by R. Stennett-Willson, MSIA. For J. Wuidart & Co. Ltd (GB). RIGHT: Venetian blown glass pitcher; applied frontal decoration in bright colours. Height 17½ inches. Designer: Dino Martens. Makers: Vetreria Aureliano Toso (ITALY)

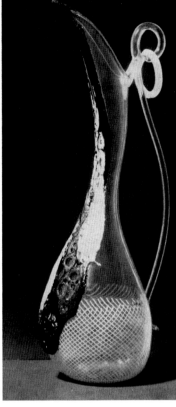

ABOVE: Clear crystal water set and bowl. Designer: Ingeborg Lundin. Makers: AB Orrefors Glasbruk (SWEDEN). BELOW RIGHT: Wheat-ear wine service and decanter in clear cut crystal. Designer: Irene Stevens, ARCA. Makers: Webb Corbett Ltd (GB). BELOW: Coloured glass tumblers, and decanters with applied decoration. Designer: Kjell Blomberg. Makers: Gullaskrufs Glasbruks AB (SWEDEN)

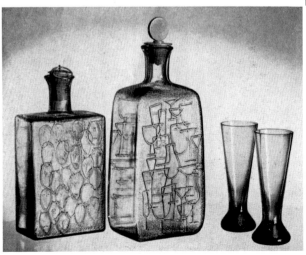

ABOVE: Blown glass tumblers and black and white opaque glass jugs. Designer: Nanny Still. Makers: Riihimaki Glassworks (FINLAND)

RIGHT: Water jug and stackable tumblers in clear and coloured glass. Designer: Saara Hopea. Makers: O/Y Wärtsilä-concern A B Notsjö Glassworks (FINLAND)

BELOW: Crystal bowl decorated in the *Graal* technique; clear crystal wine service. Designer: Edward Hald. Makers: A B Orrefors Glasbruk (SWEDEN)

ABOVE: *Vendôme* wine service in cut crystal. Designer: Georges Chevalier. Makers: Cie. des Cristalleries de Baccarat (FRANCE)

ABOVE: Venetian glass pitcher with black and white *Zanfirico* decoration. Height 19½ inches. Designer: Dino Martens. Makers: Vetreria Aureliano Toso (ITALY)

Crystal vase and bowls; colour decoration embodied in the glass by the *Kraka* and *Ravenna* techniques. Designer: Sven Palmquist. Makers: AB Orrefors Glasbruk (SWEDEN)

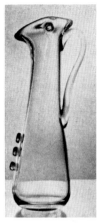

ABOVE: Clear crystal jug, one of a series representing bird shapes; colour accents on details. Designer: Lucrecia Moyano. Makers: Cristalerías Rigolleau (ARGENTINA)

FAR LEFT: *Palma* clear crystal wine service. Designer: Ie Valkema. Makers: NV Koninklijke Nederlandsche Glasfabriek Leerdam (HOLLAND) LEFT: Fruit dish and bowl smoked crystal glass. Designer Monica Bratt. Makers: Reijmyre Glasbruk AB (SWEDEN)

BELOW: Clear crystal *Kardinal* wine service. Designer:
Bengt Orup. Makers: AB Johansfors Glasbruk (SWEDEN)

ABOVE: Clear crystal wine service on heavy crystal
base. Designer: Tapio Wirkkala. Makers: Karhula-
Iittala Glassworks (FINLAND)

ABOVE: *Unica* bowl in light violet crystal with opal centre.
Designer: A. D. Copier. Makers: NV Koninklijke Neder-
landsche Glasfabriek Leerdam (HOLLAND). LEFT: Clear
crystal engraved glasses. Designer: Hilkka Liisa Ahola.
Makers: O/Y Wärtsilä-concern AB Notsjö Glassworks
(FINLAND)

The creation of decorative new designs in glass continues to challenge, as it always has, the imagination and skill of designers, chemists, glass-blowers and moulders. With virtually no change in the equipment used, variations on established techniques are under constant development and each year new forms emerge to make a contribution to the collective history of the art, perhaps after prolonged experiment and many disappointments.

There appears to be a growing interest in the possibilities of pattern, texture and colour fused into the body of the glass itself in many of the decorative pieces produced, particularly in Italy. Sometimes this achieves an opacity akin to that of ceramic ware; other times ribbons of opaque or translucent colour trace patterns on or under the surface of clear or tinted glass, attaining decorative effects which harmonise with the forms to which they are applied.

The cost of the raw material being relatively insignificant, freedom can be exercised in the amount of glass used and the pieces illustrated vary from delicate thin-walled vessels to heavy, massive forms with lenticular properties which supplement the reflections of their polished surfaces.

Whatever the form of decoration applied, glass remains a fusible material and most of the outstanding designers and craftsmen working in this medium preserve its basic characteristics in the pieces they produce. The hard, incised decoration which did much to destroy the intrinsic beauty of glass, although still practised by some of the traditional factories, has largely given way to much freer and more appropriate decorative treatments.

Sculpture in crystal in *Ariel*, *Graal*, and other techniques. Designer: Edvin Öhrström. Makers: AB Orrefors Glasbruk (SWEDEN)

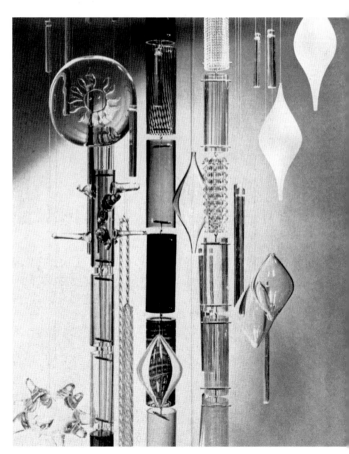

LEFT: Glassware by student designers. Clear crystal bowl by Ian Gordon, Edinburgh College of Art; red-flashed bowl with cut and engraved decoration by Charles Richards, Royal College of Art; vase with festooned thread decoration by M. Harris, Stourbridge College for Further Education (GB) (*Courtesy: Glass Manufacturers' Federation*)

BELOW: Free form, 24 inches high, in clear, high-polished crystal. Designer: Michel Daum. Makers: Daum Cristallerie de Nancy (FRANCE)

ABOVE: Bent red-flashed glass bowl with engraved decoration. Designer and maker: Geoffrey Baxter, Des.RCA, Royal College of Art (GB)

RIGHT: Heavy crystal bowl, 8 inches diameter, decorated yellow lustre. Designer: Stanislav Libensky. Makers: Zelezny Brod Glassworks (CZECHOSLOVAKIA)

BELOW: Thick crystal vase with sand-blasted decoration. Designer: Victor Berndt. Makers: AB Flygsfors Glasbruk (SWEDEN)

ABOVE AND LEFT: Hand-made *Pezza* vases, between 10 and 15 inches hig made up of small pieces of coloure Venetian spun glass blown together; bo opaque and transparent effects are obtain able in this technique. Designer: Erc Barovier. Makers: Barovier & To (ITALY)

ABOVE: *Shizuku* ('dripping') glass bowl crystal infused in a hand-made clay stone cast, producing a raindrop-lil surface pattern and diffused reflectio 8 × 5½ inches. Designer: Masakic Awashima. Makers: Awashima Glass C Ltd (JAPAN)

BELOW: *Shizuku* ('dripping') glass goblet of clay-infused crystal on clear crystal base. 6½ inches. Designer: Masakichi Awashima. Makers: Awashima Glass Co. Ltd (JAPAN)

ABOVE: Cobalt blue bubble-glass bowl and vases; 10 and 12 inches. Designer: Ercole Barovier. Makers: Barovier & Toso (ITALY). BELOW: Crystal bowls (largest 19½ inches) decorated by the artist Dubé; black aluminium base. Makers: Fontana Arte (ITALY)

ABOVE: Spun Venetian glass hand-made *Pezzati* vases in various colourings; 8 and 11 inches. Designer: Ercole Barovier. Makers: Barovier & Toso (ITALY)

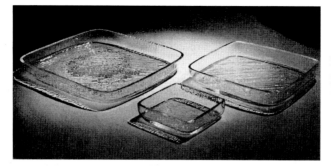

LEFT: *Shizuku* ('dripping') glass trays of crystal. The 'raindrop' surface pattern is produced by first infusing the crystal in a hand-made clay or stone cast. Designer: Masakichi Awashima. Makers: Awashima Glass Co. Ltd (JAPAN)

BELOW: Clear crystal jug and vases. 10, 8 and 9¼ inches high. Designer: Masakichi Awashima. Makers: Awashima Glass Co. Ltd (JAPAN)

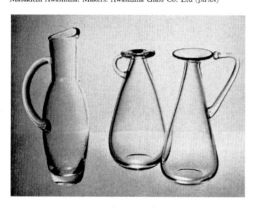

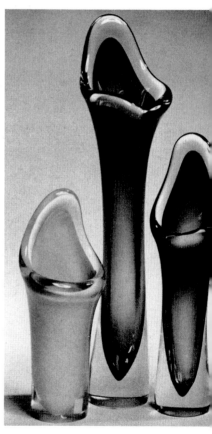

ABOVE: *Harlequin* heavy crystal vases cased in blue, green, lilac and other colours. 5¾, 11¾ and 7¾ inches high. Designer: Paul Kedelv. Makers: Reijmyre Glasbruk AB (SWEDEN). LEFT: Free form bowls in transparent coloured crystal, applied base. Lengths, 11 and 10 inches. Designers and makers: Fontana Arte (ITALY)

ABOVE: Emerald green bowl (7 inches diameter) and vase (9¾ inches high) designed by Jacob E. Bang. Makers: A/S Kastrup Glasværk (DENMARK)

RIGHT: Crystal vases with (left) sand-blasted decoration; (centre) purple base, amethyst neck; (right) vertical green threads, black base. Designed and made respectively by students Charles Richards, Robert Welch, and Jane Webster at the Royal College of Art (GB)

BELOW: Two-colour crystal plates in blue/grey, violet/grey, green/grey or greenish tones. Designer: Timo Sarpaneva. Makers: Karhula-Iittala Glassworks (FINLAND)

RIGHT: Coloured crystal vases in the cased technique in green and (right) in amethyst. Designer: Gunnar Ander. Makers: AB Lindshammars Glasbruk (SWEDEN)

ABOVE: Cut crystal ashtrays, with centres in deep violet and in dark green glass. 4¾ and 5¾ inches diameter. Designer: Saara Hopea. Makers: O/Y Wärtsila-concern AB Notsjö Glassworks (FINLAND)

LEFT: Vase and bowl in opaque grey crystal. Designer: Bengt Orup. Makers: AB Johansfors Glasbruk (SWEDEN)

ABOVE: *Aborigeni* free form hand-made vases in amber Venetian glass. Designer: Ercole Barovier. Makers: Barovier & Toso (ITALY)

RIGHT: Spun coloured glass vases, resembling ceramic ware, with applied decoration. 11 and 19 inches high. Designer: Angelo Barovier. Makers: Barovier & Toso (ITALY)

ABOVE: Coloured crystal vase with etched graduated bands.
Designer: Oysten Sandnes. Makers: Norsk Glassverk A/S
(NORWAY)

RIGHT: Venetian milk-white spun glass bottle. Height 14 inches.
Designers and makers: Venini Glassworks (ITALY)

ABOVE: Coloured unique pieces encased in clear crystal. Vase yellow, bowl in red and green; 10 and 9 inches. Designer: F. Meydam. Makers: NV Koninklijke Nederlandsche Glasfabriek 'Leerdam' (HOLLAND)

BELOW: Pale blue vases encased in heavy crystal; 7½, 5 and 11 inches high. Designer: Vicke Lindstrand. Makers: AB Kosta Glasbruk (SWEDEN)

ABOVE: Clear crystal vases, 7 inches high; etched decoration. Designer: W. Heesen. Makers: NV Koninklijke Nederlandsche Glasfabriek 'Leerdam' (HOLLAND)

BELOW: Bowl (19½ inches diameter) and vase (18 inches high) in sapphire blue glass. Designer: Flavio Poli. Makers: Seguso, s.r.l. (ITALY)

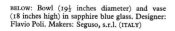

LEFT: Flower vases in clear crystal with inner holder suspended in the body of the glass. 4¾, 2 and 3¾ inches high. Designer: F. Meydam. Makers: N V Koninklijke Nederlandsche Glasfabriek 'Leerdam' (HOLLAND)

ABOVE: Classic urn with solid crystal base and teardrop finial. Height 12 inches. Designers and makers: Steuben Glass (USA). LEFT: Vase (6½ inches high) and bowl (8¾ inches diameter) in emerald-green glass. Designer: Jacob E. Bang. Makers: A/S Kastrup Glasværk (DENMARK)

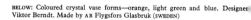

ABOVE: Coloured and clear crystal vase shapes. Designer: John Selbing. Made by A B Orrefors Glasbruk (SWEDEN)

LEFT: Carafe and bowl in green soda glass. Designer: Erik Höglund. Made by Boda Bruks A B (SWEDEN)

BELOW: Coloured crystal vase forms—orange, light green and blue. Designer Viktor Berndt. Made by A B Flygsfors Glasbruk (SWEDEN)

Tourterelles in solid crystal on clear crystal base with coloured spiral. 8 inches high. Designer: Marc Lalique. Made by Verreries de R. Lalique (FRANCE)

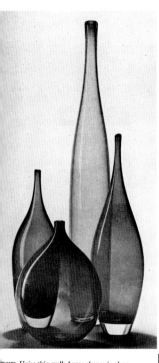

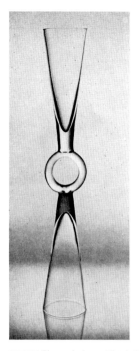

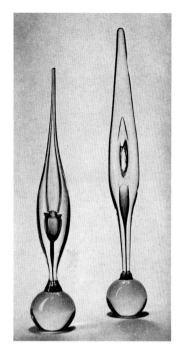

ABOVE LEFT: Ring vase in clear crystal. 24 inches high. Designer: Bengt Orup. Made by AB Johansfors Glasbruk (SWEDEN). ABOVE RIGHT: Abstract forms in clear crystal or with colour suspended in the body; about 14 inches high. Designer: A. D. Copier. Made by NV Koninklijke Nederlandsche Glasfabriek 'Leerdam' (HOLLAND). BELOW: Vase shapes in crystal. Designer: Edvin Øhrström. Made by AB Orrefors Glasbruk (SWEDEN)

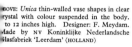

ABOVE: *Unica* thin-walled vase shapes in clear crystal with colour suspended in the body. to 12 inches high. Designer: F. Meydam. Made by NV Koninklijke Nederlandsche Glasfabriek 'Leerdam' (HOLLAND)

BELOW: *Hirondelles* in clear crystal on heavy crystal base. 8 inches high. Designer: Michel Daum. Made by Daum Cristallerie de Nancy (FRANCE)

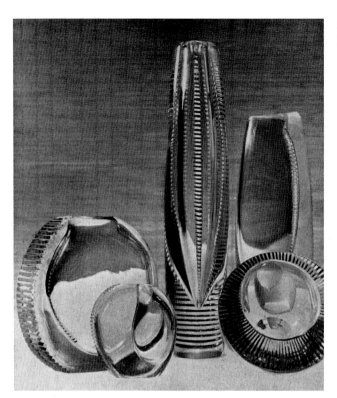

LEFT: Vases from the series *Contrast by Asymmetry* in transparent crystal with cutting on one side reflected in the whole piece. Designer: Vicke Lindstrand. Made by AB Kosta Glasbruk (SWEDEN)

ABOVE: Heavy crystal vase with cut flutes and copper wheel engraved decoration. 10 inches high. Designer David Hammond, Des.RCA. Made by Thos. Webb & Sons (GB)
BELOW: Oval bowl in crystal, 11¼ inches at widest point; applied base ornaments in a foliated pattern. Designed and made by Steuben Glass (USA)

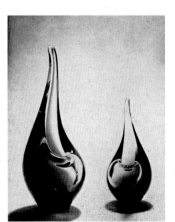

ABOVE: 'Flame' vases in pine-green encased in clear crystal, 6 and 9 inches high. Designer: Per Lütken. Made by Holmegaards Glasværk A/S (DENMARK)

ABOVE LEFT: *Unica* vases in clear crystal with colour suspended in the body of the glass. 5, 5½, and 11 inches high. Designer: F. Meydam. Made by N V Koninklijke Nederlandsche Glasfabriek 'Leerdam' (HOLLAND). ABOVE RIGHT: Vase in clear crystal with engraved decoration. Designer: Jindřich Tockstein. Made by Žel. Brod Glassworks (CZECHOSLOVAKIA)

LEFT: Engraved clear crystal vase, with inner holder suspended in the body of the glass; about 12 inches high. Designer: W. Heesen. Made by N V Koninklijke Nederlandsche Glasfabriek 'Leerdam' (HOLLAND).
BELOW: Heavy crystal vase and bowl with deeply engraved decoration. Designer: Erik Höglund. Made by Boda Bruks A B (SWEDEN)

ABOVE: *Connoisseur* wine service in clear crystal. The straw-like stem is drawn from the finely blown bowl leaving a tapered depression in the bottom of the bowl. Designer: Sven Fogelberg. Made by Thos. Webb & Sons (GB)

RIGHT: *Narcisso* wine service in clear crystal. Designer: Isabel A. M. Giampietro. Made by NV Koninklijke Nederlandsche Glasfabriek 'Leerdam' (HOLLAND)

BELOW: Ravenhead *Waterloo* suite in flint glass. Designer: A. H. Williamson, ARCA. Made by automatic process by The United Glass Bottle Manufacturers Ltd. For Johnsen & Jorgensen Flint Glass Ltd (GB)

ABOVE: Cocktail mixer and glasses in clear crystal. Designer: Monica Bratt. Made by Reijmyre Glasbruk AB (SWEDEN)

BELOW: *Sherdley* flint glass beer mugs. Designer: A. H. Williamson, ARCA. Made by automatic process by The United Glass Bottle Manufacturers Ltd. For Johnsen & Jorgensen Flint Glass Ltd (GB)

BELOW: Blown crystal vase and tumblers. Designer: Ingeborg Lundin. Made by AB Orrefors Glasbruk (SWEDEN)

ABOVE: Clear crystal decanter and goblet with flute decoration. Designed and made by David Hammond, Des.RCA, at the Royal College of Art (GB)

ABOVE: Decanter and long-stemmed wine glasses in clear crystal. Designer: Nils Landberg. Made by AB Orrefors Glasbruk (SWEDEN)

BELOW: Clear crystal cocktail set; stopper and glass base coloured green. Designers: Monica Bratt and Paul Kedelv. Made by Reijmyre Glasbruk AB (SWEDEN)

BELOW: Blown crystal Martini mixer and glasses, etched line decoration. Made in Sweden for Raymor (USA)

ABOVE: Liqueur set in clear crystal with cut decoration. Designer: Bengt Orup. Made by AB Johansfors Glasbruk (SWEDEN)

ABOVE: Blown crystal decanter and glasses. Designer: Ingeborg Lundin. Made by AB Orrefors Glasbruk (SWEDEN). BELOW: Blown crystal small decanters with moulded stoppers and decoration. Designer: Erik Höglund. Made by Boda Bruk AB (SWEDEN)

ABOVE: *Aristocrat* clear crystal decanter with sculptured stopper, and long-stemmed beer and schnaps glass. Designer: Per Lütken. Made by Holmegaards Glasværk A/S (DENMARK)

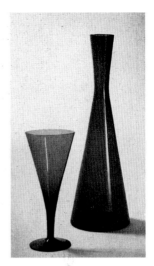

ABOVE LEFT: Bottles for water or fruit juice in white and in green glass with red and white moulded stoppers. Designer: Kaj Franck. Made by o/y Wärtsilä-concern AB Nuutajärvi Glassworks (FINLAND). ABOVE RIGHT: *Winston* decanter and wineglass in pine-green glass. Designer: Per Lütken. Made by Holmegaards Glasværk A/S (DENMARK). LEFT: Cane-bound decanter, and tumbler in emerald-green or opaline glass. Designed and made by A/S Kastrup Glasværk (DENMARK)

BELOW LEFT: Whisky decanter in clear crystal with cut decoration. Designer: Vicke Lindstrand. Made by AB Kosta Glasbruk (SWEDEN). BELOW: Wicker-covered green glass water set with raffia stoppers to jug and carafe. Designed and made by Mancioli Natale & C. (ITALY)

Vases in clear crystal. Designer: Victor Berndt. Makers: AB
Flygsfors Glasbruk (SWEDEN)

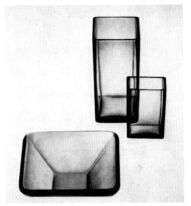

Bevel-edge coloured glass vases and 9-inch bowl. Designer:
Sven Palmqvist. Makers: AB Orrefors Glasbruk (SWEDEN)

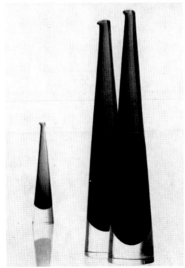

ABOVE: Vases or decanters in blue-grey glass; 8 and 12 inches.
Designer: Timo Sarpaneva. Makers: Karhula-Iittala Glassworks (FINLAND). RIGHT: *Maypole* vases in blue/green or clear
glass, red/black or green/purple 'pole'; 11½ inches. Designer:
Nanny Still. Makers: O/Y Riihimaki Glassworks (FINLAND)

Bottle vases in grey-blue glass; 15, 5 and 10
inches. Designer: Per Lütken. Makers:
Holmegaards Glasværk A/S (DENMARK)

Thick crystal vase, engraved decoration and hand-polished shaped top; 6¼ inches. Designer: G. P. Baxter, Des.RCA. Makers: James Powell & Sons (Whitefriars) Ltd (GB)

Crystal dish with curved edge and handle; length 8¼ inches. Designer: Lloyd Atkins. Makers: Steuben Glass (USA)

Thick crystal bowl; diameter 8 inches. Designer: Tapio Wirkkala. Makers: Karhula-Iittala Glass-works (FINLAND)

◀ Free form thick crystal vases with trapped bubble; 10 and 13 inches high. Designer: Vicke Lindstrand. Makers: AB Kosta Glasbruk (SWEDEN)

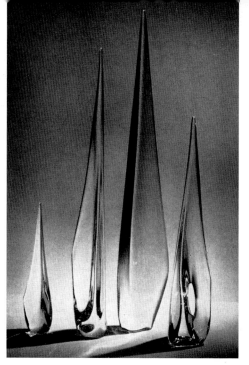

Sculptured shapes in thick crystal. Designer: Michel Daum. Makers: Daum Cristallerie de Nancy (FRANCE)

Blown Venetian glass vases in clear or opaline glass, white or coloured *Zanfirico* decoration; 20 to 22 inches high. Designer: Dino Martens. Makers: Rag. Vetreria Aureliano Toso (ITALY)

White crystal ashtrays, about 6 inches across. Designer: Aimo Okkolin. Makers: o/y Riihimaki Glassworks (FINLAND)

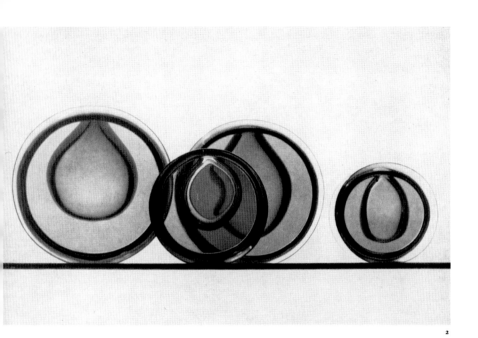

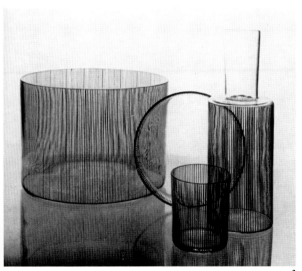

1   Crystal dense colour vases, 5 to 9½ inches high. Designer: Tappio Wirkkala. Made by Karhula-Iittala Glassworks (FINLAND)

2   *Bloc* thick crystal vases in green and purple; inner holder suspended in the body of the glass. Designer: Nanny Still. Made by O/Y Riihimaki Glassworks (FINLAND)

3   Blown glassware, painted 'Stripe' decoration. Large bowl 6 inches deep, diameter 8¼ inches. Designer: Bengt Orup. Made by AB Johansfors Glasbruk (SWEDEN)

Thinly-blown pedestal vases in coloured crystal; 15 to 25 inches. Designer: Nils Landberg. Made by AB Orrefors Glasbruk (SWEDEN)

Cocktail glass in clear crystal, base decorated white spiral. Designer: Tapio Wirkkala. Made by Karhula-Iittala Glassworks (FINLAND)

Flamingo clear crystal wine glasses. Designer: Saara Hopea. Made by O/Y Wärtsilä-concern AB Nuutajarvi Glassworks (FINLAND)

Heavy-based crystal glasses. Diamond point engraving by H. Warren Wilson (GB)

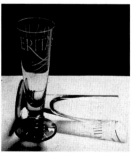

Clear crystal wine glasses from the *Saint-Rémy* service. Designer: Georges Chevalier. Made by Cie des Cristalleries de Baccarat (FRANCE)

Clear crystal wine service with handcut decoration. Designer: Nils Landberg. Made by AB Orrefors Glasbruk (SWEDEN)

White crystal table glasses on pedestal base. Designer: Nanny Still. Made by O/Y Riihimaki Glassworks (FINLAND)

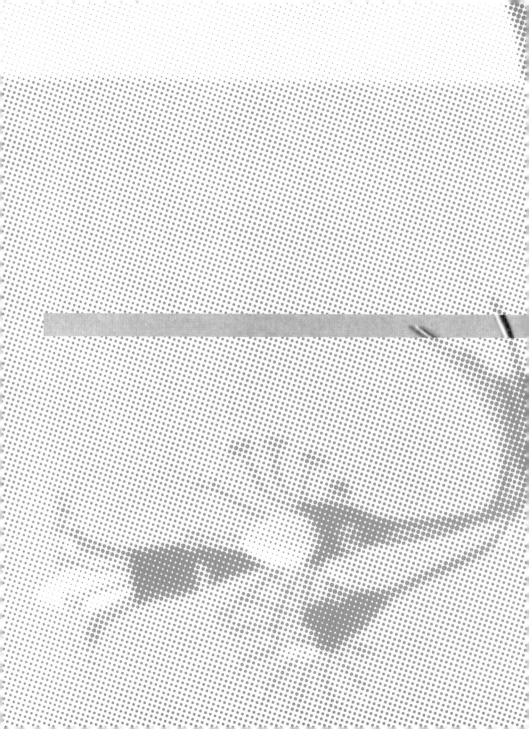

LEFT AND CENTRE: Flexible sconce with white lacquered shade of brass, and globe of matt plexiglas with details of dull brass, both designed by Hans Bergström and made by Atelje Lyktan.
BELOW: White plastic lantern designed by Esben Klint and made by Le Klint.

LEFT: Wall fixture of sandblasted glass with clear line decoration and gilt coloured cellulosed metal work designed by Loraine Read Tucker and made by Tucker and Edgar.
BELOW, RIGHT: Fawn stoneware pottery lamp with brush decoration and shade of pale aquamarine blue. Stoneware horse directly modelled in refractory clay.
Both designed and made by Reginald Marlow.

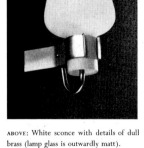

ABOVE: White sconce with details of dull brass (lamp glass is outwardly matt).
RIGHT: Table lamp of dull brass with stock of rifled teak, both designed by Hans Bergström and made by Atelje Lyktan.

CENTRE: Fitment designed by Lisa Johansson-Pape and made by Orno Metal Factory for O.Y. Stockmann A B. Outer shade is of clear glass engraved with stripes: inner shade of opal-coloured glass. RIGHT: Spotlight reflector, designed by J. A. C. Howard and made by Tucker & Edgar, cellulosed Kingfisher blue, with chromium-plated cap and universal joint.

LEFT: Three-light semi-ceiling fitting, by Best & Lloyd Ltd, with obscured and tinted glasses and reflector finished in enamel. Other metalwork cast-brass and finished French old gold or Butler's silver.

BELOW: Three lamps designed by Bertil Brisborg and made by Nordiska Kompaniet: (1) Table lamp with foot and stand of polished ash, textile shade. (2) Table lamp of dull finished brass with shades of white lacquered wire, covered with textile. (3) Floor lamp with foot and stand of mahogany, metal parts of dull finished brass.

2

1

1. Crystal glass cup under a brushed-brass reflector on a mahogany pillar and brushed-brass base designed and made by Stilnovo.
2. Brass base with glass shade and leather-covered pillar designed by Hans Bergström and made by Atelje Lyktan.
3. Black slipware base with sgraffito decoration and shade of pleated paper designed and made by Marianne de Trey.

3

4

5

4. White rope-wound stem on polished timber base with white shade sprayed primrose nylon flock on top section and gold trimmings, designed by Beverley Pick, M S I A, and made by W. S. Chrysaline Ltd
5. Brass pillar with linen shade designed by Paavo Tynell and made by O/Y Taito A B.
6. Teak pillar with brass shade and base designed by Hans Bergström and made by Atelje Lyktan.
7. Aluminium reflector on steel tubing with fire-baked enamel finish in dusk grey, sage green, terra-cotta, desert gold or coral red designed and made by Kurt Versen Lamps Inc.

6

7

8

8. Cast-stone sculptured base and lacquered vellum shade designed and made by Kyle-Reed.

9. Lemon glazed earthenware base and opaque shade edged with lemon-coloured silk cord designed by G. L. de Snellman-Jaderholm and made by Wartsila Koncernen A B Arabia.

10. Pottery base with scratched primitive figures in orange outlined in black. Fibreglass shade sprayed warm grey and wound with thin green jute string designed and made by Berrier-Gnazzo.

9

10

11

12

13

11. Brass stem and ball weight with spotlight shade in aluminium anodized silver, copper, gold or yellow, red, Portland stone, blue/grey or in white stove-enamelled finishes, and black rubber rests designed by Robert Nicholson, ARCA, and Roger Nicholson, MSIA, and made by Merchant Adventurers Ltd.

12. Brass stand with neutral green silk screening on plastic shades by Kurt Versen Lamps Inc.

13. Rosewood stem on brass base with swirl Fibreglass shade. Arm movable to any one of seven stops, the shade and socket section remaining vertically in balance. Designed by Greta von Nessen and made by Nessen Studio Inc.

1

3

1. White cotton shade and brass fitments designed by Hans Bergström and made by Atelje Lyktan.
2. 15-in. adjustable flexible tube arm in chrome or silver designed by Paul Boissevain, Dip. Arch, M S I A, and made by Merchant Adventurers Ltd. Reflector and wall plate in contrasting colours, gold or copper anodized aluminium, or cream, red, yellow, blue/grey or Portland stone stove enamelled finishes.
3. White covering with gold stars and knob designed by Beverley Pick, M S I A, and made by W. S. Chrysaline Ltd. (Chrysaline shades are built on a wire frame cellulosed white and sprayed twice cocoon-wise with plastic while they are rotated. Shrinkage while drying produces the pleasant curves between the wires).
4. *Mondolite* bracket, off-white metal-laced satin aluminium, varying lengths available, produced by Troughton & Young (Lighting) Ltd, and designed in their Design Department.

2

6

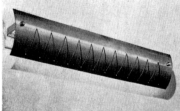

4

5

7

8

5. Aluminium shade on adjustable swivel joint designed by Paul Boissevain, Dip. Arch, M S I A, and made by Merchant Adventurers Ltd. Shade of aluminium anodized in various colours, or white stove-enamelled finish.
6. Brass bracket with white lacquered cups designed and made by Stilnovo.
7. *Mondolite* bracket, movable horizontally or vertically, metal in satin brass and off-white finishes, and shade in off-white plastic by Troughton & Young (Lighting) Ltd.
8. Wall bracket with *Tellachrome* metalwork and *Sunray* pleated shades trimmed with wine-coloured cord. Designed by Ian Henderson and produced by Tucker & Edgar.

10

11

9

9. Orange lacquered metal fitment with cream paper shades designed by Jean Royère.

o. Five-branch brass fitment with white silk lampshades designed by Hans Bergström and made by Atelje Lyktan.

1. Brass and painted aluminium ceiling fitment designed by Paavo Tynell and made by O/Y Taito A B.

13

14

12

12. *Mondolite* wall standard with satin aluminium arm horizontally adjustable to any position. Large shade in ivory or peach rimpled plastic: inverted shade in off-white grained plastic. Produced by Troughton & Young (Lighting) Ltd, and designed in their Design Department.

13. Floor lamp 4 ft. 8 in. high on mahogany or beech base with paper shade designed by Nigel Walters and made by Primavera.

14. End table, floor lamp with reed shade, and magazine rack combination in light grey mahogany designed by Arthur A. Klepper and made by Wor-De-Klee Inc.

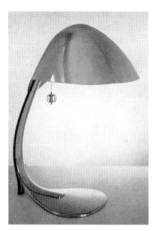

Black base and reflector, white tige, and polished brass adjustable arm. Designers and makers: Stilnovo (ITALY).

Brass reading lamp. Designer: Paavo Tynell. Makers: OY Taito AB (FINLAND).

Polished brass base and arm, white lacquered reflectors and tige. Direct and indirect light. Designers and makers: Stilnovo (ITALY).

Steel tube and rod with spun aluminium shade stove enamelled black and white. Mahogany handgrip with push button switch. Designer: Robin Day, ARCA. Associate designer: John Reid, ARIBA. Makers: Thorn Electrical Industries Ltd (GB).

Brass arm and base with modern fabric shade. Designer and producer: Hans Bergström, Atelje Lyktan (SWEDEN).

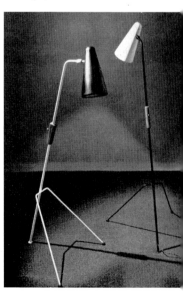

Bent black oxidized steel tubing with adjustable free-swivelling bulb cup. Fourteen-inch diameter shade finished baked parchment-toned enamel. Designer: Greta Von Nessen. Makers: Nessen Studio (USA).

...edish brass table or wall lamp with swivel shade. ...signer: Catherine Speyer. Makers: Laurel Lamp ...nufacturing Co Inc (USA).

...nic pillar and shade lacquered grey, with brass base ...d adjustable arm. Designer and producer: Hans Berg-...öm, Atelje Lyktan (SWEDEN).

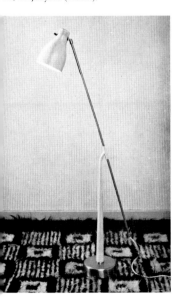

Aluminium and copper, with perforated adjustable metal shade. Designer: Paul Laszlo. Makers: Laszlo Inc (USA).

Crystal cups ringed with brass, white lacquered rod and arms. The cups can be rotated to any position. Designers and makers: Stilnovo (ITALY).

Bright lacquered brass arm with shade of cream pleated buckram and white-enamelled wall mounting boss. Adjustable vertically and horizontally. Makers: The General Electric Co Ltd, and designed in the Design Office of their Fittings Department (GB).

White reflector with adjustable green lacquered reflector on white arm. Polished brass swivel joint. Designers and makers: Stilnovo (ITALY).

Natural wax finished mahogany with adjustable stem and red Le Klint shade. Designer: Peter Brunn. Makers: Peter Brunn Workshop (GB). (*Photo: Elsam Mann & Cooper*)

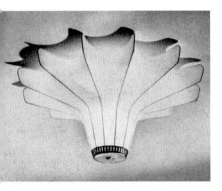

ABOVE: Champagne-coloured *Chrysaline* ceiling fitting with gilt metal end cap. Makers: The General Electric Co Ltd. Designed in their Fittings Department (GB).

RIGHT: Perforated shade, spun brass finish. Designer: Geoffrey Dunn. Makers: Dunn's of Bromley (GB).

BELOW: Natural cane screening supplied in lengths of different width, used here as lampshade and pot cover. From Dunn's of Bromley (GB).

Perforated brass shades with inner shades of light yellow silk fabric. Designer and producer: Hans Bergström, Atelje Lyktan (SWEDEN).

Hanging pendant with fabric shade. Designer and maker: Hans Bergström, Atelje Lyktan (SWEDEN).

BELOW: Stone base with Egyptian design in grey, brown and eggshell or matt black and white, mounted on a wood block, with burlap shade. Designer and maker: Raymor. From Modernage Furniture Corporation (USA).

BELOW: *The Puppy*. Base of natural birch or silver-finished oak, set on a dark oak block, with fabric-over-parchment shade. Designer: Yasha Heifetz. Makers: The Heifetz Company. Small figure on left in copper or brass by Ben Fisher (USA).

ABOVE: *Unad* adjustable lamp, walnut handgrip, feet and counterweight, with brass leg and arm, and Le Klint shade. *Unad* low wing easy chair and *Tile* textile. Designers: The Story Design Group. Makers: Story & Co Ltd (GB).

LEFT: Pottery base with nail-head design in terra cotta colour and sprayed fibreglas shade. Designers and makers: Berrier-Gnazzo (USA).

ABOVE: Underglaze decorated lampbase designed and made by John Erland with woven wicker shade designed and made by W. J. Bingham. From Annette Handcrafts of Britain. Background: *Earlston* 50-inch screen printed linen, available also in three alternative colour schemes. Designer: Mea Angerer. Producers: Donald Bros Ltd (GB).

RIGHT: White etched glass base with shade of pale blue over white organza bordered with white braid. Designer: G. L. de Snellman-Jaderholm. Makers: Iittala Glassworks (FINLAND).

Shelf, wall or table lamp, the two front legs movable along the main stem for various height adjustment. Steel stem finished dark grey with aluminium shade lacquered red, black, grey, yellow or white. Designer: Anthony Ingolia. Makers: The Heifetz Company (USA)

Table or wall lamps in wood and metal with fabric shades. Designer: Yki Nummi. Makers: O/Y Stockmann A/B (FINLAND)

Hyacinth vases and lamp base with sgraffito decoration on the white earthenware body, and a bonbonnière in pale green and white earthenware. Designer: Endre Hevezi B.Arch. Makers: Booths & Colcloughs Ltd (GB)

White marble base with polished brass tige and black reflector. Designers and makers: Stilnovo (ITALY)

White marble base with white lacquered tige, black lacquered terminal and red lacquered reflector. Designers and makers: Stilnovo (ITALY)

Sculptured walnut base, natural finish, and hand-woven shade, natural colour with cocoa and copper threads. Sculptor: F. F. Kern. Designer: Paul Laszlo. Makers: Laszlo Inc (USA)

lamp on oak base with carved walnut stem, and 'fish' lamp on carved mahogany and birch base. Designer: Nicholas Mocharniuk. Carved oak bookends by James L. McCreery. Made for Rena Rosenthal Inc (USA)

Cobalt blue glass base with shade of white *Rhodoid* edged with white cord. Designer: G. L. de Snellman-Jaderholm. Makers: Iittala Glassworks (FINLAND)

Brass stand with oiled teak feet and sprayed white plastic shade. Designer and maker: Hans Bergström, Atelje Lyktan (SWEDEN)

Pumpkin-shaped base in fine earthenware with hand-painted decoration in forest green and black or terra-cotta and black. Ivory *Crinothene* shade. Designer: Truda Carter ARCA. Makers: Carter Stabler & Adams Ltd (GB)

Lamp base designed by Esben Klint and made by Knabstrup Keramiske Industri. Pleated white paper shade designed and made by Le Klint (DENMARK)

Polished brass arm with adjustable black lacquered reflector, white-lined. Designers and makers: Stilnovo (ITALY)

Wall bracket of perforated brass sprayed with plastic. Designer and maker: Hans Bergström, Atelje Lyktan (SWEDEN)

Shade stove-enamelled off-white on specially perforated metal, fitted with two lamps. Makers: Troughton & Young (Lighting) Ltd, and designed by their Design Staff for St Bartholomew's Students' Hostel (Easton & Robertson FFRIBA, Architects) (GB)

Gilt anodized spotlight reflector mounted on arm adjustable to any position. Designer: A. B. Read RDI, FSIA, in association with Dennis Lennon MC, FRIBA. Makers: Troughton & Young (Lighting) Ltd (GB)

Wall bracket of polished aluminium. Designer: Paavo Tynell. Makers: O/Y Taito AB (FINLAND)

Wall bracket or table lamp in beech and metal with pleated white or coloured buckram shade. Designer: 'Doren'. Maker: Oswald Hollmann (GB)

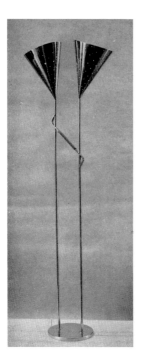

Brass floor lamp with perforated shades and centre handle covered in white leather. Designer: Paavo Tynell. Makers: O/Y Taito AB (FINLAND)

Brass ceiling fitment with perforated shade. Designer: Paavo Tynell. Makers: O/Y Taito AB (FINLAND)

Opal glass shade and painted iron stem ringed with brass. Designer: Paavo Tynell. Makers: O/Y Taito AB (FINLAND)

Hanging lamp made from thin perforated slats of polished beech plywood. Designer: E. R. Aldhouse MSIA for Primavera (GB)

Oiled teak arms with brass details and sprayed plastic shades. Designer and maker: Hans Bergström, Atelje Lyktan (SWEDEN)

All-metal ceiling lamp, 18 inches diameter, with louvres in the base, finished two colours in plain enamel or enamel combined with polychromatic copper, brass or silver. Designers and makers: Best & Lloyd Ltd (GB)

ABOVE: Hanging fitment with plastic-sprayed shades and details of blue lacquered iron and teak. Designer and maker: Hans Bergström, Ateljé Lyktan (SWEDEN)

Ceiling lamp with burnished copper base and shade. Designer and maker: Hans Bergström, Ateljé Lyktan (SWEDEN)

BELOW RIGHT: Pendant hung from teak bracket with white plastic-sprayed shades. Designer and maker: Hans Bergström, Ateljé Lyktan (SWEDEN)

Wooden wall bracket in oak, beech, walnut or mahogany with buckram shade finished in a choice of pastel colours. Designer: Rudolf Hollmann. Maker: Oswald Hollmann (GB)

ᴏᴠᴇ: Wall lamp fixed on beech block mounted on two
ᴇl pins, with wire legs in various finishes and pleated
ᴇtate shade in apricot, ivory or white. Designers: E.
ᴏke-Yarborough and Ronald Homes. Makers: Cone
ttings Ltd (ɢʙ)

ɪʜᴛ: One of five decorative wall light panels featuring
ᴡer motifs in beaten copper, finished verdigris,
ᴍed against an illuminated background of white
alite glass. Designer: Gerald Lacoste, ᴍʙᴇ, ғʀɪʙᴀ.
akers: Metalwork by Wm. Pickford Ltd. Glasswork
Troughton & Young (Lighting) Ltd (ɢʙ)

ʟᴏᴡ: Table lamps on glass bases with copper net and
ꞈstic shades. Designer: Lisa Johansson-Pape. Makers:
r Orno ᴀ/ʙ (ғɪɴʟᴀɴᴅ)

BELOW: Ceiling lamp with 14-inch
reflector coloured outside and sprayed
white inside; rise-and-fall unit case in
polished brass with ceiling plate
sprayed to match reflector. Diabolo-
shaped handgrip of beech, mahogany
or walnut. Designer: Rudolf Hollmann. Maker: Oswald Hollmann (ɢʙ)

Table lamp of dyed cane on wooden
base. Designer: Desmond Sawyer,
ʟsɪᴀ. Makers: Desmond Sawyer
Craftsmen in Cane (ɢʙ)

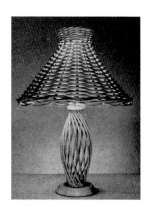

Table lamp on heavy crystal glass base with parchment shade. Designer: Michel Daum. Makers: Daum & Cie, Cristallerie de Nancy (FRANCE). FAR RIGHT: Desk lamp with shade mounted on swivel joint; finished satin silver, gold or copper anodized aluminium throughout, or with shade in stove-enamelled colour. Designer: Paul Boissevain, MSIA. Makers: The Merchant Adventurers Ltd (GB)

Table lamp, 17 inches high, on wood and metal base finished satin silver, brass or copper, with 15-inch diameter enamelled metal shade over 6-inch diameter glass cone. Designers and makers: Best & Lloyd Ltd (GB). FAR RIGHT: Lamp on black lacquered and white glass base with perforated metal shade lacquered red. Designers and makers: Stilnovo (ITALY)

FAR LEFT: Table lamp on base of etc opaque glass in two tones of wh opalescent Rhodoid shade decora with gold stars and cord edg Designer: Mrs G. L. de Snellm Jaderholm. Makers: Iittala Glasswc (FINLAND). LEFT: Table lamp on bla lacquered tripod frame, white g cylindrical diffuser and red-lacque shade. Designers and makers: Stiln (ITALY)

Lamp on brass stand with walnut hand grip; linen shade with baffle above and diffuser below. Designer: Gerald Thurston. Makers: Lightolier Inc (USA)

6½-inch diameter ball-shaped desk lamps rotating on a rubber-tipped, three-pronged base, permitting a wide range of adjustment. Available in black or white for use with a 25-watt lamp. Designer: Harry Gitlin. For Stamford Lighting (USA)

Table lamp on plastic-covered wire tripod base with pleated acetate shade in apricot, ivory or white, and grey switch lampholder. Designers: E. Cooke-Yarborough and Ronald Homes. Makers: Cone Fittings Ltd (GB)

Table lamp with white etched glass base and shade of natural linen bordered with red cotton cord and decorated with red wooden beads. Designer: Mrs G. L. de Snellman-Jaderholm. Makers: Iittala Glassworks (FINLAND)

Table lamp with effective use of 'gravity curve' as a purely decorative feature. Polished brass base and stem, mustard stove enamelled wire cage. Designers: Beverley Pick Associates. Makers: Chrysaline Ltd (GB)

Polished brass table lamp designed for diffused lighting, with white-lacquered perforated reflector and coloured top reflector. Designer: Jacques Biny. Makers: Luminalite (FRANCE)

ABOVE: (*left*): Table lamp on wire base in satin brass or colours, Chrysaline sprayed shade. Designer: Beverley Pick, FSIA. Makers: Chrysaline Ltd (GB). (*Right*): Table lamp on Australian walnut and sycamore base, plastic shade. Designed and made by A. J. Eves, BA (GB). LEFT: Beech table lamp, with reverse pleated plastic shade. Designed and made by Troughton & Young (Lighting) Ltd (GB)

BELOW (*left*): Table lamp on cross-reeded rimu wood base. Designer: John Crichton. Makers: Mount Eden Turnery. Double espartre shade made by Max Robertson (NEW ZEALAND). BELOW (*right*): Lynx table lamp on clear crystal base, raffia shade. Designed and made by Daum Cristallerie d'Art (FRANCE). RIGHT: Table lamp on white opaque etched glass base; pleated white muslin shade with pale grey border. Designer: Mrs. G. L. de Snellman-Jaderholm. Base made by Karhula-Iittala Glassworks (FINLAND)

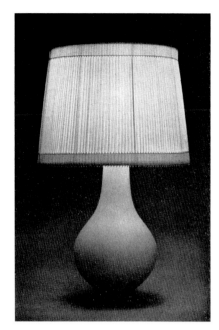

LEFT: Table lamp on clear crystal base, raffia shade. Designers and makers: Daum Cristallerie d'Art (FRANCE)

ABOVE: Table lamps on bases of walnut and polished brass; that on right is a ratchet design permitting adjustment in height from 29 to 33 inches. White translucent parchment shades mounted with light matchwood strips. Designer: Gerald Thurston. Makers: Lightolier Inc. (USA)

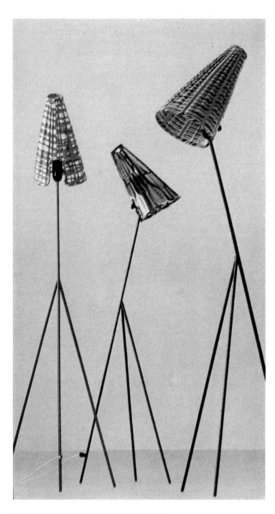

ABOVE: Combined birch standard lamp and small table; shade in shantung on a brass frame. Designer: A. A. Patijn. Makers: De Kroon (HOLLAND) BELOW (*left*): *Indilux* floor lamp on wrought-iron stem, white metal cup and reflector. Designer: Mathieu Matégot. Makers: Société Matégo (FRANCE). BELOW (*right*): Floor-lamp on iron pedestal, sprayed black, and polished brass support. Perforated metal screen, lacquered white; reflector sprayed white inside, red, green, yellow or black outside. Designers: Ateliers Pierre Disderot (FRANCE). Makers: Geni Products (GB)

Standard lamps on metal stems lacquered in various colours. The gay textile shades are movable in any direction. Designer: Hans Bergström, SIR. Makers: Ateljé Lyktan (SWEDEN)

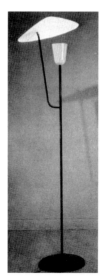

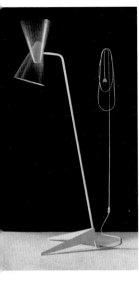

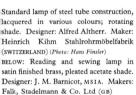

Standard lamp of steel tube construction, lacquered in various colours; rotating shade. Designer: Alfred Altherr. Maker: Heinrich Kihm Stahlrohrmöbelfabrik (SWITZERLAND) (*Photo: Hans Finsler*) BELOW: Reading and sewing lamp in satin finished brass, pleated acetate shade. Designer: J. M. Barnicot, MSIA. Makers: Falk, Stadelmann & Co. Ltd (GB)

Floor lamp on polished brass tubing double tripod frame, carrying nine individually flexible white-enamelled hoods pierced at the rim. BELOW: Combined floor lamp and table-height tray of walnut on cast brass base, with natural woven straw shade fitted with a plastic diffuser and baffle screen. Designer: Gerald Thurston. Makers: Lightolier Inc. (USA)

Floor lamp on wrought-iron base lacquered white, with pivoting brass arm balanced by a counterweight; the lacquered iron reflector is also adjustable. Designer: Jacques Biny. Makers: Luminalite (FRANCE). BELOW: Polished mahogany standard lamp with extendible satin brass tube. Designers and makers: Troughton & Young (Lighting) Ltd (GB)

Polished satin brass bracket with brass cups, lacquered yellow, red, green and blue, under Perspex reflectors. Designer: J. M. Barnicot, MSIA. Makers: Falk, Stadelmann & Co. Ltd (GB)

BELOW: Clip-on adjustable wall light for positions where no wall point exists. Dove grey, red or off-white reflector, clip and stem chromium-plated brass. Designer: J. M. Barnicot, MSIA. Makers: Falk, Stadelmann & Co. Ltd (GB)

Wall bracket of stove-enamelled wire holding basket in *House & Garden* colours. Translucent silk-screened shade in red or mustard with white decor. Designer: Beverley Pick Associates. Makers: Chrysline Ltd (GB)

Combined wall lamp and telephone shelf in polished brass and walnut. The rectangular shade is in pleated aspenslat with an inset glass baffle screen. Designer: Gerald Thurston. Makers: Lightolier Inc. (USA)

BELOW: Steel wall bracket with perforated brass cup. The curved back reflector, 15 inches wide, is in matt Perspex. Designers: Ateliers Pierre Disderot (FRANCE). Makers: Geni Products (GB)

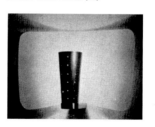

ABOVE: Wall or table lamp in satin brass with counterweight. Shade in off-white grained plastic material. Designers and makers: Troughton & Young (Lighting) Ltd (GB)

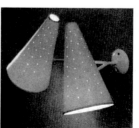

Painted white metal wall bracket carrying twin lights fitted with pierced card shades in various colours. Designer: Francis Mackmin. For Heal's of London (GB)

Lacquered metal ceiling fitting with globes of sprayed plastic over a wire armature. Designer: Hans Bergström, SIR. Makers Ateljé Lyktan (SWEDEN)

BELOW: Adjustable wall pendant on pivoting telescopic arm controlled by a counterweight. Polished brass shade. Designer: Gerald Thurston. Makers: Lightolier Inc. (USA)

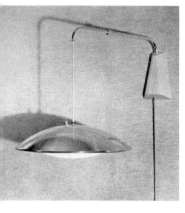

Wall lamp fitted with lacquered copper shade and reflector; olive green base and stem. Designer: John Crichton. Makers: J. E. West & Co. (NEW ZEALAND)

ABOVE: Wall bracket operating on the ball-and-socket principle, with metal perforated shade designed to give indirect patterned ceiling illumination. Designers and makers: Solec (FRANCE)

RIGHT: Wall bracket in aluminium, the reflector surfaces painted white, outer surfaces coloured or in anodised finish. Designer: Rudolf Hollman. Makers: Oswald Hollman Ltd (GB)

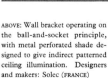

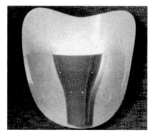

Polished brass wall bracket with striped fabric shades in rust and white, turquoise and white, or other colours. Designer: Doren Leavey. Makers: Oswald Hollman Ltd (GB)

The design of light fittings, and particularly of the free-standing type, offers much scope for decorative treatment and every year sees a host of new creations in which the only standard component is the socket for the lamp. Apart from the light-giving properties of the shaded bulb there are few functional considerations that prevent the designer from doing almost anything he fancies, and considerable freedom in the use of imagination is found in all manner of shapes made up from several kinds of material.

The resulting sculptural exercises can, and often do, run to extremes of fantasy, and they introduce a note of gay nonsense which may give pleasure to the beholder while serving the needs of room lighting to a greater or lesser degree, depending on the design of the shade and the material used. While liberties in the design of the supporting standard or bracket do not impair the efficiency of the light, the shade may not always be the most suitable for giving the desired quality or intensity of light, and appearance alone is not a sufficiently reliable guide to the choice of a fitting.

This review illustrates designs for use in various applications which call for different types of shading. The efficiency of output necessarily varies as between one design and another, but since the type of light demanded of a reading lamp, for example, is different from that required for general room illumination, shade design and shade material vary accordingly. While exploiting the decorative possibilities, designers have not overlooked the respective functional requirements of the fittings under review.

ABOVE: *Two Silhouettes* twin light fitting on cast aluminium base lacquered dark brown and light yellow; plastic shade. Designer: C. I. A. Nilsson. Makers: A/B E. Hansson & Co. (SWEDEN)

Table lamps. ABOVE LEFT: *Black Beauty* on cast aluminium base lacquered black/white, with patterned plastic shade. Designer: C. I. A. Nilsson. Makers: A/B E. Hansson & Co. (SWEDEN). ABOVE RIGHT: Base of 'Verbano' ivory porcelain, pleated Perspex shade. Designer: Guido Andlowiz. Makers: Società Ceramica Italiana (ITALY). RIGHT: Black lacquered metal base with polished crystal centre. Designer: Max Ingrand (FRANCE). Makers: Fontana Arte (ITALY)

Table lamp on natural mahogany support with polished brass tube and legs. The reflector is enamelled. Designed and made by Best & Lloyd Ltd (GB)

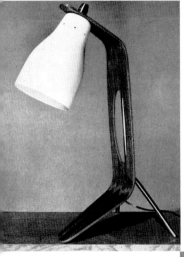

ABOVE: Table lamp on heavy crystal base; raffia shade. Designer: Michel Daum. Makers: Daum Cristallerie de Nancy (FRANCE)

ABOVE RIGHT: Table lamp on grooved base of Heart Rimu wood; white straw cloth shade. Designer: John Crichton; base made Mt. Eden Turnery, shade by Max Robertson (NEW ZEALAND)

RIGHT: Desk lamp on telescopic brass tube support. The shade and louvered diffuser are of ribbed styrene. Baked enamel finish in a choice of four colours. Designer: Gerald Thurston. Makers: Lightolier Inc. (USA)

BELOW: Reading lamp of cast aluminium, green hammer lac finish, polished brass arm balance, adjustable reflector. Designer: C. I. A. Nilsson. Makers: A/B E. Hansson & Co. (SWEDEN)

ABOVE LEFT: Table lamp on teak rod support, Perspex shade. Designer: Hans Bergström. Makers: Ateljé Lyktan (SWEDEN). ABOVE RIGHT: Table lamp. Base, reflector and shade of polished brass or black aluminium, with white underside to top reflector. Designer: Svend Aage Holm Sørensen. Makers: Holm Sørensen & Co. (DENMARK)

ABOVE LEFT: Wall light on beech mount. The arms are in polished brass, and the 13-inch shade satin opal glass. Designed and made by Best & Lloyd Ltd (GB). ABOVE RIGHT Wall light, type 'C.P.' Anodised aluminium cap and legs, polished beech mount, and pleated acetate shade, in white, ivory, or apricot; it is removable for washing. Designed by Yarborough-Homes, MMSIA. Makers: Cone Fittings Ltd (GB)

ABOVE: *Valencia* Triple light bracket in satin brass. Designed for indirect lighting by Svend Aage Holm Sørensen. Makers: Holm Sørensen & Co. (DENMARK)

BELOW: *Altair* Single light bracket on polished brass tubular frame with Perspex reflector. The aluminium cup shade is enamelled in various colours. Designer: J. M. Barnicot, MSIA. Makers: Falk, Stadelmann & Co. Ltd (GB)

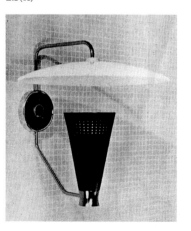

ABOVE: *Diabolo* wall bracket in enamelled aluminium and polished brass. Cherry red blue grey, and off-white reflectors. Designer J. M. Barnicot, MSIA. Makers: Falk, Stadelmann & Co. Ltd (GB)

LEFT: Wall bracket for indirect lighting i polished brass with opal glass shades in fiv different colours. Designed and made by Fontana Arte (ITALY)

ABOVE LEFT: Wall light with matt opal shade, polished brass ring and. Designed and made by Paavo Tynell (FINLAND). ABOVE RIGHT: Fluorescent tube wall fitting lacquered in various colours; allast mount lacquered black. The tube can be rotated in the ertical plane to a horizontal position. Designer: Gino Sarfatti. Makers: Arteluce Soc. Acc. (ITALY)

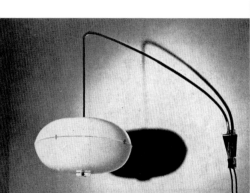

Free-swinging orientable wall lamps with up-and-down sliding movement. ABOVE: Walnut mount, polished brass arms. Walnut strips radiating from a pierced brass collar decorate the fibreglass shade. Designer: Gerald Thurston. Makers: Lightolier Inc. (USA). LEFT: Arm in polished brass; ball shade in Perspex. Designed and made by Stilnovo, s.r.l. (ITALY)

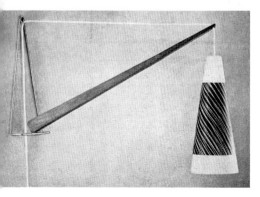

ABOVE: *Airlie* wall lamp with batten holder. The perforated reflector is in birch plywood, cellulosed in choice of colours; interior surface white. Designed and made by Alten Products (GB). LEFT: Wall bracket of polished brass tube with movable teak suspension arm. Satin opal glass shade with black-and-white plastic decoration. Designer: Svend Aage Holm Sørensen. Makers: Holm Sørensen & Co. (DENMARK)

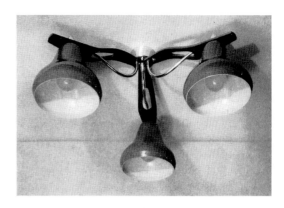

ABOVE: Ceiling pendant with enamelled reflectors on polished beech arms; tubes and ceiling plate are in polished brass. Designed and made by Best & Lloyd Ltd (GB)

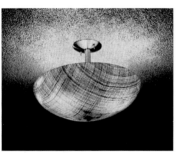

ABOVE LEFT: Ceiling fitting in lacquered metal. Blue frame, shades in white, primrose, light green. Designer: Hans Bergström. Makers: Ateljé Lyktan (SWEDEN)

LEFT: Polished brass ceiling fitting with shade of moulded fibreglass, in rattan and various other finishes. Designed by H. Gottlieb and Erich Marx. Made by Modulite Inc. (CANADA)

LEFT: White opal pendant lamps with aluminium caps enamelled in *House & Garden* colours. Suspension tubes in anodised aluminium, gilt or silver finish. Designed by Misha Black, OBE, PSIA, of Design Research Unit. For Hume Atkins & Co. Ltd (GB)

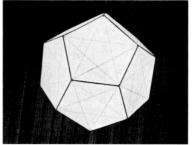

ABOVE: Pendant with oiled te suspension bracket; white o glass shades with non-glo satin finish. Designer: Sve Aage Holm Sørensen. Make Holm Sørensen & Co. (DE MARK)

LEFT: Ceiling lamp with pla sprayed wire shade. Desigr Hans Bergström. Makers: At Lyktan (SWEDEN)

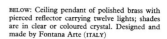

BELOW: Ceiling pendant of polished brass with pierced reflector carrying twelve lights; shades are in clear or coloured crystal. Designed and made by Fontana Arte (ITALY)

ABOVE: Ceiling pendant in polished brass with thirty-two lamps enfolded in clear and coloured crystal petal-shaped shades. Designed and made by Fontana Arte (ITALY)

ABOVE LEFT: *Three in Line* adjustable ceiling fitting. Polished brass yoke, rubber covered coil suspension; textured cloth shades. Designer: Gerald Thurston. Makers: Lightolier Inc. (USA).
ABOVE RIGHT: Shades in matt opal glass, plain or decorated. Designed by Uno Westerberg SIR. Metalwork in polished brass. Shades made in Sweden; fittings by Fredk. Thomas & Co. Ltd (GB)

FAR LEFT: Ceiling light in polished aluminium or brass with pierced baffle reflector. Available in natural finish or coloured lacquers. Designed and made by Modulite Inc. (CANADA)

LEFT: Ceiling lamp with plast-sprayed shade. Designer: Hans Bergström. Makers: Ateljé Lyktan (SWEDEN)

The means used for lighting a room continue to play an important part in its decorative scheme. Table lamps still make good wedding presents, and, whereas there are some which cannot reasonably be selected without reference to the setting in which they will appear, most of them suit a wide range of circumstances.

Generally speaking, the purer and simpler the form, the more nearly absolute will be its ubiquity. Simplicity does not, however, call for characterless or negative design; in fact, as will be seen from the illustrations, there is strength and unity in the simplest of the lamps and fitments shown.

Fixtures are of a different category. Designed for permanent siting, they can be selected in the first place to give the required amount of light where it is needed and, secondly, to fit either unobtrusively or as decorative motifs into the surrounding detail. With the possible exception of some of the shades which may have become distractingly large or elaborate and are, in any case, often supplied as separate or interchangeable items, most of the fixtures have been designed with sufficient flexibility to allow of harmonious siting in a variety of contemporary settings.

Conventional materials; ceramics, glass, wood and metal; still offer sufficient scope to meet the structural needs of most designs, but there is occasional use for plastics and, particularly where soft or semi-rigid shades are concerned, for synthetic washable materials. They can either be sponged down in situ, or removed bodily and immersed in a detergent solution.

ABOVE: Wall lamps in (*left*) black-lacquered aluminium with decorative reflector; (*right*) with teak turned ornaments and textile shade. Designers and makers: Hans-Agne Jakobsson AB (SWEDEN)

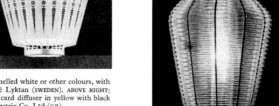

ABOVE LEFT: Tubular pendant, 28 inches long, in aluminium enamelled white or other colours, with plast glass diffusers. Designer: Hans Bergström. Makers: Ateljé Lyktan (SWEDEN). ABOVE RIGHT: White-enamelled wire lantern with polished brass relief; fitted card diffuser in yellow with black motifs. Designers: Beverley Pick Associates. Makers: General Electric Co. Ltd (GB)

ABOVE: Pendant shade, hand-woven in plastic monofilament on plastic coated wire frame. Colours: clear on red or yellow frame; all red, all yellow. Designer: Desmond Sawyer, LSIA. Makers: Desmond Sawyer Designs Ltd (GB)

FAR LEFT: Pendant of grouped aluminium cylinders lacquered black or other colours (interior white). LEFT: Ceiling lamp with balanced reflector on oxidised brass mount. The shade is in aluminium, lacquered black, with glass diffuser. Both are designed and made by Stilnovo, s.r.l. (ITALY)

ABOVE LEFT: Pendant shade of layered parchment interleaved with pressed and dried grasses and leaves. Designed and made by Birgitta Sorbon-Malmsten (SWEDEN). ABOVE RIGHT: Ceiling pendant with plast-sprayed shades; copper suspension details. Designers and makers: Hans-Agne Jakobsson AB (SWEDEN). LEFT: Floor standard, 4 feet 4 inches high, on white terrazzo base with foot-operated switch. Black stem with polished brass sleeve; black and yellow patterned shade with Perspex top diffuser. Designers and makers: Troughton & Young (Lighting) Ltd (GB). BELOW LEFT: Pendant for direct or indirect lighting with aluminium shades lacquered black or other colours; polished brass waist. Designer: Sven Aage Holm Sørensen. Makers: Holm Sørensen & Co. (DENMARK). BELOW RIGHT: Pendant with matt black decorated opal glass shade; polished brass and gold-lacquered ceiling plate and gallery, matt black suspension. Designer: J. A. C. Howard. Makers: Tucker & Edgar (GB)

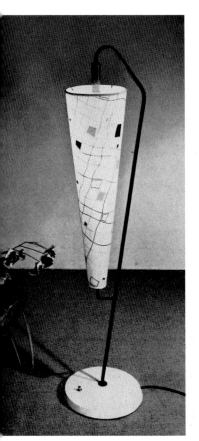

BELOW: Double standard floor lamp on polished brass base with black-lacquered brass stem and rubber-covered carrying handle. The shades (larger in Plexiglass, smaller in aluminium lacquered black and white) are carried on an extending swivel bracket and can be moved up and down and rotated. Designers and makers: Stilnovo s.r.l. (ITALY)

ABOVE: Small wall lamps with cupped shades in satin white and coloured crystal glass on hinged mount of polished brass. Designers and makers: Fontana Arte (ITALY)

RIGHT: Polished brass wall bracket with white relief; fitted 'Silverlight' candle bulbs. Designers and makers: General Electric Co. Ltd (GB)

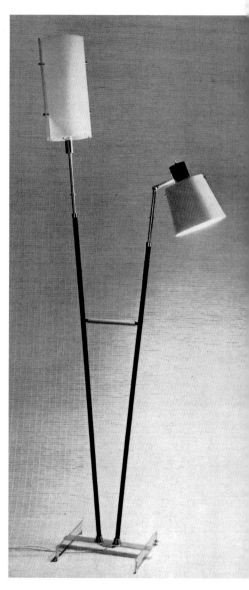

RIGHT: Wall lamp on adjustable brass mount; pierced shade in spun aluminium with pearl-grey baked enamel finish and brass finial. Designer: John Crichton. Makers: E. West & Co. (NEW ZEALAND)

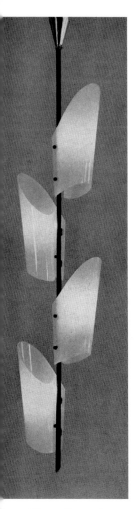

ABOVE: Satin brass wall bracket on white mount. Red silk-screened shade with white motif and gilt edge. Also available with glass shade. Designers: Beverley Pick Associates. Makers: General Electric Co. Ltd (GB)

ABOVE: Wall bracket with large opal glass shade on fancy brass mount. Designer: J. Junek. Makers: Kamenicky-Senov Chandelier Works (CZECHOSLOVAKIA)

BELOW: Wall lamp with white-lacquered brass mount held in a bronze hand; satin glass globe. Height 18½ inches. Designers and makers: Fontana Arte (ITALY)

ABOVE: *Prisma* ceiling pendant on polished brass mount; black-lacquered stem with opal Plexiglass shades. Total length: 3 feet 11 inches. Designer: Hildegard Liertz. Makers: Hesse-Lamps (GERMANY)

RIGHT: *Gala* floor standard on polished brass base with black-lacquered stems. The two lower shades are in brass lacquered electric blue; the centre shade is in polished brass. Total height: 5 feet 4 inches. Designer: Hildegard Liertz. Makers: Hesse-Lamps (GERMANY)

ABOVE: Wall bracket with polished brass and gold-lacquered arms and finial; perforated gallery in cherry or lemon chrome and white flashed opal glass shade. Designer: J. A. C. Howard. Makers: Tucker & Edgar (GB)

ABOVE: Pendant of moulded fibreglass on aluminium pulley fixture; rattan finish shade with brass or copper trimming. Designer: H. Gottlieb. Makers: Modulite Inc. (CANADA).

RIGHT: Table lamp on light ruby glass base; shade of white rhodoid with raised spots, and vieux-rose velvet ribbon binding. Designer: Mrs. G. L. de Snellman Jaderholm. Base made by Karhula-Iittala Glassworks (FINLAND)

BELOW: Table lamp on flexible brass stem; white Perspex base and shade. Designer: Yki Nummi. Makers: Stockmann-Orno (FINLAND)

ABOVE: Pendant on metal suspension with lacquered aluminium shades mounted on teak cup. Designer: Sven Middelboe. Makers: A/S Nordisk Solar Co. (DENMARK)

LEFT: Table lamp on black terrazzo base with satin brass stem and embossed linen shade. Also available with a white terrazzo base and black bronze stem. Designers and makers: Troughton & Young (Lighting) Ltd (GB)

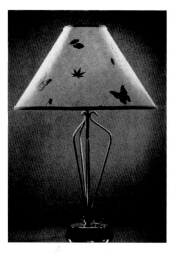

BELOW: Table lamp on polished brass base with white plast shade on 15-inch teak rod support. Designer: Hans Bergström. Makers: Ateljé Lyktan (SWEDEN)

ABOVE LEFT: Table lamp on cast iron base, dull black finish; white plastic shade with adjustable aluminium reflector lacquered black (cream underside) on polished brass arm. Designer: Sven Aage Holm Sørensen. Makers: Fog & Mørup (DENMARK). ABOVE RIGHT: Table lamp in polished brass with shade of pressed butterflies and leaves under fibreglass. Height overall 27 inches. Designer: John Crichton. Base made by E. West & Co.; shade by Max Robertson (NEW ZEALAND)

BELOW LEFT: Table lamp in polished brass, or with black lacquer finish; white satin glass diffuser. Designers and makers: Fontana Arte (ITALY). BELOW RIGHT: Table lamps on teak base with hand-painted multi-colour decoration; matt white shade. Height 13½ inches. Designers and makers: Hans-Agne Jakobsson A B (SWEDEN)

BELOW: *Terrazze* pendants in opal glass; single or tiered aluminium shades lacquered black, orange, or red. Designer: Jørn Utzon. Makers: A/S Nordisk Solar Co. (DENMARK)

ABOVE: Wire frame globe pendants, 19½ to 27 inches diameter, printed textile shades; suspension details in maple. Designers and makers: Hans-Agne Jakobsson AB (SWEDEN). BELOW: Triple pendant of adjustable multicolour art glass shades with brass accents; the white plastic suspension cord runs through a brass divider with inner rods in correlated colours. Custom made in Denmark for Raymor (USA)

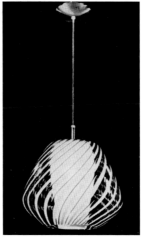

ABOVE: *Mondolite* pendant, white satin finish opal glass shade, black and yellow line decoration; suspension, satin black finish, or polished brass. Designers and makers: Troughton & Young (Lighting) Ltd (GB)

ABOVE: Glass-in-glass ceiling pendant, opal inner cylinder, clear glass outer shade with etched swirl and fine mauve line decoration. From the *Capri* collection by Lightolier Inc. (USA)

BELOW RIGHT: *Granada* pendant in clear glass with white and violet stripes, inside sand-blasted. BELOW: Wall bracket *Parma* clear glass shade with matt white stripes. Both are designed by A. F. Gangkofner. Made by Peill & & Putzler GmbH (GERMANY)

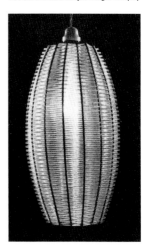

ABOVE: Pendants with globe shades of white plastic ribbon. Designer: Antti Nurmesniemi. Made by Artek (FINLAND)

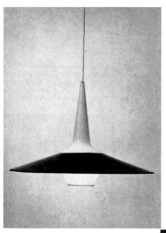

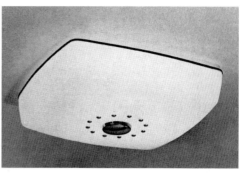

ABOVE: Pendant globe in plastic with lacquered metal shade. Designer: Bertil Roos. Made by Livoflex GmbH (SWITZERLAND)

BELOW: *Orno* pendant for diffused lighting, brass-finish sprayed aluminium shade. Designer: Lisa Johansson-Pape. Made by O/Y Stockmann AB (FINLAND)

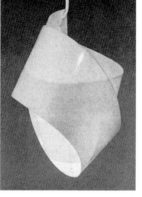

ABOVE: Pendant shade of twisted plast strip about 12 inches wide. Designer: Hans Bergström. Made by Ateljé Lyktan AB (SWEDEN)

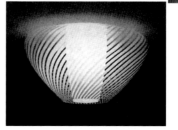

ABOVE: Pendants in satin brass with satin etched opal glass diffuser; the bulb is adjustable to change the light distribution. Designer: Birger Dahl. Made by Sønnico (NORWAY)

LEFT: Ceiling fitting *Toledo*: clear glass shade with striped decoration embodied in the glass; opal glass inner diffuser. Designer: A. F. Gangkofner. Made by Peill & Putzler GmbH (GERMANY)

RIGHT: Wall lamp on extensible swivel arm in polished brass; white and black lacquered aluminium reflector on pulley slide fitting. Designed and made by Stilnovo s.r.l. (ITALY)

ABOVE: Wall lamps for use with candelabra bulb; white or yellow Bonoplex glass shade, polished oak detail. Designers and makers: Hans-Agne Jakobsson AB (SWEDEN)

BELOW: Single and twin-bracket wall lamps on polished brass mount; matt white glass shades. Designers and makers: Hans-Agne Jakobsson AB (SWEDEN)

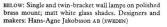

LEFT: White pinspot Perspex wall light. It is clipped to a metal mount and can be inverted. Designed and made by Troughton & Young (Lighting) Ltd (GB)

ABOVE: Wall bracket with cupped shade in white Plexiglass on bronze mount. Designed and made by Ilum (ARGENTINA)

Adjustable wall bracket from the *Harlequin* range. Satin finish white flashed opal glass shade; also available with metal reflector in black, white, or four colours; or decorated glass. Designed and made by Troughton & Young (Lighting) Ltd (GB)

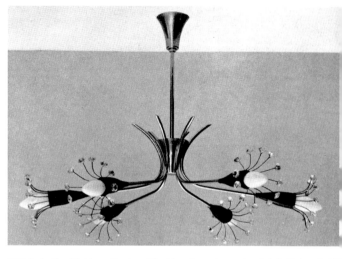

ABOVE: Pendant in polished brass with cut crystal bead decoration to the cupped candle bulbs. Designer: Rudolf Hollman. Made by Oswald Hollman Ltd (GB)

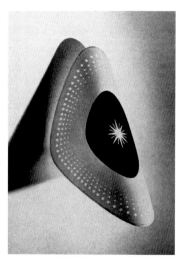

ABOVE: Wall fitting intended for use where a normal bracket is not available; shield shade in card, decorated in red and black. Designed and made by The General Electric Co. Ltd (GB)

LEFT: Table lamp with adjustable bar mounted on smoked oak support and black-lacquered metal base; pleated shade in plastic-coated paper. Designer: Wilhelm Wohlert. Made by Le Klint (DENMARK)

ABOVE: Table lamp in white glass with copper base and top. Designed and made by Solec (FRANCE)

LEFT: Floor lamps on black tubular steel tripod base with spun plastic globes over wire frame. Designed by Isamo Nouguchi (JAPAN). For Gösta Westerberg AB (SWEDEN)

RIGHT: Standard lamp with black perforated metal shade set on an iron stand; white fibreglass inner diffuser. Designer: John Crichton. Made by H. J. Murray (NEW ZEALAND)

BELOW: Table lamp in white and black Plexiglass mounted on black oxidised brass stand. Designed and made by Stilnovo, s.r.l. (ITALY)

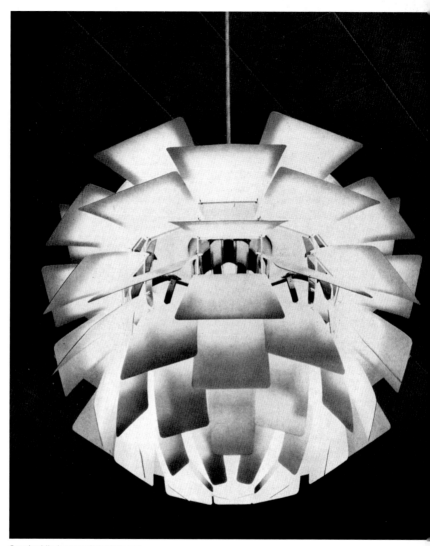

Cone chandelier in copper, for 300/400 watt lamp;
outside matt-brushed, inside white. Diameter 28½
inches. Designer: Poul Henningsen. Makers: Louis
Poulsen & Co. (DENMARK)

Avocado pendant in pleated plastic, lacquered metal details. Designed and made by Le Klint (DENMARK)

ABOVE: Multiple pendant on flexible suspension with brass arms; reflectors satin black or coloured. Made by Troughton & Young (Lighting) Ltd (GB). RIGHT: White Chrysaline pendant, card shade in red, citron, or black. Designer: Beverley Pick, FSIA. Makers: W. S. Chrysaline Ltd (GB)

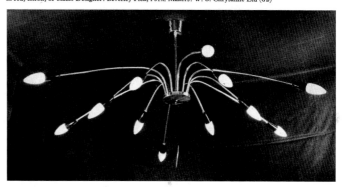

White opal cone pendants with outer shade of coloured glass. Designer: Carl Fagerlund. Makers: AB Orrefors Glasbruk (SWEDEN)

Candle-bulb multi-spray metal pendant, finished polished brass with black-sprayed spun aluminium lamp housings. Designer: W. E. Summers. Makers: Courtney Pope (Electrical) Ltd (GB)

Etched glass pendants in orange/yellow, amber/grey, and blue/acquamarine. Designer: Dino Martens. Makers: Vetreria Rag. Aureliano Toso (ITALY)

ABOVE: *Yankee* white opal glass pendant with lacquered aluminium shade. Designer: Sven Middelboe. Makers: A/S Nordisk Solar Co. (DENMARK)
RIGHT: Triple brass-tube pendant with spun aluminium shades sprayed black. Designed and made for fluorescent lighting by Svend Aage Holm Sørensen (DENMARK)

LEFT: Floor lamp with swivelling reflectors on adjustable polished brass white-lacquered stem; black base. Made by Stilnovo, s.r.l. (ITALY)

CENTRE: Floor lamp with plastic-coated cottonweave shade on wire frame; brass rod support on steel tube stem, cast base lacquered black

RIGHT: Floor lamp on conical steel legs with teak points; shade, opaline glass on spun brass ring. Both these designs are made by Svend Aage Holm Sørensen (DENMARK)

LEFT: *Osaka* table or low floor lamp; black balsa frame, white plastic ribbon-strip shade. Designed and made by Heal's of London (GB)

CENTRE: Teak tripod floor lamp with white nylon cylinder shade. Custom-made in Denmark for Raymor (USA)

RIGHT: Floor lamp with twin shades in red and light green plexiglass, and white-lacquered turnable reflector; black-lacquered stem and white marble base. Made by Stilnovo, s.r.l. (ITALY)

An all-metal table lamp with base in black iron tubing; lacquered reflector and cup. Designed by Martin Eisler in collaboration with Susy Aczel. Made by Ilum (ARGENTINA)

Table lamp on teak tripod base; white, red, or curry colour pleated plastic shade and brass details. Custom-made in Denmark for Raymor (USA)

Rimu wood table lamp on copper base, white fibreglass shade. Designer: John Crichton. Base by Mt. Eden Turnery; shade by Max Robertson (NEW ZEALAND)

Table lamp on polished brass base; red, black, green or yellow-lacquered metal reflector and matching candle-bulb shade. Made by Homeshade Company Ltd (GB)

Metal wall bracket with expanded aluminium diffusing screen in lemon-chrome
or cherry-red finish. Designed and made by
Teeanee Ltd (GB)

Plexiglass wall lamp on teak
mount. Designer: C. I. A. Nilsson. Makers: Lindeberg & Roos
AB (SWEDEN)

◀ 'Pin-up' bracket with adjustable
mahogany arm on matt black
mount; washable Chrysaline
shade, brass top cone. Designer:
Beverley Pick, FSIA. Makers:
W. S. Chrysaline Ltd (GB)

▲
Wall bracket in
satin opal glass on
polished brass
mount. Made by
Hailwood & Ack-
royd Ltd (GB)

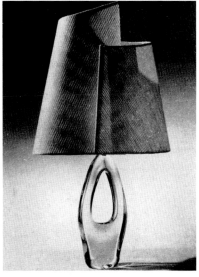

White frosted glass table lamps 14 and 16
inches high; perforated metal details in
brass or copper. Designed and made by
Hans-Agne Jakobsson AB (SWEDEN)

Box table lamp in Acririte, which is
semi-opaque and gives a diffused light.
Designed and made by Yasushiro
Hiramatsu (JAPAN)

Table lamp on lead-crystal base; shade of
figured fabric flashed onto parchment.
Made by Daum Cristallerie de Nancy
(FRANCE)

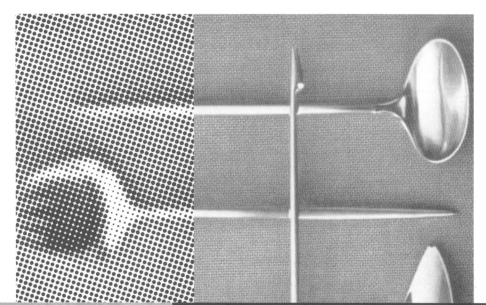

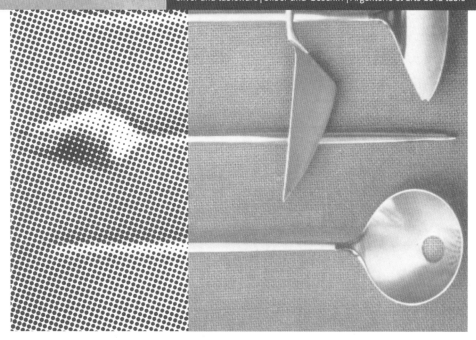

silver and tableware | Silber und Geschirr | Argenterie et arts de la table

ABOVE: Tea-set in 'polka dot' pattern produced by T. G. Green & Co Ltd, available in liberty green and maroon. Breakfast, dinner sets and jugs are also produced in this design. (Photo: Courtesy of *The Pottery Gazette*).

RIGHT: *Magnolia* tea and coffee service printed in grey, with motif in pale yellow and white with green leaves. Background groundlaid in pale green with a fine green line on outer edge. Designed by S. C. Talbot and made by A. E. Gray & Co Ltd.

ABOVE: *Ludlow* dinner-ware designed by S. C. Talbot and made by A. E. Gray & Co Ltd. Decorative border is printed in green with a pale green groundlaid surround extending to the green off-edge line; centre motif hand-painted in pink, lilac, blue, cerise, yellow, red and green. LEFT: Tea and coffee service made by Porzellanfabrik Langenthal A G.

Part of a dinner service in fine earthenware called 'LA' designed by Stig Lindberg and made by AB Gustavsberg Fabriker.

BELOW: *Sherborne* tea-set with coloured slip facing in celadon green or shell pink designed by John Adams, ARCA, and produced by Carter Stabler and Adams Ltd, makers of Poole Pottery. The knobs and handles are ivory white.

RIGHT: Dinner-ware designed by Susie V. Cooper, RDI, and made by The Susie Cooper Pottery Ltd. Plate on left has a wide mahogany-coloured band with a sgraffitto motif accentuated by black free-hand painting interspersed with small circles and finished with a narrow band of fern green in the well. Plate, soup bowl and saucer on right show the same motif freehand painted on a cream ground.

Part of a dinner service in bone china, known as 'LB' and designed by Stig Lindberg. Made by AB Gustavsberg Fabriker.

BELOW: *Sherborne* coffee-set to match tea-ware illustrated on the opposite page, designed by John Adams, ARCA, and produced by Carter Stabler and Adams Ltd.

Gray Lines tableware in white earthenware designed by Wilhelm Kåge and made by AB Gustavsberg Fabriker.

Stainless steel Gense tableware
designed by Folke Ahrström.

Silver coffee pot,
hot-milk jug and sugar bowl
with ebony knobs and handles
designed by Sven-Arne Gillgren
and made by Guldsmeds Aktiebolaget
i Stockholm.

Silver rose bowl designed by A. G. Styles and
made by S. J. Sparrow of R. E. Stone for The
Goldsmiths & Silversmiths Co Ltd., and RIGHT,
octagonal-shaped silver tea-set designed by F.
Cobb and made by The Goldsmiths and Silversmiths Co Ltd.

Silver Ice Pail, Spoon, Tongs and Cups
designed by Sigvard Bernadotte
and made by Georg Jensen.

RIGHT, ABOVE: Silver sugar bowls and jug
designed by Karl Gustav Hansen
and made by Hans Hansen Solvsmedie A/S.

RIGHT, BELOW: Silver coffee ware designed
and made by Frantz Hingelberg.
The coffee pot has an ivory handle and
knob, and its shape makes an interesting
comparison with a similar set below.

LEFT TO RIGHT: Silver coffee ware designed and made by Frantz Hingelberg. Silver teapot designed by
Magnus Stephensen and made by Kay Bojesen. Silver candleholder designed by Ole Hagen and made
by A. Michelsen.

Cocktail set of spun silver
designed by Erik Fleming
and made by Atelier Borgila, A B.
The handgrip is of gold, as is also
the stirring spoon.

BELOW: Silver bowl
designed and made by
Margret Craver.
(Purchased by Newark Museum
for their permanent collection.)

BELOW: Silver tea-kettle
designed and made by
Karl Gustav Hansen.

Chased silver bonbonnière.
Knob set with agates,
designed by Arne Erkers
and made by Guldsmeds
Aktiebolaget i Stockholm.

Pitcher in aluminium
by a staff designer for
The Aluminium Company
of Canada Ltd.

Hand-wrought sugar sifter
designed and made by
Margret Craver.

Stainless steel sauce bowl
designed by Sigurd Persson,
and made by AB Silver och Stål.

Bowl suitable for
chocolates or cigarettes
designed by Helge Lind-
gren, and made by
K. Anderson

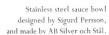

Hand-made silver wine jug
designed and made by
Sigurd Persson.

Prototype in silver of 1½-pint
tankard to be made in
pewter or stainless steel,
matt finish, designed by
Milner Gray, RDI, FSIA,
of The Design Research Unit
and made by A. Carter,
of D. & J. Wellby Ltd.

Silver bowl
and fluted flower vase
designed by Sven-Arne Gillgren.
Made by the designer
and Guldsmeds
Aktiebolaget i Stockholm.

Prototype of another silver
tankard, one-quart size,
designed by
Milner Gray, RDI, FSIA,
and made by A. Carter.
(See illustration above
for additional details.)

1. *Tudor.* Ivory dinner ware, copper-plate engraved, printed in royal blue with blue inner line, silver edges and handles, designed by S. C. Talbot and produced by A. E. Gray & Co. Ltd.

2. *Westover.* Fine bone china dinner, tea and coffee ware designed by Millicent Taplin and produced by Josiah Wedgwood & Sons Ltd. The design is in grey and robin's egg blue.

3. Earthenware in grey, brown and blue designed by Edwin and Mary Scheier.

4. Luncheon service of dark brown bisque stoneware with speckled tan glaze linings, and hand-wrought sterling silver flatware all designed and made by F. C. Ball.
(Photo: Stone & Steccati.)

5. Black and cream slipware jug and mugs designed and made by Marianne de Trey.
6. Earthenware chocolate set, mottled brown, gold and grey glaze with subdued red, blue, green and violet reflections, designed and made by Herbert H. Sanders. *(Photo: George E. Stone & H. W. Wichers.)*
7. Beer mugs produced by Josiah Wedgwood & Sons Ltd. Shape designed by Keith Murray, R D I, and 'resist' decoration in gold or silver by Millicent Taplin.

8. Earthenware bowls fitted with lids designed by Stig Lindberg and produced by Gustavsberg Fabriker A B.
9. Tableware in sea green and oyster white designed by Simon Slobodkin and made by Senegal China Institute Inc.

1. *Tulip* pattern *Streamline* coffee ware, hand-painted in two shades of green on a pale celadon green ground, or in two shades of red on a shell-pink ground, both with 'crystal' colourless glaze. Designed by John Adams, A R C A, and produced by Carter Stabler & Adams Ltd. Knobs, handles and linings are in the ivory white body.

2. *Sandringham*. Fine bone china tea-set printed in brown with flowers and ribbon in either blue, pink or yellow. Designed by Victor Skellern, A R C A, and produced by Josiah Wedgwood & Sons Ltd.

3. *Cockerel*. Dinner and tea ware in black and gold on white, designed by Walter Dorwin Teague, and made by Taylor, Smith & Taylor Co.
(*Photo; Lucas & Monroe.*)

4. *Cobalt* pattern in Franciscan fine china with deep cobalt band, edged with burnished gold. Shape designed by Mary K. Grant. Produced by Gladding McBean & Co.

1

2

3

4

5. Early morning tea-set in highly-fired copper-red stoneware with matt celadon linings, designed by Donald Mills and produced by Donald Mills Pottery Ltd. (*Photo: Ducrow.*)

6. Tableware designed and made especially for a reception attended by H.R.H. the Princess Elizabeth given by the Royal Designers for Industry. Designer: Susie V. Cooper, R D I. Producers: Susie Cooper China Ltd. (*Courtesy: Royal Society of Arts.*) Wallpaper background produced by The Wall Paper Manufacturers Ltd.

5

6

7

9

10

8

7, 8. Tea services with sgraffito decorations designed by Susie V. Cooper, R D I. Pink set produced by Susie Cooper China Ltd. Green set by Susie Cooper Pottery Ltd. *(Colour photos: McLeish & Macaulay.)*

9, 10. Tea service with sea-anemone design in jade, fern or bright green, Indian red, Sèvres blue or grey-blue, with gold finish on handles. Designed by Susie V. Cooper, R D I, and made by Susie Cooper China Ltd. Fabrics in top illustration by Loom Art Ltd, *see page 60.*

11. *Carnation.* Jug and plate with hand-painted white 'resist' decoration on a sage green stippled lustre ground, designed by S. C. Talbot and produced by A. E. Gray & Sons Ltd.

11

12

12. Tea ware in soft shell pink or Sèvres blue with gold white-circled stars, designed by Susie V. Cooper, R D I, and made by Susie Cooper China Ltd. Background: *Mull* printed linen designed by Marion Hoffer and produced by Donald Bros Ltd.

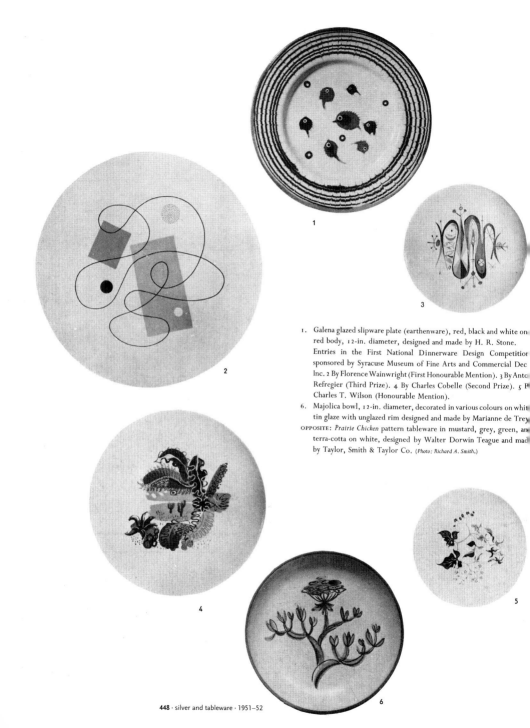

1. Galena glazed slipware plate (earthenware), red, black and white on red body, 12-in. diameter, designed and made by H. R. Stone.
   Entries in the First National Dinnerware Design Competition sponsored by Syracuse Museum of Fine Arts and Commercial Dec Inc. 2 By Florence Wainwright (First Honourable Mention). 3 By Anto Refregier (Third Prize). 4 By Charles Cobelle (Second Prize). 5 P Charles T. Wilson (Honourable Mention).
6. Majolica bowl, 12-in. diameter, decorated in various colours on whit tin glaze with unglazed rim designed and made by Marianne de Trey
OPPOSITE: *Prairie Chicken* pattern tableware in mustard, grey, green, an terra-cotta on white, designed by Walter Dorwin Teague and mad by Taylor, Smith & Taylor Co. *(Photo: Richard A. Smith.)*

1

2

3

4

1. Stoneware coffee jugs with celadon glaze designed and made by Gutte Eriksen.
2. Majolica coffee-set decorated in pink and brown on an off-white glaze designed and made by Marianne de Trey.

3. Condiment set and sugar castor in bone china designed by Stig Lindberg and made by Gustavsberg Fabriker A B.
4. Highly-fired celadon stoneware condiment bottles with blue decoration designed by Donald Mills and made by Donald Mills Pottery Ltd. *(Photo: Ducrow.)*

5

6

Stoneware tea-set glazed with white inside cups and pot, and brown matt finish outside. Designed and made by Laura Andreson.

Stoneware tea-set and matching vase designed and made by Laura Andreson. Large plate with pink matt glaze: remainder white with red clay emphasizing texture.

7

8

Meadow Tree cup and saucer; *Cockerel* coffee pot; *Day Lily* cream jug; *Oak Leaf* cereal dish; and *Autumn Leaves* sugar bowl all designed by Walter Dorwin Teague and made by Taylor, Smith & Taylor Co.
(*Photo: Lucas and Monroe.*)

Encanto pattern in fine bone china designed by Mary K. Grant and produced by Gladding McBean & Co.

1. Silver-plated candlesticks, approximately 11½ in. high, designed by Aage Helbig Hansen and made by Alfenide Ltd, Dansk Forsølvnings Anstalt.

2. Silver-plated candle holders for candles of different thicknesses, or for use as flower bowls. Designed by Aage Helbig Hansen and made by Alfenide Ltd, Dansk Forsølvnings Anstalt.

3. Silver candelabra designed by T. Trier Morch and made by A. Michelsen.

4. Silver candelabra designed by Henning Koppel and made by Georg Jensen.

5. Brass candleholder, designed by Paavo Tynell and made by O/Y Taito A B.

6. Silver bread dish, candlestick and water pitcher with ivory handle designed by Svend Weihrauch and made by Frantz Hingelberg.

7. Silver candlesticks, chased and engraved, designed and made by R. E. Stone for The Goldsmiths & Silversmiths Company Ltd.
(Courtesy : Design and Research Centre for the Gold, Silver and Jewellery Industries.)

5

6   7

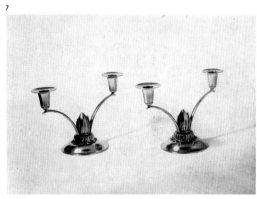

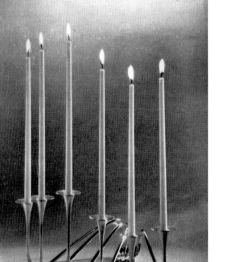

8. Silver condiment set designed by F. Piret and made by Adie Bros Ltd. Salt and mustard lined with blue glass. Ivory handle to mustard.

8

9. Silver candelabra designed by T. Trier Morch and made by A. Michelsen.

9

5. Silver-plated combined corkscrew and bottle-opener designed by Napier Associates and made by The Napier Company.

6. Silver tableware designed by Jacob Prytz and made by Tostrup.

1. *Loewy Modern* pattern stainless steel grade-rolled flatware designed by Raymond Loewy Associates and made by Diamond Silversmiths Ltd, a subsidiary of Ekco Products Company. (*Photo: Allen, Gordon, Schroeppel & Redlich Inc.*)

2, 3. Silver condiment set and sugar caster designed by Ib Bluitgen, and table silver designed by Harald Nielsen. Both made by Georg Jensen.

4. Silver-plated one-handed 'party servers,' each with a spoon for juices and either a flat side for serving sandwiches or a fork for straining liquids. Designed by Napier Associates and made by The Napier Company.

7 *Lily of the Valley* silver tableware, part of a large set in the same pattern, designed by H. Russell Price, and made by The Gorham Company. Grey *Feather* china with white motif, made by Glidden Pottery Inc.

8. Hand-made silver tableware designed by Sigurd Persson.
9. Stainless steel tableware, part of a 50-piece set, designed by Aage Helbig Hansen and made by Alfenide Ltd, Dansk Forsølvnings Anstalt.
10. Silver table spoons and forks designed by Svend Weihrauch and made by Frantz Hingelberg.

8

9

10

1. Silver vegetable dish with ivory-knobbed lid designed and made by Inger Moller.

2

2. Handwrought silver three-sided bowl designed and made by William De Hart.

3. Stainless steel cake dish designed by Sigurd Persson and made by AB Silver & Stål.

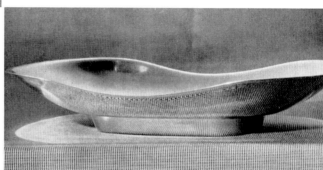

4

4. Silver bowls designed by Sven-Arne Gillgren and made by Guldsmeds Aktiebolaget i Stockholm, G A B.

3

5

5. Silver bowl and bonbonnière with ivory-knobbed lid, both designed by Karl Gustav Hansen and made by Hans Hansen Sølvsmedie A/S.

6. Silver and ivory dish with cover, carrot dish, sauce pitcher and ladle designed by Svend Weihrauch and made by Frantz Hingelberg.

6

7

7. Free form handwrought silver bowl on ebony feet designed and made by Frederick Miller.

8

8. Silver cake plate designed by H. P. Jacobsen and made by Carl M. Cohr's Sølvvarefabriker A/S.

9

9. Silver dish designed by H. P. Jacobsen and made by Carl M. Cohr's Sølvvarefabriker A/S.

10

10. Free form silver plate designed by H. P. Jacobsen and made by Carl M. Cohr's Sølvvarefabriker A/S.

1. Silver water pitcher with ivory handle designed by C. J. Antonsen and made by C. Antonsen.

2. Silver water pitcher 11 in. high with ivory handle designed by Sven Weihrauch and made by Frantz Hingelberg.

3. Silver coffee pot with wooden handle designed by H. P. Jacobsen and made by Carl M. Cohr's Sølvvarefabriker A/S.

2

1

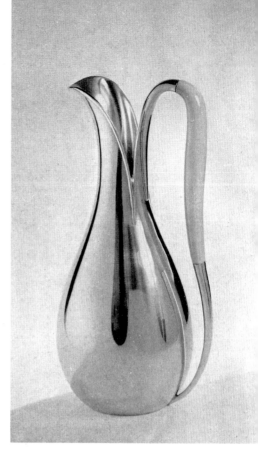

3

4. Hand-raised silver jug, natural grey finish, designed by W. P. Belk and made by Roberts & Belk Ltd.
   (Courtesy: Design and Research Centre for the Gold, Silver and Jewellery Industries.)

5. Silver sauceboat with ivory handle designed by H. P. Jacobsen and made by Carl M. Cohr's Sølvvarefabriker A/S.

4   5

6. Silver teapot with wicker handle and silver water jug designed by Karl Gustav Hansen and made by Hans Hansen Sølvsmedie A/S.

7. Silver demitasse coffee set, the pot with an ebony handle, designed by Karl Gustav Hansen and made by Hans Hansen Sølvsmedie A/S.

7

8

8. 1½-pint silver and ebony tea set designed by A. Edward Harvey, ARCA, LRIBA, and made by Hukin & Heath Ltd. (*Photo: B. P. Arnold, RBSA.*)

9. Silver tea caddy and combined teapot and hot-water jug designed by M. L. Stephensen and made by Kay Boyesen.

10. Silver tea set, the pot with plastic handles, designed by Arne Korsmo and made by Tostrup.

11. Silver coffee set with ebony handles and feet designed by Åge Erhard and made by Folmer Dalum of A. Dragsted A/S.

9

10   11

RIGHT: Polished brass centrepiece. Designer: Tommi Parzinger. Makers: Dorlyn (USA).

BELOW: Silver bowl, 15½ in. diameter. Designer: Henning Koppel. Maker: Georg Jensen (DENMARK).

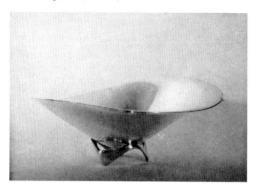

BELOW: Silver cigar and cigarette box engraved and engine-turned, with two cedar-lined compartments and ivory *Prometheus* figure. Designer and sculptor: A. Lucas. Makers: E. Silver (Bond Street) Ltd (GB).

Hand-made silver vase. Designer and maker: Sigurd Persson (SWEDEN).

Enamelled bowl decorated in transparent and opaque red. Designer and maker: Sigurd Persson (SWEDEN).

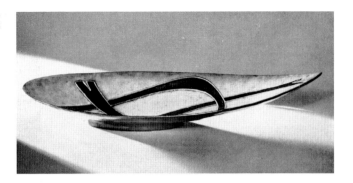

Enamelled bowl decorated in green and blue. Designer and maker: Sigurd Persson (SWEDEN).

BELOW: Silver candelabrum. Designer: E. C. Clements. Makers: Padgett & Braham Ltd (GB). (*Courtesy : Design and Research Centre for the Gold, Silver and Jewellery Industries.*)

Hand-made silver cigarette casket with engraved decoration, lined inside with black macassar ebony. Designer and maker: Robert E. Stone (GB).

Earthenware beer set in brown, yellow and black, the design inlaid. Designer and maker: Rachel Warner. Fabric in background designed and printed by Susan Warner (GB).

RIGHT: Silver jug. Designer: Henning Koppel. Maker: Georg Jensen (DENMARK).

BELOW: Glazed stoneware beer set, black, rust and oatmeal. Designer: Bernard Leach. Makers: The Leach Pottery team (GB).

White porcelain *Columba* ware. Designer: Arthur Percy. Makers: Upsala-Ekeby AB, Karlskrona Factory (SWEDEN).

Biscuit box, wine pitcher with ebony handle, and cups with blue enamel linings, all in sterling silver. Designer: Sven Weihrauch. Maker: Frantz Hingelberg (DENMARK).

LEFT: Sugar castor, whisky flagon and flower vase in highly-fired tin-glazed stoneware with blue, rust, yellow and green decoration. Designers: Donald and Jacqueline Mills. Makers: Donald Mills Pottery Ltd (GB).

BELOW: Silver cream and sugar set. Designer: A. Edward Harvey, ARCA, LRIBA. Prototype made by Mrs Maughan Harvey (GB). (Photo: B. P. Arnold, RBSA.)

Silver candelabrum designed by Karl Gustav Hansen.
Makers: Hans Hansen Sølvsmedie A/S (DENMARK)

Silver ice bucket. Designer: Sigvard Bernadotte.
Makers: Georg Jensen Silversmiths Ltd (DENMARK)

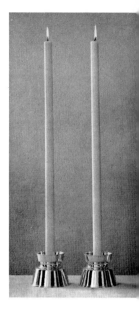

BELOW: Golden melon colour *Interplay* ovenproof china, *Arabesque* pattern, made by Iroquois China Company combined with *Etiquette* glass by Imperial Glass Corporation, *Bamboo* silver by Langbein & Co., and nasturtium orange napkins by John Matouk on a redwood table by Van-Kepple Green. Chairs by Fulbright Industries (USA)

Hand-made silver candlesticks. Designer and maker: Sigurd Persson (SWEDEN)

Trend sterling silver candlesticks usable singly or mounted one upon another. Designed by Gorham Designers. Makers: The Gorham Company (USA)

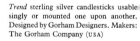

laque painted in gold and purple lustre with
n glaze. Designed and painted by Doris
arton MSIA (GB)

Dessert set in fine earthenware with hand-painted motif in copper,
green and grey or fawn and grey. Designer: Truda Carter ARCA.
Makers: Carter Stabler & Adams Ltd (GB)

Contemporary silver, china and Russel Wright's *Flare* pattern
tumblers available in four different colours and three sizes made by
Imperial Glass Corporation (USA)

ilver bowls designed by Karl Gustav Hansen.
Makers: Hans Hansen Sølvsmedie A/S (DENMARK)

Silver and ivory tea and coffee set. Designer:
Ibi Trier Morch. Maker: A. Michelsen
(DENMARK)

Silver and ebony tea and coffee set. Designer:
Karl Gustav Hansen. Makers: Hans Hansen
Sølvsmedie A/S (DENMARK)

ABOVE AND BELOW:
Silver Jugs. Designer: Henning Koppel.
Makers: Georg Jensen Silversmiths Ltd
(DENMARK)

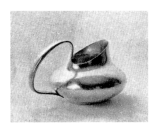

Interplay coffee set in fine china, available in two solid colours and three different patterns. ABOVE: *Charcoal* jug and saucers used with *Arabesque* cups. Makers: Iroquois China Company (USA)

LEFT: Faience tableware for everyday use, yellow on cream glaze. Designer: Nils Thorsson. Makers: The Royal Copenhagen Porcelain Factory (DENMARK)

BELOW: Heat-resistant *Princess* tableware of thin lightweight opal glass. Makers: Corning Glass Works (USA)

Silver sugar sifter and condiment set. Designer: Ib Bluitgen. Makers: Georg Jensen Silversmiths Ltd (DENMARK)

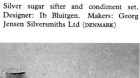

ABOVE: Denby ovenware available in meadow green with cream glazed interior, cottage blue with yellow glaze, and mahogany brown with pale lavender glaze. The complete set of eighty-six pieces (all sold singly) covers a wide range from casseroles and serving dishes to plates, cups and saucers, all usable from oven to table. Makers: Joseph Bourne & Son Ltd (GB)
(*Photo: Courtesy of Harrods Ltd.*)

Streamline tableware in fine earthenware finished *Twintone* two-colour eggshell glaze, available in various colour combinations. Plates in background designed by Poole Design Unit. Other pieces by John Adams ARCA. Makers: Carter Stabler & Adams Ltd (GB)

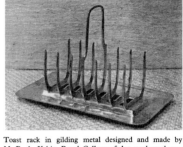

Tin-glazed plaque painted in blues, green and orange with gold outline, motif based on Persian paintings. Designer: Doris Parton MSIA. Makers: T. G. Green & Co. Ltd (GB)

BELOW: *Sienna* dinnerware, translucent white tin glaze over red-brown clay body intentionally left exposed on the rims. Makers: Keramik Manufaktur Kupfermuehle. (GERMANY) *U.S.: Frasers Inc.*

ABOVE: *Vogue* pattern earthenware with coffee brown or mist green glaze. Designer: Alf Rosen. Makers: Universal Potteries (USA)

Silver tureen with bound white plastic handles. Designer: Arne Erkers. Makers: Just Andersen A/S (DENMARK)

BELOW: *Twin Oaks* dinner and tea service. White china with the motif in two shades of green, pink and brown. Makers: The Edwin M. Knowles China Company (USA)

Cider jar, 14 inches high, buff body with iron brush decoration, inside glazed. Designer and maker: F. G. Cooper (GB)

BELOW: Coffee pot, cup and saucer, flat-sided vase and small dish in fine earthenware with copper carbonate glaze (green breaking to metallic black). Designer: Murray Fieldhouse. Makers: Pendley Pottery (GB)

Stoneware teapot with wood ash glaze. Designer and maker: H. R. Stone (GB)

Photo: F. Hague

Pewter jug designed by Ellen Schlanbusch.
Makers: Just Andersen A/S (DENMARK)

Early morning teaset, resist white stripe on
solid bronze ground. Designer: S. C. Talbot.
Makers: A. E. Gray & Co Ltd (GB)

Earthenware teapot, cream glaze with iron
slip-trailed decoration. Designer and maker:
F. G. Cooper (GB)

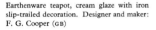

ABOVE: Pewter tea and coffee service. Designer: Ellen Schlanbusch. Makers: Just Andersen A/S (DENMARK)

LEFT: Sauce and salt boats, sterling silver exteriors and gilt
interiors. Designer and maker: E. G. Clements, Royal College
of Art (GB)

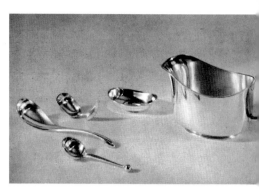

Sterling silver ladles, sweet dish and sauce boat with insulated cane handle. Designer: Karl Gustav Hansen. Makers: Hans Hansen Sølvsmedie A/S (DENMARK)

Amulett dinner set in white earthenware with blue or red decoration. Designer: William Kåge. Makers: A B Gustavsberg Fabriker (SWEDEN)

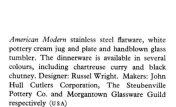

Dana stainless steel child's spoon, fork and pusher. Designer: Aage Helbig Hansen. Makers: A/S Alfenide, Dansk Forsølvnings Anstalt (DENMARK)

American Modern stainless steel flatware, white pottery cream jug and plate and handblown glass tumbler. The dinnerware is available in several colours, including chartreuse curry and black chutney. Designer: Russel Wright. Makers: John Hull Cutlers Corporation, The Steubenville Pottery Co. and Morgantown Glassware Guild respectively (USA)

Stoneware oil or vinegar bottle with ground stopper. In celadon, black or grey-blue glazes. Designers: Harry and May Davis. Makers: Crowan Pottery (GB)

BELOW: White porcelain plates, hand-decorated by Leone Plard on a white muslin tablecloth. Stainless steel cutlery with Plexiglass handles. Gilded copper candle holders, green metal centrepiece and green glassware. Setting arranged by Colette Gueden for Primavera (FRANCE)

Stainless steel fork, knife and spoon, also made in silver or electroplate. Their size is unusual—between dinner and dessert length. Designer: Voss. Maker: C. Hugo Pott (GERMANY)

Silver spoons, knife and fork. Designer: Ole Hagen. Makers: A. Michelsen (DENMARK)

Stainless steel flatware. Designer: Sigurd Persson. Makers: Silver & Stål (SWEDEN)

Brass candlesticks with foliage decoration. White porcelain doves. White porcelain dinner service by Gustavsberg Fabriker and glasses by Strömbergshyttan. Silver cutlery with ebony handles; rush mat table cover. Table decorations and cutlery designed and made by Svenskt Tenn AB (SWEDEN)

Silver condiment set. Designer: Ib Bluitgen. Makers: Georg Jensen Silversmiths Ltd (DENMARK)

Gold-tooled leather napkin rings on metal bases. Designer and maker: James S. Taylor, ARCA (GB)

ABOVE: The *Holiday* ceramic pepper mill and salt shakers, hand-painted in dark green, chartreuse or burgundy on a cream ground, tops of stainless steel. Designer: Olde Thompson. Makers: George S. Thompson Corporation (USA)

Bread trays carved in light maple, available with movable or fixed handles. Designer and maker: Laur. Jensen (DENMARK)

LEFT: Spun silver wine goblets and silver condiment set with fluted covers. Designer and maker: Robert G. Clark, Des. RCA, MSIA (GB)
(*Courtesy: Mr. and Mrs. George Clark*)

Plate from the *Forest Glade* dinner, tea or coffee set in fine bone china with slightly conventionalized flower design in natural colours. Designer: Eric W. Slater. Makers: Shelley Potteries Ltd (GB)

Leaf pattern plate available in dinner, tea or coffee ware in pastel shades of grey-green, chrome-green or pink, the surround hand done on the wheel in grey-green, and the outline of the leaf accentuated in the same colour. Designer: Eric W. Slater. Makers: Shelley Potteries Ltd (GB)

LEFT: Prototype muffin dish in gilding metal with rosewood insulated handle incorporating decorative use of rivets, and above it a silver sauceboat with carved rosewood handles. Designers and makers: Eric G. Clements, Des. RCA, MSIA, T. J. Boucher and H. A. Lock (GB)
(*Photo: Peter Parkinson*)

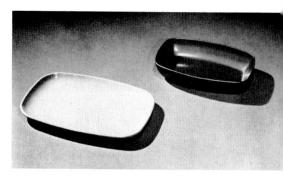

ABOVE : Melamine plastic *Maplex* or *Evermaid* serving platter in chartreuse and vegetable bowl in dark green. Both available in other colours. Designers and makers : Maple Leaf Plastics Ltd (CANADA).

BELOW : Silver flower or fruit bowl with candle-holders. Designer: Arne Erkers. Makers: Just Andersen A/S (DENMARK)

Salier china dinner service hand-decorated in gold, turquoise and grey-violet by Sigrid von Unruh. Shape designed by Siegmund Schütz. Makers: Staatliche Porzellan-Manufaktur Berlin (GERMANY)

Gratina ovenware designed by Gunnar Nylund and made by A B Rörstrands Porslinsfabriker (SWEDEN) Background fabric is an all-cotton screen print, *Hedgerow*, with nigger brown motif on piece-dyed grounds in colour shown, or on green, mulberry or grey. Designer: Mary Beard. Makers: Scatchard's Fabrics Ltd (G B)

Stainless steel fruit or bread servers. Designer: Folke Arström. Makers: A/B Gense (SWEDEN)

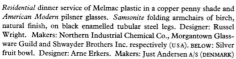

Residential dinner service of Melmac plastic in a copper penny shade and *American Modern* pilsner glasses. *Samsonite* folding armchairs of birch, natural finish, on black enamelled tubular steel legs. Designer: Russel Wright. Makers: Northern Industrial Chemical Co., Morgantown Glassware Guild and Shwayder Brothers Inc. respectively (USA). BELOW: Silver fruit bowl. Designer: Arne Erkers. Makers: Just Andersen A/S (DENMARK)

Gabriella faience dinner, coffee and tea ware with blue outer band and centre motif. Designer: Nils Thorsson. Makers: The Royal Copenhagen Porcelain Factory (DENMARK). BELOW: Vases in sterling silver with engraved lineal designs. Designed and made by Barbro Littmarck for W. A. Bolin (SWEDEN)

Gold-rimmed *Vintage* china on *Accent* shape in burgundy and grey with sepia tracing. Designed and made by The Edwin M. Knowles China Company (USA)

Dana stainless steel candelabra. Designer: Aage Helbig Hansen. Makers: A/s Alfenide, Dansk Forsølvnings Anstalt (DENMARK)

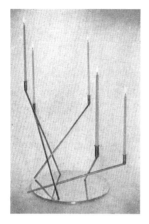

Stoneware sweetmeat dishes with pale blue ash glazes. Designer and maker: Eleanor Whittall (GB)

Salt and pepper set in sterling silver, the handle tops inset with moonstones and topaz. Designer and maker: Birger Haglund (SWEDEN)

Circular footed bowl and dessert plates finished in *Alpine* semi-matt off-white glaze. Hand-painted decorations in the Delft technique. Half of the set in green and grey, remainder in coral pink and grey. Designer: Truda Carter, ARCA. Makers: Carter, Stabler & Adams Ltd (GB)

Shelley china tankard and ashtray with sgraffito design on various coloured grounds and burnished gold tracing on handle and foot of tankard. Designer: Eric W. Slater. Makers: Shelley Potteries Ltd (GB)

Spiral fern leaf decoration in avocado green on tea and dinner ware. Designer: Susan V. Cooper, RDI. Makers: The Susie Cooper Pottery Ltd (GB)

Dana stainless steel dish with teak handles. The lid can also be used as a dish. Designer: Aage Helbig Hansen. Makers: A/s Alfenide, Dansk Forsølvnings Anstalt (DENMARK)

Pottery beer mugs available in black, dark brown, light brown, green or blue. Designer: G. Beaudin. Makers: Decor Pottery Reg'd (CANADA)

Sterling silver coffee set, the handles of the coffee
pot bound with plastic. Designer: Sigvard Bernadotte. Makers: Georg Jensen Silversmiths Ltd
(DENMARK)

Stainless steel pitcher. Designer: Folke Arström.
Makers: A/B Gense (SWEDEN)

Hand-made silver coffee service, including a
square sugar box. The handle of the pot is
mahogany. Designed and made by Sigurd
Persson (SWEDEN)

Dana stainless steel coffee set with teak handles.
Designer: Aage Helbig Hansen. Makers: A/S
Alfenide, Dansk Forsølvnings Anstalt (DENMARK)

Contour silver candlesticks, sugar bowl, cream pitcher and beverage server with black polystyrene handle. Designer: John Van Koert. Makers: The Towle Silversmiths (USA)

BELOW: Silver iced-water jug with ebony handle. Designer: Sigvard Bernadotte. Makers: Georg Jensen Silversmiths Ltd (DENMARK)

Sterling silver tea set with handles of wicker. Designer: Henning Koppel. Makers: Georg Jensen Silversmiths Ltd (DENMARK). RIGHT: One of a pair of silver coffee pots with handle bound in leather. Designer and maker: Eric G. Clements, Des. RCA, MSIA (GB) (*Photo: Peter Parkinson*)

LEFT: Plain shapes in celadon, lavender, or Windsor grey self-coloured fine earthenware. Makers: Josiah Wedgwood & Sons Ltd (GB). BELOW: *Pastella* fine domestic earthenware in blue, green or yellow glazes. Designer: Stig Lindberg. Makers: AB Gustavsberg Fabriker (SWEDEN)

ABOVE: *Krokus* coffee service in white porcelain rimmed with gold or purple. Designer: Hubert Griemert. Makers: Staatliche Porzellan-Manufaktur Berlin (GERMANY). RIGHT: *Script* tea and dinner plates from the new range of *Continental* porcelain tableware made in four harmonious and interchangeable designs. Designers: Raymond Loewy Associates. Makers: Rosenthal-Porzellan AG (GERMANY) for the Block China Corporation of New York (USA)

LEFT: Soup cup and saucer, and pint beer mug in fine earthenware with mushroom and white glazes breaking to red body combination. Designer: Murray Fieldhouse. Makers: Pendley Pottery (GB) *(Photo: Pottery Quarterly)*

BELOW: *Residential* dinnerware, sea mist colour, made of Melmac plastic by Northern Industrial Chemical Co; *Flare* glasses made by Imperial Glass Corporation; and *American Modern* stainless steel flatware made by John Hull Cutlers Corporation. All designed by Russel Wright (USA)

Walnut salad bowl, 12 inches wide, on brass stand 7 inches high. Designer: Tommi Parzinger. Makers: Dorlyn Silversmiths (USA). BELOW: Hand-decorated salad service caddy, chrome details, white enamelled iron rack. Designer: Olde Thompson. Makers: George S. Thompson Corporation (USA)

Serving spoons and forks in teak and beech. Designed and made by Nanny Still (FINLAND)

Silver salt and pepper shakers. Designer: Hans Henriksen. Makers: Georg Jensen Silversmiths Ltd (DENMARK)

Silver condiment set. Designed and made by K. W. Lessons at the Royal College of Art (GB). (*Courtesy: The Worshipful Company of Goldsmiths*)

Silver-topped condiment set in blue crystal glass. Designed and made by Robert Welch at the Royal College of Art (GB) (*Courtesy: The Worshipful Company of Goldsmiths*)

Beaten silver engraved sugar sifter spoons. Designed and made by Robert Welch (GB) *(Courtesy: The Worshipful Company of Goldsmiths)*

Prototype stainless steel knife, fork and spoon, with black plastic handles. Designed by H. Batelaan (HOLLAND)

RIGHT: Silver hors d'oeuvre set designed by Magnus Stephensen. Makers: Georg Jensen Silversmiths Ltd (DENMARK)

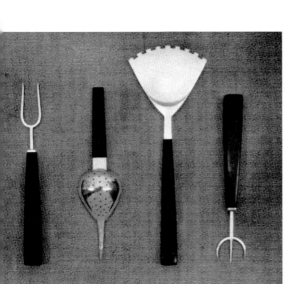

Table silver with palissander handles. Designer: Bertel Gardberg (FINLAND)

Stainless steel flatware. Designer: Acton Bjørn. Makers: Dansk Knivfabrik (DENMARK)

Double tea jugs in faience, decorated in black, grey and blue. Designer: Stig Lindberg. Makers: AB Gustavsbergs Fabriker (SWEDEN)

BELOW: Earthenware jugs and small mug in green, yellow and blue glazes; hand decorated white jug. Designer John Andersson. Makers: Andersson & Johansson (SWEDEN)

ABOVE: Sterling silver teapot with shaped buffalo-horn handle, and matching sugar basin and milk jug. Designer: Karl Gustav Hansen. Makers: Hans Hansen Sølvsmedie A/S (DENMARK)

ABOVE: 'LF' coffee set in white bone china. Designer: Stig Lindberg. Makers: AB Gustavsbergs Fabriker (SWEDEN)

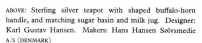

LEFT: Stainless steel coffee set with ebony handles. Designer: Magnus Stephensen. Makers: Georg Jensen Silversmiths Ltd (DENMARK)

LEFT: Coffee pot, cup and saucer in undecorated feldspar china. Designer: Carl-Harry Stålhane. Makers: AB Rörstrands Porslinsfabriker (SWEDEN).

Earthenware teapot, black glaze, with twin jampot and 'television' cup, saucer and plate combination in white and yellow. Designed and made by Axel Brüel (DENMARK)

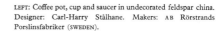

BELOW: Porcelain tea- and coffee-ware in ivory or celadon green. Designers and makers: Porzellanfabrik Langethal AG in collaboration with the Schweizer Werkbund (SWITZERLAND) (*Photo: Hans Finsler*)

White porcelain coffee set with underglaze *Cornflower* decoration in blue and black. Designer: Ebbe Sadolin. Makers: Bing & Grøndahls Porcellænfabrik A/S (DENMARK). BELOW: Silver and ivory coffee set designed by Svend Weihrauch. Makers: Frantz Hingelberg (DENMARK)

Sterling silver wine pitchers. Designer: Svend Weihrauch. Makers: Frantz Hingelberg (DENMARK). RIGHT: Fine bone china coupe shape rimless plate. Grey on-glaze print and freehand platinum decoration *Wild Oats*; available in tea, dinner or coffeeware. Designer: Victor Skellern. Makers: Josiah Wedgwood & Sons Ltd (GB)

Gold-rimmed fine bone china coupe-shaped dinner plate from the *Pinehurst* service, decorated grey on-glaze print and free-hand gold painting. Designer: Millicent Taplin, MSIA. Makers: Josiah Wedgwood & Sons Ltd (GB)

ABOVE: Decorated earthenware dishes in blue and white: fish dish with majolica decoration in brown, yellow and green. Designed and made by Audrey Samuel (GB)

Sterling silver vases and/or candleholder. Designed by Arne Erkers—those at FAR LEFT in collaboration with Ellen Schlanbusch. Makers: Just Andersen A/S (DENMARK)

Queensware *Travel* dinner service decorated black print and hand enamelling. Designer: Eric Ravilious. LEFT: *Partridge in a Pear Tree*. On-glaze litho print and gold hand enamelling on white coupe shape. Both sets are made by Josiah Wedgwood & Sons Ltd (GB). BELOW: White earthenware *Moderne* shape, black print and hand-painted decoration. Designer: S. C. Talbot. Makers: A. E. Gray & Co. Ltd (GB)

BELOW: *Spisa-Terma* coffee pot in flame-proof earthenware. Designer: Stig Lindberg. Makers: AB Gustavsbergs Fabriker (SWEDEN)

ABOVE: *Classic Modern* china-porcelain tableware decorated in various motifs; shown is *Plaza*. Designers: Raymond Loewy Associates. Makers: The Rosenthal-Block China Corporation (USA)

ABOVE: *Contemporary* Hand-decorated ovenproof kitchenware. Colours: Bluish-green on grey with white. Designer: Charles Murphy. Makers: Red Wing Potteries (USA)

ABOVE: Earthenware tableware in plain black and green, or with yellow/grey pattern on a white body. Designer: Carl-Harry Stålhane. Makers: AB Rörstrands Porslinsfabriker (SWEDEN)

Black slipware; turquoise, yellow or white stripes. Designer: Peter Draper. Makers: The Milton Head Pottery (GB)

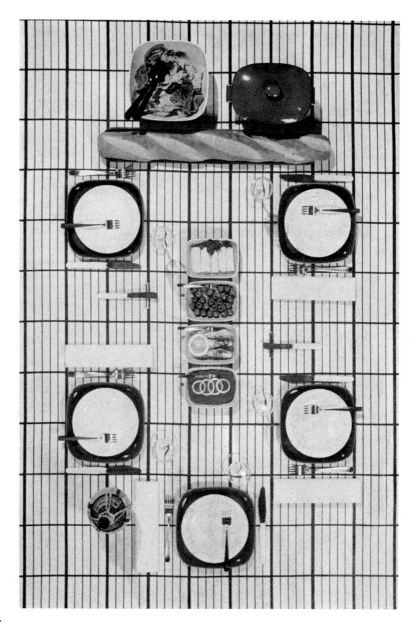

RIGHT: Luncheon table set with
Gratina, *Arena* and *Dala* fine
earthenware plates and dishes.
Designer: Gunnar Nylund.
Makers: AB Rörstrands Pors-
linsfabriker (SWEDEN)

Stylecraft salad ware in semi-porcelain Staffordshire china, underglaze decoration. Shapes designed by Roy Midwinter; decoration by Terence Conran. Makers: W. R. Midwinter Ltd (GB)

BELOW: 'Hen' casserole in earthenware, brown glaze with raised yellow spots. Designer: Kaarina Aho. Makers: O/Y Wärtsilä-concern AB Arabia (FINLAND)

LEFT: Fine china salad service, black and white glaze. Designer: Trude Petri-Raben. Makers: Staatliche Porzellan-Manufaktur Berlin (GERMANY)

ABOVE: White porcelain tableware, on glaze decoration in matt gold. Shape designed by Dr. H. Gretsch (GERMANY); decoration by Jean Luce (FRANCE). Makers: Porzellanfabrik Arzberg (GERMANY). RIGHT: Hard-fired kitchenware, yellow or manganese brown glazes. Designer: John Andersson. Makers: Andersson & Johansson AB (SWEDEN)

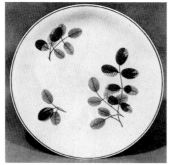

A table is laid with a mixture of breakables and unbreakables. The breakables need periodical replacement, either piecemeal or in sets, whereas the steel and silver pieces are far more likely to survive as eventual heirlooms. This need not imply that cutlery is immune to design changes whereas china is not, but it does point to inevitable differences in design outlook. Knives, forks and spoons must be given long-term consideration if they are to harmonise with whatever the future may bring to the design of the breakable pieces destined to accompany them.

Because of the more rapid turnover in chinaware, it would appear that greater scope exists for changes in design than with cutlery, and yet the silver of today has moved a long way from the traditional outlook which has characterised so much of the recent output, particularly in Britain. Nevertheless in Britain, too, there appears to be a growing realisation that the heirlooms of tomorrow will be the designs of today and not the rehashed legacies of yesterday. Several young designers are showing considerably more enterprise than in the immediate past, but they still have some way to go before they are likely to challenge the supremacy of a country like Denmark.

Virility in design should not ignore tradition but, by pursuing it, it will cease to be virile. The receptiveness of the eye changes with time and environment, but the design, even of traditionally based crafts such as tableware, must feed the eye with what it needs. There is always scope at least for subtle variations of shape conditioned by environment while allied to the infinite possibilities of surface treatment, and these are the designers' main weapons for enhancing the pleasures of dining.

ABOVE RIGHT: *Summer Sky* fine earthenware (Queen's Ware) pale blue and white dinner service in the Barlaston shape. The pieces are made from two-colour clays permanently fused in the firing. Designers and makers: Josiah Wedgwood & Sons Ltd (GB)

RIGHT: Milk glass tableware, ashtray and sweet dish with heart pattern border. Designer: Gunnar Ander. Makers: AB Lindshammars Glasbruk (SWEDEN)

ABOVE: Salad servers in black Melamine. Designer: Herbert Krenchel. Makers: Torben Ørskov & Co. (DENMARK)

ABOVE: Stainless steel knife and tea-spoon; enamel inlay to handles. Designer: Arne Korsmo, Arch. MNAL. Makers: Cathrineholms Emaljefabrik (NORWAY)

ABOVE: Silverplated tableware with hollowed-out handles. Designer: Arne Korsmo, Arch. MNAL. Makers: Tostrup (NORWAY)

BELOW: Hand-carved scoops and mixing spoon in holly. Designer and maker: Robert J. Martin (GB)

ABOVE: Ovenproof earthenware dishes and casseroles in dark red and yellow glazes. Designer: Sven Erik Skawonius. Makers: The Upsala-Ekeby Group, Ekebybruk (SWEDEN)

Salt and pepper shakers and mustard pot; tin glazed, with majolica decoration in soft olive-green and fine black stripes. Designed and made by Powell & Wells Studio Pottery (GB)

One-and-a-quarter and two-quart jugs in aluminium, bakelite handles. Designer: Erik Herløw, Arch. m.a.a. Makers: Dansk Aluminium Industri A/S (DENMARK)

ABOVE: *Black Princess* dinner service in stoneware, black/white glaze. Designer: F. Meydam. Makers: Kunstaardewerkfabriek 'Regina' (HOLLAND)

Taverna fine earthenware dinner service with on-glaze printed decoration, and matt green casserole. The coffee cup and saucer are from the *Inca* service in feldspar china. Designer: Carl-Harry Stålhane. Makers: AB Rörstrands Porslinsfabriker (SWEDEN)

ABOVE: *Blanca* undecorated dinnerware in white feldspar china. Designer: Carl-Harry Stålhane. Makers: AB Rörstrands Porslinsfabriker (SWEDEN). BELOW: Fine bone china teaware decorated black print *Prelude* on Sapphire shape, with matt black saucer. White sculptural form vase with black decoration. Designers and makers: Ridgway Potteries Ltd (GB)

ABOVE: Ivory porcelain dinner service with fine gold rim and gold monogram. The square-based *Bandol* glasses are in clear crystal. Designers and makers: Maison Rouard (FRANCE)

Stainless steel toast rack. Designer: Robert Welch, Des.RCA, MSIA. Makers: J. & J. Wiggin Ltd (GB)

RIGHT: Salad servers, potato spoon, and forks for cold meats, in stainless steel. Designer: Magnus Stephensen. Makers: Georg Jensen Silversmiths Ltd (GB)

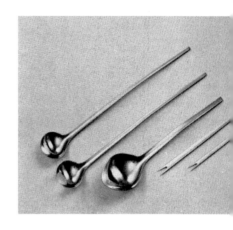

BELOW: Hand-wrought sterling silver engraved wine bowl and serving spoon; the lower part of the bowl is gilded and burnished. Designer and maker: Birger Haglund (SWEDEN)

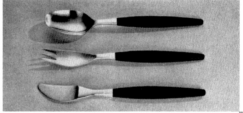

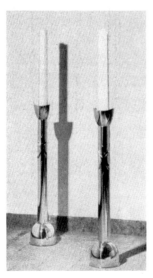

ABOVE: Stainless steel flatware with black nylon handles. Designer: Folke Arström. Makers: AB Gense (SWEDEN). RIGHT: Hors-d'œuvre fork in silver and rosewood. BELOW LEFT: Fish knife and fork in silver. Designer and maker: Bertel Gardberg (FINLAND). BELOW RIGHT: Flatware in stainless steel. Designer: Magnus Stephensen. Makers: Georg Jensen Silversmiths Ltd (DENMARK)

ABOVE: Floor candlesticks of smooth-ground brass. Designer: Arne Nilsson. Makers: Hans-Agne Jakobsson AB (SWEDEN)

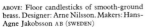

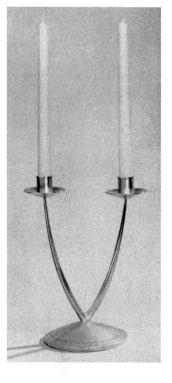

ABOVE: *Kongelys* silver-plated cutlery with engraved tapered handle ends. Designer: Henning Seidelin. Makers: A/s P. C. L. Frigast Sølvvarefabrik (DENMARK)

LEFT: *Charlotte* cutlery in sterling silver. Designer: Karl Gustav Hansen. Makers: Hans Hansen Sølvsmedie (DENMARK)

ABOVE: Branched candleholder in sterling silver, engraved base. Designer and maker: Gerald Benney (GB) (*Courtesy: The Worshipful Company of Goldsmiths*)

Ultra flatware in sterling silver. Designer and maker: Sigurd Persson (SWEDEN)

Black-glazed earthenware coffee jug, with television set in grey tin glaze. Designed and made by Axel Brüel (DENMARK)

ABOVE: Hand-wrought coffee set in sterling silver; handle in rosewood. Designer and maker: Sigurd Persson (SWEDEN)

BELOW: Fine earthenware coffee pot and plate with hand-painted majolica decoration in lime, blue, tan and fine black lines on tin glaze. Designed and made by Powell & Wells Studio Pottery (GB)

Inca coffee service in white feldspar china with dark green—almost black—decoration. Designer: Carl-Harry Stålhane. Makers: AB Rörstrands Porslinsfabriker (SWEDEN)

RIGHT: *Select* undecorated white feldspar china coffee service. Designer: Sylvia Leuchowius. Makers: AB Rörstrands Porslinsfabriker (SWEDEN)

White porcelain jug and beaker/plate combination, hand-decorated in black, green, blue and other colours. Shape designed by Sven Erik Skawonius; decoration by Eva Bland. Makers: The Upsala-Ekeby Group, Karlskrona Factory (SWEDEN)

ABOVE: Television set, sugar bowl, and stacking teapots in multi-coloured faience. Designer: Stig Lindberg. Makers: AB Gustavsbergs Fabriker (SWEDEN)

RIGHT: Hand-thrown earthenware early morning tea set; white tin glaze, turquoise decoration. Designed by Brigitta Appleby. Made by Briglin Pottery Ltd (GB)

ABOVE: Teaware in white porcelain with slight flute decoration. Designer: Sigvard Bernadotte. Makers: A/S Bing & Grøndahls Porcellænsfabrik (DENMARK)

ABOVE: Hand-thrown stoneware coffee and teapot in greenish russet and brick red/russet ash glazes on dark body. Designed and made by Dorothy Kemp (GB)

ABOVE: Fine earthenware coffee service, off-white semi-matt glaze, sepia contrast; *Blue Tulip* in-glaze decoration in blue, grey and brown designed by Truda Carter, ARCA and Ruth Pavely. Makers: Carter, Stabler & Adams Ltd (GB)

Hand-thrown early morning teaset; white tin glaze with black oxide contrast. Designer: Brigitta Appleby. Made by Briglin Pottery Ltd (GB)

BELOW: Coffee or tea service in polished brass or pewtertone finish, with metal-lined lids in 'Wengee' wood to match tray. Custom made in Denmark for Raymor (USA)

ABOVE: Coffee service in silver plate with plastic bound handle to pot. Designer: Heinz Decker. Makers: C. G. Hallbergs Guldsmeds AB (SWEDEN)

ABOVE: *Siam* tea service in red clay ware; cup glazed white with yellow band decoration. Designer: Carl-Harry Stålhane. BELOW: *Rosmarin* tea service in earthenware; pink exterior glaze, white inside. Designer: Hertha Bengtson. Both designs are made by AB Rörstrands Porslinsfabriker (SWEDEN)

LEFT: Porcelain teaware, colourless glaze, hand-decorated onglaze in black and white with orange cup. Designed and made by D. Duszniak, Warsaw Institute of Industrial Design (POLAND)

RIGHT: Stoneware teapot, celadon glaze. Designer: Jørgen Mogensen. Makers: The Royal Copenhagen Porcelain Manufactory A/S (DENMARK)

LEFT: Stoneware teapot. White glaze with onglaze red iron brush decoration. Designed and made by F. G. Cooper, MSIA (GB)

BELOW: *Gourmet* ovenproof earthenware; white, with 'grill' decoration in green, yellow or brown. Designers: Stig Lindberg and Bibi Breger. Made by AB Gustavsbergs Fabriker (SWEDEN)

ABOVE: Dinner service in white feldspar china, 'ripple' decoration. Designer: Sven Erik Skawonius. Makers: The Upsala-Ekeby Group, Ekebybruk (SWEDEN)

ABOVE: *Krenit* steel enamelled frying pan with detachable Bakelite handle. Made in three sizes: 6, 8 and 10-inch diameter, and in different colour combinations for each size. Designed and made by Herbert Krenchel (DENMARK). LEFT: *Patella* ovenproof porcelain in yellow, rusty brown and speckled brown glazes. Designer: Magnus Stephensen, MAA. Makers: The Royal Copenhagen Porcelain Manufactory A/S (DENMARK)

LEFT: Aluminium saucepan with black-anodised lid; lid knob in white bakelite, handle in black. Designer. Erik Herløw, M A A. Makers: Dansk Aluminium Industri A/S (DENMARK). BELOW LEFT: Hand-made stainless steel fruit dish, 7½ × 9 inches. Designed and made by John Grenville (GB). (*Courtesy: The Worshipful Company of Goldsmiths*). BELOW CENTRE. Flatware in stainless steel. Designer: Arne Jacobsen, M A A. Makers: A. Michelsen (DENMARK)

Candlestick in silver or in polished brass, on teak base. Designer: Sven Aage Holm Sørensen. Made by Holm Sørensen & Co. (DENMARK)

Hand-thrown salad bowl, 14 inches diameter; quart soup flagon, with matching soup cup and saucer. Designed and made by Susan Lane at Ways Ware Pottery (GB)

LEFT: Lobster fork in stainless steel. Also made in sterling or plated silver. Designer: Sigurd Persson (SWEDEN). Makers: Württembergische Metallwarenfabrik (GERMANY)

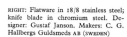

RIGHT: Flatware in 18/8 stainless steel; knife blade in chromium steel. Designer: Gustaf Janson. Makers: C. G. Hallbergs Guldsmeds AB (SWEDEN)

LEFT: Flatware design No. 2722 in 18/8 stainless steel. Designer: Carl Pott. Makers: C. Hugo Pott (GERMANY)

RIGHT: Silver-plated dessert and table spoons. Designed by Bertel Gardberg. For Hackmann & Co. (FINLAND)

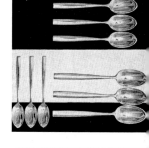

LEFT: *Pilét* kitchen knives: mirror-polished stainless steel, serrated edge; rosewood handles assembled by expansion rivets to an inseparable unity with blade. In three sizes and, alternatively, for left-hand use. Designer: Henning Nørgaard. Makers: Raadvad Cutlery Works Ltd (DENMARK)

LEFT: *Eton* flatware in 18/8 stainless steel, knife in chromium steel; celluloid handles in ivory or other colours, or in imitation mother-of-pearl, or pallisander wood. Designer: Henning Nørgaard. Makers: Raadvad Cutlery Works Ltd (DENMARK)

RIGHT: Engraved punch ladle in sterling silver and whalebone. Designed and made by K. W. Lessons at the Royal College of Art (GB)

LEFT: Flatware design No. 111 in sterling silver. Designer: Henning Koppel. Makers: Georg Jensen Sølvsmedie A/S (DENMARK)

RIGHT: Silver-plated flatware. Designed by Bertel Gardberg. For Hackmann & Co. (FINLAND)

LEFT: Condiment set in stainless steel. Designer: Robert Welch, Des.RCA, MSIA. Made by J. & J. Wiggin Ltd (GB) (*Photo: C.o.I.D.*)

RIGHT: Serving set in sterling silver with black lignum vitae handles. Designer: Mauno Honkanen. Made by Koruteollisuus Tillander (FINLAND)

LEFT: Hors d'oeuvres set in sterling silver, including mayonnaise spoon, herring fork, sardine server, salmon fork, olive spoon and tomato knife. Designer: Vagn Åge Hemmingsen. Made by Franz Hingelberg (DENMARK)

RIGHT: Steel knife with glass handle and gilt mounts. Designed and made by Robert Welch, Des.RCA, MSIA (GB) (*Courtesy: The Worshipful Company of Goldsmiths*)

LEFT: Soup serving spoon in stainless steel. Designed by Bertel Gardberg. For Hackmann & Co. (FINLAND)

RIGHT: *Pilét* kitchen forks in mirror-polished stainless steel with rosewood handles; of similar construction to knives shown opposite. Designer: Henning Nørgaard. Makers: Raadvad Cutlery Works Ltd (DENMARK)

ABOVE: Stainless steel casserole with copper bottom and ebony handle; capacity 4 pints. Designer: Magnus Stephensen. Makers: Georg Jensen Sølvsmedie A/S (DENMARK)

Fiesta moulded Melmex tableware in 'House & Garden' colours. Designed with heavy sections and tapered edges, it is of pleasant weight and good appearance. Designer: Ronald E. Brookes, MSIA. Makers: Brookes & Adams Ltd (GB)

ABOVE: Queen's Ware permanently fused two-colour tableware, *Summer Sky* (blue and white) and *Havana* (lilac brown and white) in the Barlaston shape. Designer: Norman Wilson. Makers: Josiah Wedgwood & Sons Ltd (GB)

Handmade sterling silver beakers, height $5\frac{1}{2}$ inches, chased decoration filled with multicoloured enamels. Designer: Barbro Littmarck. Makers: W. A. Bolin (SWEDEN)

Oven-proof individual soup bowl in stoneware; unglazed exterior with iron decoration, interior white or grey-green glaze. Designed and made by Harry and May Davis at Crowan Pottery (GB)

Vegetable dish in stainless steel, 9-inch diameter. It is made in eight different sizes. Designer and maker: S. A. Sartel (BELGIUM)

BELOW: Mottled green/white hand-thrown beaker; oxide decoration under white tin glaze. Height: 5 inches. Designer: Brigitta Appleby. Made by Briglin Pottery Ltd (GB)

ABOVE: *Form 2000* white porcelain tableware with gold trim and rose silhouette printed decoration in sepia. Designer: Raymond Loewy. Made by Rosenthal-Porzellan AG (GERMANY). BELOW: *Waterflowers* onglaze enamel screen transfer decoration in yellow, new-leaf green, beige, dark grey-green and peat-brown on fine white earthenware. Designed and executed by Johnson, Matthey & Co. Ltd (GB)

◀ Yellow-glazed earthenware curry bowls designed by Hertha Bengtson. Makers: AB Rörstrands Porslins-fabriker (SWEDEN)

Earthenware 'Fish' plates, hand-painted multicolour decoration. Designed by Gunvar Olin. Makers: O/Y Wärtsilä-concern Arabia (FINLAND)

Cayenne red clay ovenware; reddish-brown and black exterior glaze, bone-white interior glaze. Designer: Hertha Bengtson. Makers: AB Rör-strands Porslinsfabriker (SWEDEN)

Fine earthenware plates with hand-painted underglaze decoration; centre plate, yellow; those at left, lilac-brown and brown-black; right-hand plate, blue-white. Designed by Stig Lindberg. Makers: AB Gustavsbergs Fabriker (SWEDEN)

Casserole dish in 18/8 stainless steel. Designer: Dick Simonis. Makers: NV Gerofabriek (HOLLAND)

Silver pipkin designed by Søren Georg Jensen. Made by Georg Jensen Solvesmedie A/S (DENMARK)

Glass hors-d'œuvre or butter dish in iron frame holder with wicker- or plastic-covered grip designed by G. L. de Snellman-Jaderholm. Dish by O/Y Wärtsilä-concern AB Nuutajarvi Glassworks (FINLAND)

Coffee service in sterling silver with heat-resistant plastic handle; moonstone stopper. Designer: Helge Lindgren. Makers: A/B Hovjuvelerare K. Anderson (SWEDEN)

Hand-carved salad servers in acajou. Designed
and made by A. Van Itterbeeck (BELGIUM)

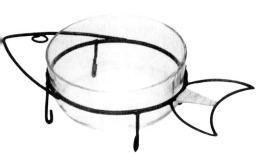

Cane core bread basket designed and made by
Lauris Lønborg (DENMARK)

Columbia anodised aluminium coffee maker
◀ with nylon handle. Designer: Kås Claesson.
Makers: Peter Bodum A/S (DENMARK)

Sugar, salt and pepper pourers in 18/8 stainless
steel, plastic base. Designer: Pierre Forssell. ▶
Makers: AB Gense (SWEDEN)

2

4

3

1 Flatware in silver. The fork is from the
   Hopea Siipi (Silver Wing) service, the knife
   and spoon from *Tapio*. Both are designed
   by Tapio Wirkkala and made by
   Kultakeskus O/Y (FINLAND)

2 *Caravel* flatware service in silver. Designer:
   Henning Koppel. Makers: Georg Jensen
   Solvsmedie A/S (DENMARK)

3 Flatware in sterling silver, serrated knife
   blade. Designer: Marco Lugherra. Made
   by Sola Besteckfabrik AG (SWITZERLAND)

4 Flatware design No. 2723 in 18/8 chrome
   nickel steel, with stainless steel knife blade.
   It is made in a size between the usual dinner
   and luncheon sizes. Designed by Dr. Josef
   Hoffman of Vienna. Made by C. Hugo Pott
   (GERMANY)

RIGHT: Red earthenware plate, 12½-in. diameter,
decorated by feather combing in red and cream slip on a black slip ground
and glazed with a transparent galena glaze.
Designed and made by H. R. Stone.
BELOW: Unglazed stoneware inlaid with chamotte clay in different colours
designed by Axel Salto and made by The Royal Copenhagen Porcelain Factory.

Cream stoneware bulb bowl
with blue underglaze decoration
and cream stoneware dish
with black slip decoration,
both designed and made by Eleanor Whittall.

Unic stoneware vases in *sang de boeuf*, yellow-green and black-brown glaze designed by Carl Harry Stahlhane and made by
A B Rorstrand Porslinsfabriker.
RIGHT: Galena glazed plate, 12½ in. diameter,
designed and made by H. R. Stone.
Red earthenware clay, decorated by feather combing in red and black slip on a cream slip ground.

EXTREME RIGHT: Earthenware plate, one of a series of biblical subjects, 16 in. diameter, in black, brown and grey, designed and made by Edwin and Mary Scheier.

Handthrown flower-pot, 8 in. high, earth-pink matt glaze on brown body,
and vase, 16 in. high, with figures in mulberry brown against grey matt glaze,
both designed and made by Nancy Wickham; prizewinners in competition sponsored by
The Syracuse Museum of Fine Arts and The Onondaga Pottery Co. (Photo: Syracuse Museum of Fine Arts)

LEFT, from top to bottom — 1: handthrown stoneware bowl with cream and brown decoration,
sgraffito technique, designed and made by Marguerite Wildenhain.
2: oval pinched footed bowl, velvet-yellow matt glaze vase, and blue Pompeian lava glaze vase,
grey reduction glaze with melt craquelé.
3: bowl, dove-grey reduction glaze with melt craquelé, and bottle-shaped vase, tiger-eye reduction glaze.
4: cylindrical vase, grey reduction glaze with melt craquelé;
plate, eggshell matt glaze with mineral deposits and square pinched bowl, flame-red matt glaze.
2, 3 and 4 designed and made by Gertrud and Otto Natzler.

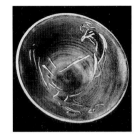

TOP LEFT: Grey-green stoneware bowl
with brush drawing in iron oxide
designed and made by H. F. Hammond.
CENTRE: *Fighting Cock* earthenware bowl
in sgraffitto on iron slip: designed and made
by Rachel Warner. (Photo: J. G. Restall)
ABOVE: Earthenware tray
with underglaze decoration in blue and
purple, designed by Birger Kaipiainen
and made by Arabia Porcelain and
Earthenware Factory.
BELOW: Vase in cream colour and celadon slip
with hand-turned 'runner' bead decoration
designed by Keith Murray, RDI,
and made by Josiah Wedgwood & Sons Ltd.

LEFT: Vase of the Evangelists, reminiscent
of Byzantine and early-Christian
bas-reliefs in ivory
yet modern in colour and form.
Designed by Endre Hévézi and Dr Gyula Bajo
and made by Booths & Colcloughs Ltd, Hanley.
Background: *Ormiston* 50-in. printed
linen designed by Marion Mahler
and made by Donald Bros Ltd. Four other
colour schemes on white grounds available:
duckegg, cyclamen or jade, each with dark and
light grey; yellow, cinnamon and chocolate.

Unic stoneware in grey-white, olive-green and ivory glaze, designed
by Carl Harry Stahlhane and made by A B Rorstrand Porslinsfabriker.

Vase and bowl of stoneware with *sang de bœuf* glaze designed by Toini Muona and made by Arabia Porcelain and Earthenware Factory.

BELOW, RIGHT: Cream glaze stoneware vase with golden yellow brush decoration, designed and made by Constance Dunn, ARCA.

LOWER: Group of Unic stoneware miniatures, with white, brown and blue flame glaze, designed by Gunnar Nylund and made by AB Rorstrand Porslinsfabriker.

1. *Veckla*. White stoneware designed by Stig Lindberg and made by A B Gustavsbergs Fabriker. 'Pinching' the soft clay before firing has enhanced the characteristics of the material.

2. *Vinda*. White stoneware designed by Stig Lindberg and made by A B Gustavsbergs Fabriker.

3. Translucent pale pink bowl and white vase of unfired thin china clay designed by Aune Siimes and made by Wartsila-Koncernen A B Arabia. The pattern is introduced by varying the thickness and thus changing the opacity.

OPPOSITE: *Våga*. White stoneware designed by Wilhelm Kåge and made by A B Gustavsbergs Fabriker. The wavy edges are reminiscent of underwater forms.

1. Unic stoneware vases with turquoise and brown glazes designed by Stig Lindberg and made by A B Gustavsbergs Fabriker.

2. *Frozen Music*. Vases of highly-fired stoneware with contrasting matt glazes designed by Carl Harry Stålhane and made by A B Rörstrands Porslinsfabriker.

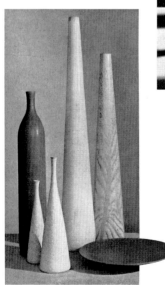

3. Faiences designed by Stig Lindberg and made by A B Gustavsbergs Fabriker.

4. Handmade stoneware vases, 7 in. and 16 in. high, designed by Meindert Zaalberg and made by Potterij Zaalberg. *(Photo: A. Dingjan.)*

5. Stoneware vases with white and green glazes, and bowl with white glaze, designed by Kyllikki Salmenhaara and made by Wartsila-Koncernen A B Arabia.

6. Vases of highly-fired stoneware with various matt glazes designed by Carl Harry Stålhane and made by A B Rörstrands Porslinsfabriker.

7. Stoneware vases and bowl with *sang de bœuf* glaze designed by Toini Muona and made by Wartsila-Koncernen A B Arabia.

1. White stoneware designed and made by Eleanor Whittall. Dish with decoration in black slip, and stemmed cup with blue decoration.
2. Vase of stoneware-chamotte with decorations in grey, black and white, designed by Carl Harry Stålhane and made by A B Rörstrands Porslinsfabriker.
3. Stoneware bowl with *sang de bœuf* glaze, and vase with white and eau-de-nil glaze, designed by Friedl Kjellberg and made by Wartsila-Koncernen A B Arabia.
4. White china miniatures with gold-painted decorations designed by Maria Hackman and made by A B Rörstrands Porslinsfabriker.

7

5. Stoneware vase and bowl with black decoration on turquoise glaze designed by Nils Thorsson and made by The Royal Copenhagen Porcelain Factory.

6. Vase with multi-coloured decoration on grey and white glaze designed by Poldi Wöjtek and made by A/S Michael Andersen & Son.

7. Dish of stoneware with black decoration on turquoise glaze designed by Nils Thorsson and made by The Royal Copenhagen Porcelain Factory.

8. Handmade pottery with rich cream-coloured slip decoration and amber glaze on red clay designed by Peter Holdsworth and made by Holdsworth Pottery.

8

ABOVE: Dull earthenware plate decorated in grey and black. Designer and maker: Marciano A. Longarini (ARGENTINA).

BELOW: Black and white slipware dish, diameter 18 in. Designer and maker: William Newland (GB).
(Collection: Arthur Lane).

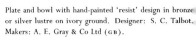

Plate and bowl with hand-painted 'resist' design in bronze or silver lustre on ivory ground. Designer: S. C. Talbot. Makers: A. E. Gray & Co Ltd (GB).

RIGHT: Underglaze plate with black, grey and citron yellow decoration on ivory coloured clay, diameter 24 in. Designer and maker: Margaret D. Hine (GB).

ABOVE: Glazed plate, the figures in blue on a white ground. Designer and maker: Marciano A. Longarini (ARGENTINA).

RIGHT: Faience plate decorated in red, blue, green, yellow and mulberry, and vase in black and grey. Designed and painted by Stig Lindberg. Makers: AB Gustavsbergs Fabriker (SWEDEN).

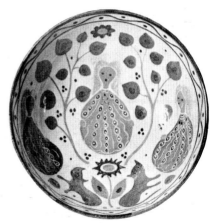

ABOVE: Three Girls. Earthenware plate painted in oxides of cobalt, iron, nickel and chrome. Designer and maker: Henry Clante (DENMARK).

LEFT: One of a series of twelve plates depicting New England industries, printed in sepia on Wedgwood cream colour *Queensware*. Designer: Clare Leighton. Makers: Josiah Wedgwood & Sons Ltd (GB).

Ceres vase. Celadon green porcelain with relief decoration, exterior unglazed. Designer: Siegmund Schütz. Makers: Staatliche Porzellan-Manufaktur Berlin, Werk Selb (GERMANY).

ABOVE: *Mathaeus* vase. Stoneware, celadon glaze with relief decoration. Designer: Jais Nielsen. Makers: The Royal Copenhagen Porcelain Factory (DENMARK).

LEFT: *Crown* bowl, white matt-glazed porcelain. Designer: Gunnar Nylund. Makers: A B Rörstrands Porslinsfabriker (SWEDEN).

OPPOSITE: Stoneware vase. Designer and maker: Stig Lindberg, AB Gustavsbergs Fabriker (SWEDEN). Now in the Trondheim Museum, Norway.

Terra-cotta vase with black, brown and white decoration, and terra-cotta bowl decorated in turquoise, cobalt, black and white. Designer and maker: Emanuel Romano. Background of handwoven pure silk Honan designed by Hugo Dreyfuss and printed in brown on natural ground by Kagan-Dreyfuss Inc (USA).

Stoneware vases with bone yellow glaze, signed 'Stig L'. Designer: Stig Lindberg. Makers: A B Gustavsbergs Fabriker (SWEDEN).

Toy Ocarinas. Faience with polychrome decorations. Designer: Stig Lindberg. Makers: A B Gustavsbergs Fabriker (SWEDEN).

LEFT: Stoneware bottles with green and brown glazes. Designer: Kyllikki Salmenhaara. Makers: Wärtsilä-koncernen A B Arabia (FINLAND).

Faience with decorations in green, yellow, blue, red and black on white glaze. Designed and painted by Stig Lindberg. Makers: AB Gustavsbergs Fabriker (SWEDEN)

RIGHT: Grey stoneware with the decoration incised through the glaze. Designers and makers: Edwin and Mary Scheier (USA)

BELOW: *The Nest*. High relief wall plaque. Designer: Gunnar Nylund. Makers: AB Rörstrands Porslinsfabriker (SWEDEN)

RIGHT: Unique high-fired stoneware. Tall vases of blanc de chine, and small vase with black-brown iron glaze. Designer: Carl Harry Stålhane. Makers: AB Rörstrands Porslinsfabriker (SWEDEN)

Small green and grey pottery vases designed to hold orchids. Designer and maker: Käte Weinreis (GERMANY)

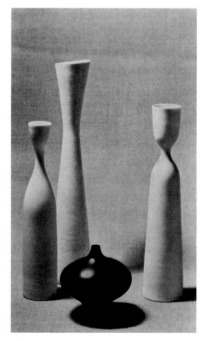

LEFT: Unique high-fired stoneware. Bowl with uranium yellow glaze and black crystals; vase with black-brown iron glaze. Designer: Carl Harry Stålhane. Makers: AB Rörstrands Porslinsfabriker (SWEDEN)

BELOW: Stoneware bottles, six inches high. Left: black glaze on buff body; right: cobalt blue glaze breaking to black. Designer and maker: Christopher Russell at the Purbeck Pottery (GB)

Blue-green and grey floor vases. Designer and maker: Käte Weinreis (GERMANY)

LEFT: Grey earthenware vases and bowl, and blue lamp base, all with the design incised through the glaze. Designers and makers: Edwin and Mary Scheier (USA)

Grey stoneware vase with black decoration. Designer and maker: Anders Liljefors of AB Gustavsberg Fabriker (SWEDEN)

Sagoland. Plate from a nursery set in earthenware with blue underglaze decoration. Designer: Stig Lindberg. Makers: AB Gustavsberg Fabriker (SWEDEN)

Bowl of white feldspar porcelain decorated in the filigree technique. Designer: Maria Hackman-Dahlén. Makers: AB Rörstrands Porslinsfabriker (SWEDEN)

Faience bowl and vases with polychrome decoration. Designer:
Stig Lindberg. Makers: AB Gustavsberg Fabriker (SWEDEN)

RIGHT: Tan stoneware vase with sgraffito decoration in black
slip and unglazed exterior. Designer and maker: H. H. Sanders
(USA) (*Photo: Robert Fritz*)

Unique stoneware. Group of three miniatures designed by Gunnar Nylund. *Coral* vase with red iron glaze, and *Ciel Noir* vase, 'uranium' with silver spots, by Carl Harry Stålhane. Bowl with onion decoration by Hertha Bengtson. Makers: AB Rörstrands Porslinsfabriker (SWEDEN) *(Courtesy: Svenska Hem)*

Stoneware vase with celadon glaze. Designer and maker: Christopher Russell at the Purbeck Pottery (GB)

Grecian style vase with sgraffito decoration through olive-green to the cream body, 15 inches high. Designer and maker: Christopher Russell at the Purbeck Pottery (GB)

Matt white pot, bowl with rust brown glaze inside, and jug with dark celadon glaze, all with iron brushwork decoration. Stoneware designed and made by William Ruscoe (GB)

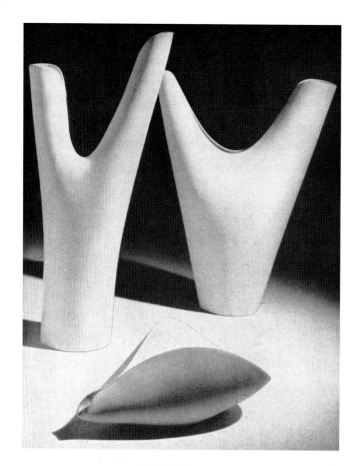

Veckla. White stoneware in which the basically symmetrical form is given a free shape by cutting and turning in the top edges. The tall vases are suitable for pouring through either 'branch' while offering a comfortable hold. Designer: Stig Lindberg. Makers: A B Gustavsberg Fabriker (SWEDEN)

BELOW: Thrown and cut earthenware bowls with grey-green opaque glaze. Designer and maker: K. I. C. Clark (GB)

White china coffee pot, and part of an earthenware dinner service designed by Arthur Percy; ceramic figure by Mari Simmulson; and white china vase by S. E. Skawonius backed by ceramic tiles by T. Kaasinen. All made by Upsala Ekeby AB (SWEDEN) *(Courtesy: Svenska Hem)*

ABOVE: Hard earthenware pot, ochre ground decorated in black-and-white slip and copper and iron oxides. Designer and maker: Honorah M. French (GB)

ABOVE: Earthenware vases from the new *Marselis* range made in a variety of different coloured glazes with incised decoration. Designer: Nils Thorsson. Makers: The Royal Copenhagen Porcelain Factory (DENMARK)

RIGHT: Earthenware vase and shallow bowl; grey, black and white, with sgraffito decoration. Designer and maker: Marianne de Trey (GB)

ABOVE: Carafes in fine earthenware, hand thrown and finished with semi-matt egg-shell glazes. Colours include mushroom, sepia, magnolia white, ice green, mist blue. Shapes designed by Poole Design Unit. Makers: Carter, Stabler & Adams Ltd (GB)

High-fired hand-thrown porcelain bowl, 14 inches diameter and pitcher 20 inches high, finished grey-white matt and reduction glazes. Small brown stoneware bowl in centre. Designer: Meindert Zaalberg. Makers: Potterij Zaalberg (HOLLAND) (*Photo: A. Dingjan*)

Fantasia. 2⅛-inch diameter cigarette cup and 4¾-inch diameter ashtray decorated copper - plate printing on light grey body in red and green. Designer of shape: Jacob E. Bang. Decoration: Paul Høyrup. Makers: Nymolle Ceramic Works, A/S Rafa (DENMARK)

RIGHT: Black and silver lacquered vase, 9 inches high. Designer and maker: Mitsusuke Tsuji (JAPAN)

LEFT: Hand-thrown glazed stoneware pitchers and bowls. Red or white body decorated majolica or tin glaze painting or underglaze painting. Designers and makers: Krystyna Sadowska and Konrad Sadowski (CANADA)

BELOW: *Italia.* Vase 9¼ inches high decorated with copper-plate printing on light grey body in red, green or brown. Designer of shape: Jacob E. Bang. Decoration: Paul Høyrup. Makers: Nymolle Ceramic Works, A/S Rafa (DENMARK)

Hand-thrown ceramics (*left*) with iron glaze, (*centre*) with sulphur lava glaze, and (*right*) with black-and-white crater glaze. Designers and makers: Gertrud and Otto Natzler (USA) (*Courtesy: Dalzell Hatfield Galleries*)

ABOVE: High-fired hand-thrown porcelain vase, 20 inches high, with grey-white ash finish; unglazed black stoneware vase, 10 inches high, with white sgraffito decoration. Designer: Meindert Zaalberg. Makers: Potterij Zaalberg (HOLLAND) (*Photo: A. Dingjan*)

RIGHT: Hand-thrown clay vases baked to 1,000°C resulting in a grey bark-like effect. Three are glazed with a transparent syrup-brown glaze, while the fourth is covered with a transparent glaze over a light blue angobe. Designer and maker: Grete Möller (SWEDEN)

Rust-Farsta stoneware vase. Designer: Wilhelm Kåge. Makers: AB Gustavsberg Fabriker (SWEDEN)

ABOVE: Pottery vase, approximately 10½ inches high, lacquered yellow, with decoration in black lacquer. Designer and maker: Mitsusuke Tsuji (JAPAN)

'Egg-shell-thin' china bowls in white and white-and-dark-blue chequer-board design. Designer: Anne Sümes. Makers: Wärtsilä-koncernen AB Arabia (FIN-LAND)

Unique multicoloured stoneware bowls, hand-painted decoration under transparent lead glaze. Round bowls 6–7 inches diameter, fishbowl 12 inches long. Designer: Hertha Bengtson. Makers: AB Rörstrands Porslinsfabriker (SWEDEN)

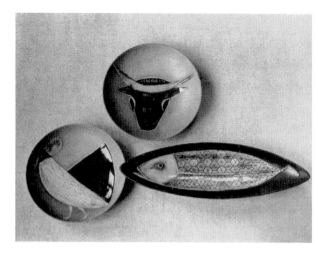

ABOVE: Translucent porcelain *Cintra* bowls. White, blue and greyish-brown glazes. Tallest, 8 inches high. Designer: Wilhelm Kåge. Makers: AB Gustavsbergs Fabriker (SWEDEN)

RIGHT: Black clay vase and bottle-vase, decorated blue-green angobe; light blue slipware plate, hand-painted decoration in black. All fired to 1000°C; transparent lead glaze. Designer and maker: Tom Möller (SWEDEN)

Beaten gold lacquerware. Makers: Technical Division, Industrial Arts Institute, Tokyo (JAPAN)

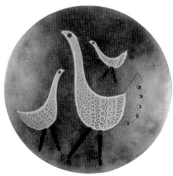

10-inch plate, enamels on copper. Birds pale opaque blue decorated black and gold, on golden-brown transparent base. Designer and maker: Françoise Desrochers-Drol (CANADA) (*Photo: Omer Parent*)

BELOW: Pottery jug and mugs in green, stone-black and sky-blue glazes, and white-glazed combined fruit dish and candle-holder with on-glaze dull green decoration. Designer and maker: Marciano A. Longarini (ARGENTINA)

ABOVE: Tigo Ware in black/white. Transparent glaze, slip decorated with matt finish. Background: *Tok* (Marrow), *Retek* (Radish); Foreground: *Harcsa* (Carp), *Csuka* (Bream), *Fogas* (Whiting). Designer: Tibor Reich, FSIA. Prototypes developed in co-operation with Gordon Burley at Alderminster Pottery (GB) (*Photo: Council of Industrial Design*)

Stoneware in brown, blue and white glazes, with incised decoration. Designer: Karin Bjorqvist. Makers: AB Gustavsbergs Fabriker (SWEDEN)

BELOW: Vases in grey grogg-clay, fired to 1000°C, transparent glaze. Interior decorated blue and brown angobe. Designer and maker: Grete Möller (SWEDEN)

Stoneware wine pitcher, celadon glaze. Height 18 inches. Designer: Hans H. Hansen. Makers: The Royal Copenhagen Porcelain Co. Ltd (DENMARK)

ABOVE: Stoneware vases in grey-brown and grey-white glazes. Designer: John Andersson. Makers: Andersson & Johansson AB (SWEDEN)

Stoneware vase, 7½ inches high, 'rabbit pelt' glaze, and miniatures (one-of-a-kind), in charcoal black, matt white, and blue, green and brown glazes. Designer: Gunnar Nylund. Makers: AB Rörstrands Porslinsfabriker (SWEDEN)

Stoneware covered jar, and bowl, red-brown glaze, with design scratched through slip. Designed and made by Edwin and Mary Scheier (USA)

Rust-Farsta tubular ornamental fish, 20 inches high. Designer: Wilhelm Kåge. Makers: AB Gustavsbergs Fabriker (SWEDEN)

Stoneware vases in charcoal black and matt white glazes (one-of-a-kind). The tallest is 16 inches high. Designer: Carl-Harry Stålhane. Makers: AB Rörstrands Porslinsfabriker (SWEDEN)

Unique stoneware in turquoise, brown, and yellow glazes. Designed and made by Stig Lindberg (SWEDEN)

BELOW: Grey earthenware bowls with exterior decoration scratched through the glaze to the body. Designed and made by Edwin and Mary Scheier (USA). RIGHT: Clay vase 12 or 16 inches. Grey/white, turquoise or black. Designer: Bruno Platten. Makers: Tonwarenfabrik-Aedermannsdorf AG (SWITZERLAND)

In addition to the balance and harmony of their shapes, ceramics
derive so much of their beauty from the combined effects of glaze,
decoration and texture that the ceramic artist enjoys an immense
field of research and a reward proportionate to the manner in which
he makes use of it.

That research should never lose sight of the tradition from which
the craft grows is, however, an axiom particularly of ceramic art,
which maintains closer contact between hand and material, during
the making, than any other craft and is therefore one of the most
satisfying.

And yet the many exquisite pieces shown here are not only of the
past, in the sense of exhibiting the best traditions of a centuries-old
medium, but are at the same time vital expressions of our age in
which new techniques and new conceptions add their contributions
to the perpetual growth of ceramic art.

ABOVE: Earthenware vase in two colours designed by Maria Campi. For Società
Ceramica Italiana (Italy). BELOW: Vases and candlesticks in matt black glaze, and
in white glaze with dark blue decoration. Vases range in size from 6½ to 10 inches.
Designer: John Andersson. Makers: Andersson & Johansson A B (SWEDEN)

ABOVE: Earthenware Vases. In-glaze decoration on matt white glaze. Black/white motifs on Purbeck grey/lupin blue/bracken brown, or charcoal/tropic turquoise/grey stripes. Others grey/yellow or charcoal/terra-cotta bands. 5½–17 inches high. Shapes designed by A. B. Read, Lucien Myers and Guy Sydenham. Decorations by A. B. Read, RDI, ARCA. Makers: Carter, Stabler & Adams Ltd (GB). RIGHT: Black/white glazes. Vases 19½ and 13 inches, dish 16⅞ inches long. Designer: Arthur Percy. Makers: Upsala-Ekeby Group (SWEDEN). BELOW: Ivory body, black underglaze decoration. 7 and 11 inches. Designer and maker: Z. D. Kujundzic (SCOTLAND)

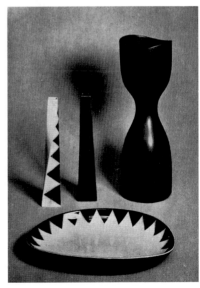

Earthenware vases. RIGHT: White glaze, decoration in black/ violet and black/pink; height 22 inches. Designed and decorated by Antonia Campi. For Società Ceramica Italiana (ITALY). BELOW: Decoration in dark blue on white glaze; tallest vase 23 inches. Designed by John Andersson. Made by Andersson & Johansson A B (SWEDEN)

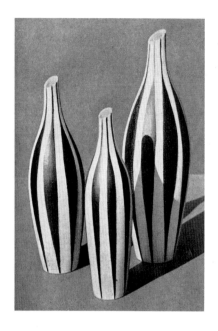

LEFT: Black-and-white striped earthenware bottles, 14¾ inches high, with red-lacquered cork stoppers. Designed by Orvokki Laine. Made by Kupittaan Saviosakeytio-Turku (FINLAND). BELOW: White porcelain vase with bluish-black decoration under transparent glaze; height 9 inches. Designed by Erik Reiff. Made by Bing & Grøndahls Porcellænsfabrik (DENMARK)

Earthenware lamp base, grey crystalline glaze; 21 inches high. Designed and made by Guido Andlowiz. For Società Ceramica Italiana (ITALY)

Terra-cotta water jugs, bottle, vase and pitcher, hand decorated, in copper, manganese, cobalt oxides, and raw umber glazes on tin glaze base. 12 to 16½ inches high. Designed and made by Krystyna and Konrad Sadowski (CANADA)

ABOVE: Stoneware bottle, with brushwork decoration in brown pigment on an oatmeal ground. Height: 15 inches. Designed and made by Bernard Leach (GB)

FAR LEFT: Earthenware bottles, 12 inches high; black, grey and white sgraffito through black slip and white glaze. LEFT: 9-inch bottle flattened both sides, pattern scratched through glaze; grey, white and brown. All designed and made by Marianne de Trey (GB)

Translucent porcelain *Cintra* bowls on chamotte mount. Designed and made by Wilhelm Kåge. For A B Gustavsbergs Fabriker (SWEDEN)

ABOVE: Stoneware salad bowl with white feldspathic glaze and sgraffito decoration. White on mottled brown ground. Diameter 11¾ inches. Designed and made by Irwin Hoyland (GB) *(Photo: David Galloway)*

RIGHT: High-fired stoneware vases, *Solfatara* uranium yellow glaze. 8 and 17 inches high. Designed by Axel Salto. Made by The Royal Copenhagen Porcelain Factory (DENMARK)

BELOW *(left and right)*: High-fired stoneware vases, *Solfatara* uranium yellow glaze. Height 15 inches; *(centre)* oxidised-fired vase, iron oxide crystal glaze. Height 14 inches. Designed by Axel Salto. Made by The Royal Copenhagen Porcelain Factory (DENMARK)

BELOW: Stoneware vase, *Sung* glaze. Height 17 inches. Designed by Axel Salto. Made by The Royal Copenhagen Porcelain Factory (DENMARK)

As in the case of glass, the ceramic artist needs to be something of a chemist; probably more so, for the shaping of a bowl, however pleasurable an exercise, is merely a preliminary to the firing and glazing which transforms it from meekness to magnificence.

It is said that organic chemistry knows no boundaries, whereas inorganic, which is the potter's chemistry, has definite limitations. Nevertheless, its applications to ceramic art are proved each year to be capable of extension, and the potter's repertoire continues to grow as his experiments with glazing and firing enlarge the scope of his knowledge and experience.

Within the framework of decorated ceramics two schools of thought and practice emerge; the one which seeks absolute control of decorative effect and the other which grants a certain licence to the forces of nature and evokes results which are not entirely predictable. It is not feasible to set one against the other. Both have their respective merits and there is no compulsion, other than personal preference and a sense of appropriateness, to be persuaded either way. Examples of both schools are illustrated as well as those exhibiting a preponderance for form in which the eloquence of the glaze is used to underline shape rather than as supplementary decoration.

ABOVE: White earthenware table lamp, clay-brown angobe decoration, interior turquoise enamel. Designed and made by José Maria Lanús (ARGENTINA)

ABOVE: Stoneware bowl, 8-inches diameter. Exterior unglazed with incrusted white slip decoration; interior dark brown glaze. Designed and made by Edgar Böckman (SWEDEN)

LEFT: Unglazed stoneware vases; sgraffito, and iron oxide decoration. Centre vase 15 inches high. Designed and made by Waistel Cooper. For Heal's of London (GB)

ABOVE: Unglazed red-brown *Terra-Farsta* stoneware vase. Height 13½ inches. Designed and made by Wilhelm Kåge. For AB Gustavsbergs Fabriker (SWEDEN)

ABOVE: Earthenware group. White glaze, banded decoration in blue, grey and yellow; linear in grey and turquoise. Vases from 7⅝ to 16 inches high; dish 11¼ inches. Designer: Mari Simmulson. Makers: The Upsala-Ekeby Group, Ekebybruk (SWEDEN). RIGHT: Stoneware vase, 7¾ inches diameter. Outside unglazed, inside green glaze. Designed and made by Lisa Larson. For AB Gustavsbergs Fabriker (SWEDEN). BELOW: Earthenware bowl and 8-inch modelled vase with copper oxide green decoration on oatmeal semi-matt glaze. Designed and made by Z. D. Kujundzic (GB)

ABOVE: Earthenware vase, scored decoration on fused manganese and turquoise blue ground; height 16 inches. Designed and made by G. F. Cook (GB)

ABOVE: One-of-a-kind stoneware vases and bowl from the *Magnific* series designed by Carl-Harry Stålhane. Made by AB Rörstrands Porslinsfabriker (SWEDEN)

BELOW: Stoneware bowls, rich brown mottled glaze; diameter 9¼ inches. Designer: Francesca Lindh. Made by O/Y Wärtsilä-concern AB Arabia (FINLAND)

ABOVE: Earthenware fruit bowl, wax-resist decoration in blue, green, yellow and brown under white tin glaze; diameter 11 inches. Designed by Eileen Lewenstein. Made at Briglin Pottery Ltd (GB)

LEFT: Condiment sets in earthenware, wax-resist decoration combined with tin glaze. Designed by George Dear. Made at Briglin Pottery Ltd (GB)

ABOVE: Stoneware vases, dark brown mottled glaze; height 12 inches. Designer: Richard Lindh. Made by O/Y Wärtsilä-concern AB Arabia (FINLAND)

BELOW: Earthenware bottle vase, applied and scratched decoration on a grey matt glaze; height 37 inches. Small stoneware pot, yellow and brown matt glaze. Designed and made by Edwin and Mary Scheier (USA)

ABOVE: Stoneware serving plate, brush decoration in black, orange, rust and white. Designed and thrown by Olea Davis. Earthenware bowl, incised decoration, by Kathleen McKim (CANADA)

LEFT: White porcelain branch vase with fine scalloped rim; height 9 inches. Designer: Tapio Wirkkala (FINLAND). Made by Rosenthal-Porzellan AG (GERMANY)

Dark brown stoneware bowl, scratched exterior decoration, inside turquoise blue glaze. Diameter 19 inches. Designer: Nils Kähler. Made by A/S Herman A. Kähler (DENMARK)

TOP: Stoneware, one-of-a-kind; unglazed wholemeal outside. Beakers, rich sienna temmoku and cream Bristol glaze inside; dish, black temmoku. 4, 6, and 4½-inch diameter. Designed and made by Murray Fieldhouse at Pendley Pottery (GB). ABOVE: Stoneware bottle jars, about 12 inches high, blue, green and uranium glazes, cut decoration; pot, yellow-brown. Designed and made by Finn Lynggaard (DENMARK)

ABOVE: Stoneware group. Jar, 11 inches high, wax-resist decoration under green-brown glaze; centre bowl, yellow-green uranium glaze; left-hand bowl, black-red ironglaze. Designed and made by Finn Lynggaard (DENMARK)

ABOVE: Stoneware bowl, olive-green and silver-grey speckled glaze. Diameter 6 inches. Designed and made by F. G. Cooper, MSIA (GB)

RIGHT: Porcelain bottles, green crackle and green reduction glazes. Designed and made by Mary B. Dickenson (CANADA)

LEFT: High-fired stoneware barrel vases, decorated black slip with white snowflake pattern, or deep tur-quoise with figure '8s'; interior white. $8\frac{1}{2}$, 26, and $16\frac{1}{2}$ inches. Designed by David Gil. Made at Bennington Pottery. For Raymor (USA)

ABOVE: Denby *Asphodel* earthenware vases; oyster, Mendip brown, lime-green and glossy black glazes. 5 to 12 inches. Designer: Kenneth Clark. Makers: Joseph Bourne & Son, Ltd (GB)

RIGHT (*left to right*): Stoneware bottle, green glaze, by Sybil Laubenthal; earthenware branch vase, iron chrome pebble glaze, by Alma and Ernst Lorenzen; stoneware vase, salt glaze, by Dorothy Dodman (CANADA)

BELOW: Earthenware bottles and deep bowl, oxide exterior decoration on the raw body, interior white tin glaze; centre bottle 11 inches high, bowl 6½ inches. Designed by Eileen Lewenstein. Made at Briglin Pottery Ltd (GB)

ABOVE: Earthenware vase, white feldspathic glaze inside, sgraffito exterior decoration through black to white; about 8½ inches. BELOW: Cylindrical plant container, sgraffito exterior decoration in mushroom and deep brown; about 6½ inches. Both are designed and made by Irwin Hoyland (GB)

ABOVE: Stoneware vase, brownish glaze and haut-relief decoration; about 12 inches. Designer: Ebbe Sadolin. Made by A/S Bing & Grøndahls Porcelænsfabrik (DENMARK). LEFT: Stoneware, incised and sgraffito decoration: tall vase (22 inches), red and white glaze; bottle, pale blue neck, unglazed dark clay base; large pot, dark grey/blue; small pot, unglazed dark clay, grey glazed decoration. Designed and made by M. Wildenhain (USA)

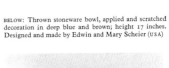

BELOW: Thrown stoneware bowl, applied and scratched decoration in deep blue and brown; height 17 inches. Designed and made by Edwin and Mary Scheier (USA)

ABOVE: Earthenware chalices, copper reduction glazes. 6 and 5½ inches high. Designed and thrown by Gertrud and Otto Natzler (USA) (*Courtesy: Dalzell Hatfield Galleries*)

BELOW: Earthenware vases, incised decoration hand-painted in green, orange, yellow and black on mustard-biege body; 11 and 8 inches. Custom-made in Italy for Raymor (USA)

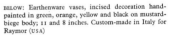

ABOVE: Red clay fan-shaped vases, transparent tin glaze, black slip and sgraffito, or oxide brush decoration. Made in various sizes, centre vase 12 × 7½ inches. Designed and made by Mary Gibson-Horrocks (GB)

ABOVE: 'Sprouting' stoneware vase, *Fang* glaze; 24 inches high. Designed and made by Axel Salto at The Royal Copenhagen Porcelain Manufactory A/S (DENMARK)

Stoneware vase, *Rutil* blue glaze; 20 inches high. Designed and made by Axel Salto at The Royal Copenhagen Porcelain Manufactory A/S (DEN-MARK). RIGHT: High-fired raw clay vase, 44 inches high. Designed and made by Meindert Zaalberg at Potterij Zaalberg (HOLLAND)

Stoneware miniatures, and tall vases in green copper glazes—from light turquoise to black-green; heights, up to 20 inches. Designed and made by Stig Lindberg at AB Gustavsbergs Fabriker (SWEDEN)

ABOVE: Earthenware vase, green crystal glaze; pedestal bowl, deep red glaze; small bowl, mystic blue glaze. Designed and thrown by Gertrud and Otto Natzler (USA)
(*Courtesy: Dalzell Hatfield Galleries*)

Earthenware. Wine Jar, matt grey glaze over red body, inside bluish-white tin glaze: height 15 inches; tin-glazed bowl, sgraffito decoration through copper pigment: width 16 inches; storage jar, tin glaze inside with manganese decoration on unglazed body: height 7 inches. All hand-thrown and decorated by P. F. Rushforth, Sydney School of Art (AUSTRALIA)

High-fired stoneware vase, decorated sgraffito through dark matt glaze; height 20 inches. Hand-thrown by M. Wildenhain (USA)

INDEX
Designers and architects
Designer und Architekten
Designers et architectes

Credits
Bildnachweis
Crédits

Bonhams, London: 24
Christie's Images, London: 11, 24
Christina & Bruno Bischofsberger Collection, Zürich: 4–5
Fiell International Ltd., London: (photos: Paul Chave): 8, 21, 22, 23 left;
9 right, 14, 23 right (Ross & Miska Lovegrove Collection);
16, 17 (Mithra Neuman Collection)
(photos: Paul Hodsoll): 10, 12
Fritz Hansen, Copenhagen: 13, 25
Louis Poulsen, Copenhagen: 19 left
Sotheby's, London: 15, 20

Designs for life

From eco-design to design-art

Selected designers and design-led companies featured in the book: **Ronan & Erwan Bouroullec, Ecotricity, Naoto Fukasawa, Zaha Hadid, Intelligent Energy, Jonathan Ive & Apple Design Team, LOT-EK, Ross Lovegrove, Marine Current Turbines, Jasper Morrison, Marc Newson, POC, Philips Design, Seymourpowell, Tokujin Yoshioka**

DESIGN NOW!

Eds. Charlotte & Peter Fiell / Hardcover, format: 19.6 x 24.9 cm (7.7 x 9.8 in.), 560 pp.

**ONLY € 29.99 / $ 39.99
£ 24.99 / ¥ 5,900**

Not only an in-depth exploration of contemporary design practice, this book is also a rallying call for a more sustainable approach to product design of every type, from lighting and furniture design to consumer electronic equipment, transportation, product architecture, and environmental design. Visually stunning and highly informative, *Design Now!* illustrates the latest work by 90 of the world's leading designers and design-led manufacturing companies, while also featuring in-their-own-words statements that give a unique insight into the nature of 3-dimensional design today. Additionally, the editors' introductory essay authoritatively outlines the main issues facing designers, manufacturers and con-

sumers, and offers a perceptive vision for a better way forward that focuses on the need to reduce, reuse, and recycle. *Design Now!* is essential for anyone interested in design and the road towards a greener future.

The editors: **Charlotte J. and Peter M. Fiell** run a design consultancy in London. They have lectured widely, curated a number of exhibitions, and written numerous articles and books on design, including TASCHEN's *1000 Lights, 1000 Chairs, Design of the 20th Century, Industrial Design A-Z, Scandinavian Design, Graphic Design for the 21st Century* and *Designing the 21st Century*.